THE COMPLETE CHORAL CONDUCTOR

DATE			

THE COMPLETE CHORAL CONDUCTOR

Gesture and Method

BRIAN R. BUSCH
University of Miami

SCHIRMER BOOKS
A Division of Macmillan, Inc.
NEW YORK

Collier Macmillan Publishers
LONDON

Schirmer Books
A Division of Macmillan, Inc.
866 Third Avenue, New York, N.Y. 10022

Collier Macmillan Canada, Inc.

Library of Congress Catalog Card Number: 83-3035

Printed in the United States of America

printing number
2 3 4 5 6 7 8 9 10

Library of Congress Cataloging in Publication Data

Busch, Brian R.
The complete choral conductor.

Includes index.
1. Conducting, Choral. I. Title.
MT85.B925 1984 784.9'63 83-3035
ISBN 0-02-870340-5

To
R. B. Walls
who gave me a chance
to "stand on my head"

Contents

Preface and Acknowledgments

Many conducting textbooks on the market do not seem appropriate for the students beginning the study of choral conducting. The musical examples in many instrumentally oriented conducting books are either not appropriate or too difficult for students to learn. Other books demand an accomplished accompanist to play the exercises.

How does this book differ from other conducting books?

1. Over 130 diagrams help explain hand and arm movement.
2. Many photographs, including two sequences of mirror-image photos, show hand and arm position. The student can use the mirror-image photos by placing the book against a mirror, then comparing his or her mirror image with the mirror image in the book.
3. Fermatas are dealt with in some detail.
4. Advanced conducting techniques are included in Part II.
5. Basic knowledge for the choral conductor—intonation, audition procedures, advanced rehearsal techniques, music selection, vocal exercises, programming, balance, and blend—is stressed in Part III.
6. The musical exercises are all melodically conceived and should be singable by any beginning conducting class. The exercises are purposely left wordless so that students can supply their own syllables for singing. The melodies are, for the most part, diatonic and without complexity. Each exercise contains a conducting problem. It is intended that students will spend time learning to conduct, not learning complicated musical examples. It is hoped that the musical exercises will be learned easily, thereby motivating students to practice more often.

The musical exercises can be adequately performed by two or three students in the class. An accomplished accompanist also is not necessary.

Supplementary conducting exercises have been included to give the student additional practice in developing necessary technique.

Techniques for daily practice of the conducting gestures, the development of musical intensity, practical considerations for the teacher-conductor, and the psychology of the final release are other topics considered in this book.

Specific points that are important for students to remember have been placed in sections entitled *Nota Bene* or *To the Student.* Some of the exercises ask students to use their imagination and ability to improvise appropriate melodies for conducting purposes. Students will also have the opportunity to experiment with alternate approaches to solving conducting problems, thereby developing a larger vocabulary of expressive gestures.

There are also lists of music appropriate for beginning and advancing conducting students. These lists are by no means comprehensive, but they do provide a point of departure when the teacher wants to introduce the full score to the students. Works suggested for beginning conductors are appropriate for choirs of elementary school and junior high school age, mostly unison, two-part, and SSA works. Recommended works for advancing conductors are more appropriate for advanced junior high, high school, and university choral groups. For those students who will go on to teach choral music, these works will serve as an introduction to appropriate literature for schools and church.

A book like this is usually the result of efforts by many people. I offer my thanks to:

Don Oglesby, assistant professor of conducting at the University of Miami, for providing much constructive criticism of technical matters, format, and matters of clarity.

Alice Gollan, a beleaguered conducting student, for her careful editing, as well as her viewpoint "from the other side of the desk," which proved to be invaluable.

Lillian Myer, a successful schoolteacher, for her editing and comments on Part III.

Marsha Athens, Lynne Auerbach, and Bill May, in the University of Miami Graphic Section of the Division of Communications Services, for their production of the original versions of the diagrams.

Roy Carpenter, in the University of Miami Photography Section of the Division of Communications Services, for his willingness to assume unusual postures to insure appropriate photos for this book.

Lee Kjelson, chairman of the University of Miami Department of Music Education, for his constant encouragement.

Mary Towne, for her professional typing and proofreading of the original manuscript copy.

Kip Irvine, for copying musical examples and exercises.

The University of Miami, which awarded me an Instructional Improvement grant that provided subsistence for my family while I completed the initial draft of Part I of this book.

A special thanks to my wife for her constant support throughout.

PART I

The Mechanics of Conducting

1 The Body in Preparation

This book examines conducting from the standpoint of clarity, position, direction, and appropriateness of gesture. The book will also help beginning conductors establish criteria so that they can make valid judgments about their conducting. In many instances several different gestures aimed at achieving the same result are discussed. The musician learning to conduct can try all of these techniques, eventually settling on the one which feels most comfortable and achieves the best results.

Posture

Posture transmits the positiveness, strength, and self-confidence of the conductor to the ensemble. The stance should thus appear solid, but not overly forced or rigidly locked into position.

As you assume the conducting stance, your feet should be approximately 12 to 18 inches apart. One foot may be slightly in front of the other. Your body weight should be distributed evenly in the hips. Your legs should be straight, but not locked at the knees. The chest should be held high, with shoulders slightly back. Your head should remain in vertical alignment with the body, neither tilted to one side nor jutting forward.

Beginning conductors should remember that assuming certain postures involves habit formation. At first this suggested stance may feel strange and awkward. Practice involves doing certain actions over and over again until they feel natural. Conducting is an activity which involves the entire body. Effective practice will teach your body to feel comfortable when conducting.

Your posture must show that you are in command of the situation, that you know what to do. As a conductor you are a leader. Those you lead must have confidence in you. Your posture alone can do much to communicate this sense of leadership.

The conductor's body must show *nonverbally* all the majesty and grandeur, grace and eloquence, which music is capable of expressing. Throughout this book you will be asked to rely on your imagination and your ability to act expressively. Many of the exercises are designed to give you an opportunity to explore your feelings as you stand on an imaginary stage before an imaginary ensemble. Being able to perceive yourself as a conductor through your imagination and ability to act expressively will help develop necessary attributes common to successful conductors.

Exercise 1-1 Stretch your arms high over your head. Note how your entire body feels in this position. Leaving your chest and shoulders in this raised position, drop your arms. Be sure your weight is distributed in the hips. Review this posture in a mirror: feet apart, weight evenly distributed, chest high, shoulders slightly back, head aligned vertically with the body.

Exercise 1-2 You are a dignitary ready to disembark from your personal jet in London. You are being honored by a full military review and a 21-gun salute. Prepare to walk through the open door of the jet and view the huge crowd awaiting you. Now take five steps through the doorway and stand at the top of the stairs viewing the waiting multitude of dignitaries below. How do you feel? What is distinctive about your posture as you stand at the top of the stairway?

Exercise 1-3 The Robert Shaw Chorale and the Philadelphia Orchestra are onstage for a performance of the Berlioz *Requiem* under your conductorship. The lights dim and you prepare to walk out onto the stage. How do you feel? You walk across the stage and turn to face this superb ensemble of musicians. How do you feel now? What is distinctive about your posture? Your facial expression?

Hand and Arm Position

As you raise your arm into conducting position the elbow should be forward of the body, not cramped against it. The position of hand and arm may best be demonstrated by shaking hands with someone. The position of the elbow, approximately six to eight inches in front of the body, will also pull the upper arm forward, allowing the shoulder, elbow, wrist, and finger joints to move freely. The entire arm should be directly out in front of the shoulder. The angle of forearm to upper arm is also important. For some conductors the forearm may be parallel to the ground, as if completing a handshake (Figure 1-1a). Other conductors will raise the forearm slightly so that the hand is approximately mid-chest high (Figure 1-1b).

The conductor's height may determine which forearm position is most appropriate. Shorter conductors may have to raise the gesture slightly to be sure the entire gesture can be seen by the ensemble. No portion of any gesture should be hidden behind a music stand, piano, or podium.

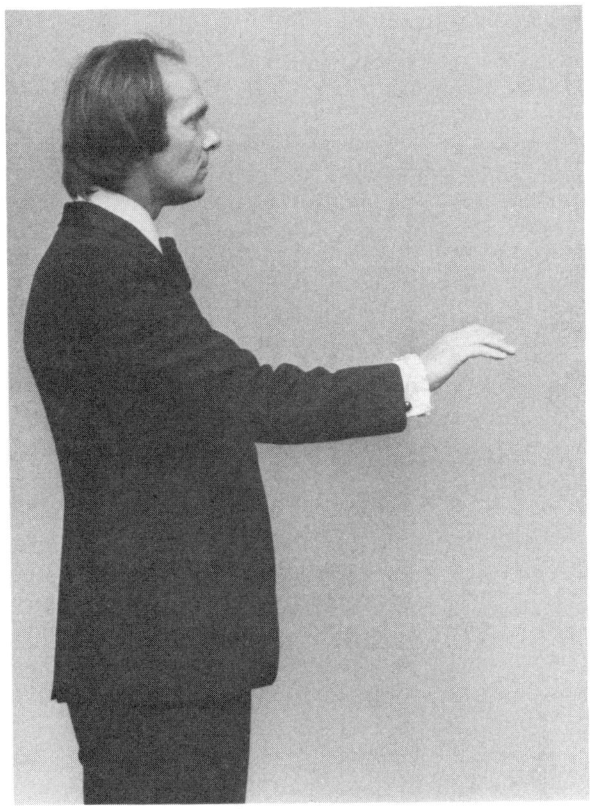

Figure 1–1a. Forearm parallel to ground.

Figure 1–1b. Forearm raised, hand mid-chest high.

As can be seen in Figures 1-1a and 1-1b, the hand should be slightly above the wrist at all times. The exception to this rule will be discussed in Chapter 2.

You may conduct with palm slightly open to the side (Figure 1-2a) or with palm down (Figure 1-2b). The difference between palm open and palm down is very slight. In any case, the palm should not show fully to the side.

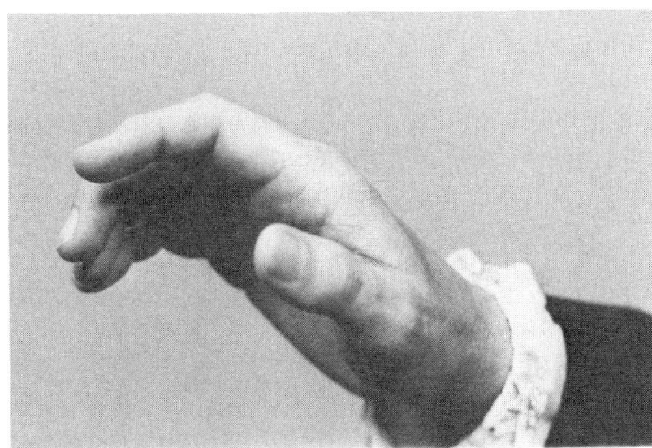

Figure 1–2a. Palm open.

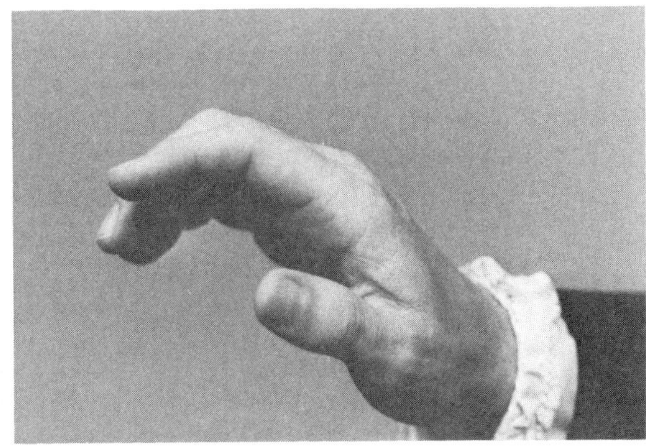

Figure 1–2b. Palm down.

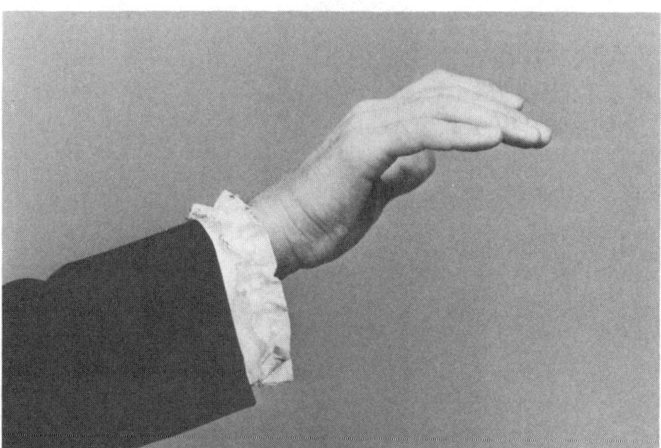

Figure 1–3. Curve of fingers.

The fingers of the hand should be slightly curved, much as if you were shaking hands or holding a chalkboard eraser diagonally across the palm (Figure 1-3). Fingers should not be held tightly together or spread too far apart. The thumb should be in a moderate position, neither sticking straight up or out nor held too tightly against the hand. The little finger should not protrude excessively, but should join the gentle curve of the rest of the fingers.

• To the Student

The suggestions for conducting stance and hand and arm position should be practiced in front of a mirror. You are seeing what your ensemble will see. Do you like what you see? Do your initial stance and conducting position convey confidence and assurance? Does the gesture look comfortable? Would you be encouraged to perform for the conductor you see in the mirror?

Compare your position with those shown in Figures 1-1a through 1-3. Experiment with hand and finger positions to find the one that fits you best. Continually check your posture.

Excessive tension in the arm and wrist should be avoided. The position of body, hand, arm, and wrist must appear natural. Elimination of excessive tension or rigidity is essential.

• Nota Bene*

Remember that the audience will be viewing you from the back. Consider the fact that the appearance of some conductors—their physical stance, arm position, excessive motion, and dress—sometimes becomes more interesting to the audience than the music being produced.

TO DETRACT FROM THE MUSIC IS A PROFESSIONAL SIN.

---

*"Nota bene" is Latin, meaning "note well." Throughout this book nota bene will be used to point out important aspects of conducting to which the students should pay careful attention.

Use of the Baton

The baton, commonly used by instrumental conductors and many choral conductors, is an extension of the arm. Conducting gestures may be executed cleanly and precisely with a baton. When using a baton, the palm of the hand should be down, with the baton held between thumb and forefinger. The baton, gripped firmly, should lie across the first joint of the forefinger with the ball of the baton resting comfortably in the palm of the hand. Holding the baton too tightly usually locks the wrist and restricts flow of movement. Holding the baton too loosely results in loss of control and ill-defined gestures.

CONTROL OF THE BATON IS ABSOLUTELY NECESSARY.

All beginning conductors should experience the baton. They should become familiar with its feel in the hand. They should experiment with the baton, noting that a small wrist gesture will move its tip a considerable distance.

Because the baton is an extension of the arm, the baton's tip should be out in front of the body (Figure 1-4). The tip should not be angled too sharply toward the center of the body, nor should it be pointed too high.

Figure 1–4. Proper position of baton.

On Practicing Conducting

When a musician practices conducting, he does not have his instrument, the ensemble, before him. When he practices singing or playing an instrument, however, the sound and resulting feeling give him immediate feedback, telling him what is correct and what needs additional practice. When practicing the physical gestures of conducting, the aural feedback is obviously missing, since there is no ensemble responding to the conductor and his gestures. How can the conductor determine if what he is doing is correct? How can he know he is establishing solid, basic conducting habits?

Initially there is only the visual aspect by which to judge: How does the gesture look when compared to criteria established both by conducting convention and a conducting teacher? Conductors must critically evaluate themselves and their conducting gestures in terms of clarity, position, direction, and appropriateness.

The following discussion on practicing conducting will serve as a guide throughout the book.

In the Beginning

Practice Time. As you begin practicing conducting, do so for short periods of time, perhaps five to ten minutes, several times each day. Gradually increase your stamina so that you can conduct for longer periods of time. Ideally you should practice several times each day.

Procedure. Unfocused practice of any skill wastes time. You should practice at a time when you can concentrate on the task to be accomplished. To practice conducting effectively, establish a routine which will give your work a focus, a positive direction.

PRACTICE IN FRONT OF A MIRROR EVERY DAY. REMEMBER: WHAT YOU *SEE* IS YOUR ONLY POSITIVE FEEDBACK WHEN YOU PRACTICE CONDUCTING.

Because practice relies on visual feedback, begin your sessions by reviewing the criteria of a good conducting gesture *in your mind* before you actually make any physical motion. Remember these general considerations:

1. Assume a correct conducting stance. Check the position of your feet, your balance, your weight distribution, and your head, chest, and shoulder positions.
2. Check your hand and arm position for general appearance and correct position in relation to the body.
3. Perform the gesture slowly. *Observe your hand and arm.* Analyze your gesture, consciously using the criteria to be discussed in class and in this book.
4. Ask yourself the following questions:
   a. Do I like what I see?
   b. Is my posture correct? solid? positive? confident?
   c. Is the position of my hand and arm appropriate?
   d. Is my gesture unmistakably clear? If I were in the ensemble, would I understand the gesture?
5. Close your eyes and mentally see yourself conducting the "perfect" gesture.
6. With your eyes open, conduct the gesture as you saw yourself do mentally. Repeat steps 5 and 6 several times.
7. The next step is to practice conducting music. Use a familiar tune or improvise a melody which will allow you to practice the specific movement.

Sing the melody as you conduct. Concentrate on being expressive. Watch yourself carefully in the mirror. In addition to the questions listed in step 4, ask yourself the following:

a. Is my gesture appropriate for the music?
b. Is my gesture expressive? Does it speak eloquently?

8. While either humming or singing silently in your mind, conduct the melody again, noting the change in your facial expression. Since you will not always be singing with the ensemble or even mouthing the words, your facial expression must complement your conducting gestures in animation and expressiveness.

• To the Student

Work with another conducting student. Conduct for each other; critique each other.

It is also possible to practice your conducting movements while you do other things—as you walk between classes, eat lunch, or talk on the telephone. Performing two different activities at the same time demands concentration and helps develop your body's capacity to do more than one thing at a time. This is a skill which conducting demands.

Practicing any type of skill takes self-discipline. Repetition is often boring, although very necessary. To make your practice more interesting, create new melodies to conduct, practice surreptitiously while talking with friends, practice mentally, and practice conducting appropriate recorded works. Practice a gesture with both right and left hands so that you develop flexibility and coordination. Try to conduct expressively with your feet, elbows, and head. The entire body must become expressive, animated, and dynamic. Creative thought will make the practice of conducting more interesting.

Being Expressive

The impact of choral music relies on the way in which the text is expressed. The sung word has musical powers capable of providing humanity with deep aesthetic experiences. As a conductor you must be willing to seek the power of this experience personally. You must understand the text and explore the many ways it can be expressed. Each word, when expressed with different inflection and mood, takes on new meaning. You must practice exploring the emotions of various words. How many different ways can you say "love" or "consideration"?

Exercise 1-4 Select a word and express that word verbally three different ways. Consider articulation and mood. Note what happens to the body and face as you (1) prepare to express the word, (2) actually deliver the word, and (3) follow through until the impact of delivery is complete. What "musical" elements do you explore during delivery of each expression?

Exercise 1-5 Select another word. Write it in big block letters on a piece of paper. Then think of a way you wish this word to be expressed. Show the word to the group. You may use any type of body, hand, or arm gesture in order to get the ensemble to perform the word the way you wish it expressed. You may *not* speak during the time you are the conductor. All efforts as conductor must be nonverbal. You will be allowed three consecutive attempts to achieve the desired results.

Analyze what each conductor does to achieve results. What type of preparation is necessary? What role does breath play? What importance does body position or body attitude have in terms of ensemble response? How important are the face, eyes, mouth, and forehead in expressing a verbal concept? How does one "turn the ensemble off"?

2 Pulse and Preparation

The Basic Pulse

The relationship of hand, arm, and wrist can best be experienced by laying your forearm on a flat surface with palm down and fingers gently curved (Figure 2-1a).

With the hand and arm in this position, raise the hand to approximately shoulder height. The arm should be extended in front of the shoulder, with the elbow six to eight inches in front of the body (Figure 2-1b).

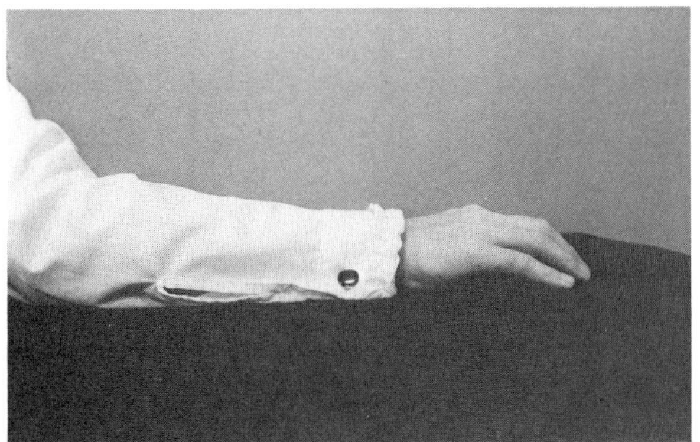

Figure 2–1a. Position of hand, arm, and wrist.

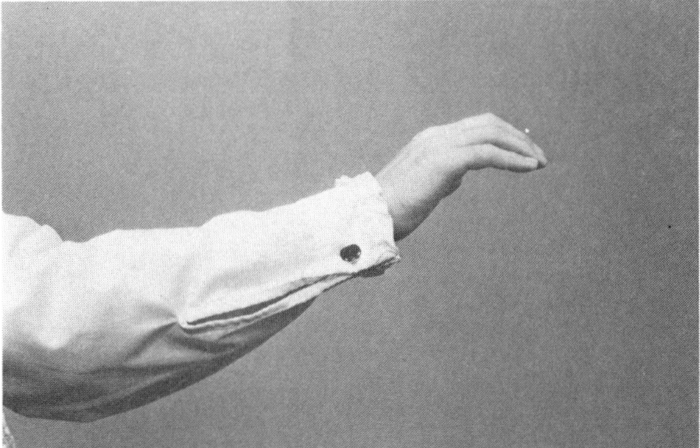

Figure 2–1b. Arm raised from surface to conducting position.

The basic pulse, or downbeat, is straight down. If your feet are approximately 12 to 18 inches apart with toes perpendicular to the body, the basic pulse will be straight down toward the toes of the right foot. Drop the hand slowly straight down. Note that the wrist slightly precedes the hand. Just before the moment of pulse, or *ictus* (From the Latin *icere,* "to strike"), the hand begins to speed up, passing the wrist. As the wrist "breaks," the fingertips (or the tip of the baton) define the exact moment of pulse at the bottom of the gesture. The range of ictus placement for the basic pulse may be from the bottom of the sternum (breastbone) to the belt line (Diagram 2-1).

Diagram 2–1

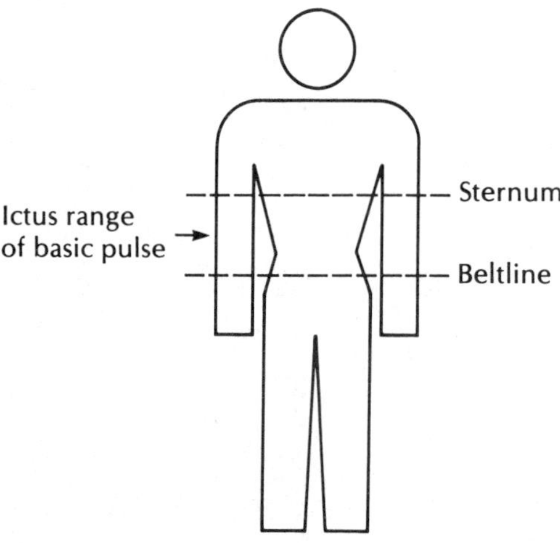

• To the Student

The illustrations in Figures 2–2a through 2–2g showing the entire sequence of the downbeat are paired. The left-hand figure shows the right hand making the gesture. The right-hand plate shows the same gesture simulated in mirror form. Use these mirror images by propping the book up in front of a mirror, assuming the conducting position being shown in the figure, and then comparing what you see in the mirror with the right-hand mirror image.

The portion of the gesture following the defining of the ictus is known as the *rebound.* It is a straight-up movement following the path the hand took as it descended. The rebound usually should not be greater than one-half the distance of the downward motion.

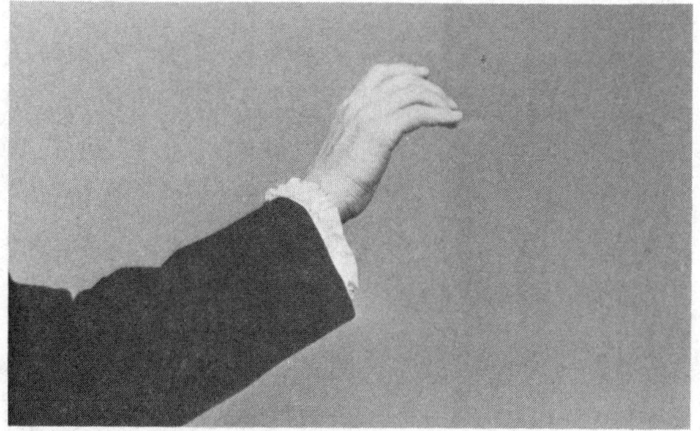

Figure 2–2a. The forearm and hand are in beginning position, with the hand approximately at shoulder level.

Figure 2–2b. The forearm falls; the wrist slightly precedes the hand.

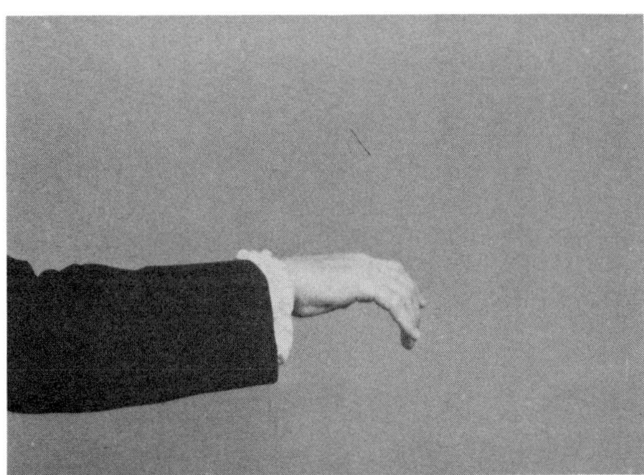

Figure 2–2c. Wrist, hand, and forearm are parallel to the ground.

Figure 2–2d. The wrist "breaks" and the hand drops below the wrist. The tips of the fingers define the ictus, or exact point of pulse.

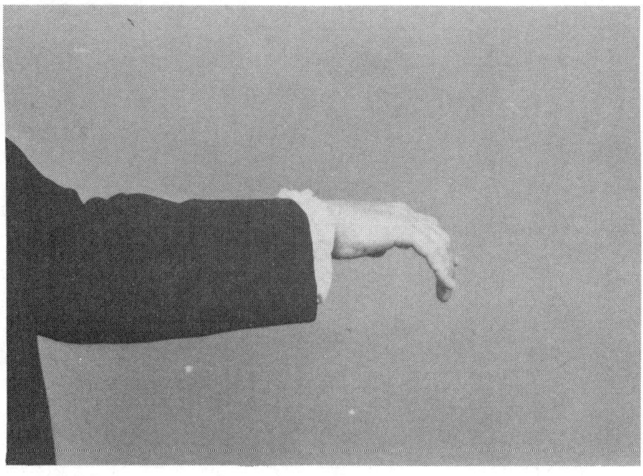

Figure 2–2e. After the tips of the fingers define the ictus, the hand begins to move straight up until hand, wrist, and arm are parallel to the ground again.

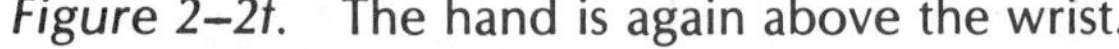

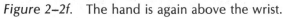

Figure 2–2f. The hand is again above the wrist.

Figure 2–2g. The hand reaches the top of the rebound.

Exercise 2-1 Practice giving this basic pulse many times. With your hand in conducting position, drop the forearm, being sure the hand stays slightly above the wrist until just before the moment of ictus. The forearm may drop to a position just below the sternum (breastbone) before the hand begins to catch up and then move below the wrist. Let the hand bounce slightly at the moment of ictus. Some conductors have described this bounce as "flicking" water off the end of the fingertips or baton. For now this should be a gentle movement. Work on a smoothly coordinated gesture involving elbow, forearm, wrist, and hand. Even as you practice this gesture, note your posture. Make the motion with eloquence and grace.

• **Nota Bene**

The rebound should not be more than half the distance of the downward motion. The elbow stays at approximately the same distance from the body during the entire gesture. Do not reach out or pull the arm back to make this basic pulse gesture. The arm should drop in a controlled fall. The fingers should not move, but should stay in the relaxed, curved position they were placed in before movement began.

DO NOT FLEX THE FINGERS.

If this is a problem, hold a chalk eraser diagonally across the palm while making the gesture. Remember: The entire gesture is straight down and straight back up.

Preparatory Gesture I (The Initial Preparation)

A preparatory gesture precedes each pulse. The primary purpose of this preparation is to communicate to the ensemble how the music which occurs on the next pulse is to be performed. The preparation must be in the exact tempo of the pulse that follows. This gesture tells the performers the character of the music and indicates the dynamic and intensity levels at which the performers should enter.

Of critical importance, the initial preparatory gesture also tells the ensemble when to take its "performance" breath. Before the conductor gives the initial preparation, he or she must look directly at the ensemble, then breathe deeply as the preparation motion is given. The importance of eye contact and the initial breath cannot be stressed strongly enough. Eye contact, the conductor's breath, and the preparatory gesture signal the ensemble to breathe before beginning.

REMEMBER: THE DOWNBEAT IS ALWAYS DOWN.

In order to prepare the ensemble for the downbeat, begin by placing the hand about shoulder-high and approximately eight inches to the right of the position for the basic pulse gesture you practiced in Exercise 2-1. For most practical purposes this eight-inch distance will be adequate for the preparation. Come to a complete stop. Then make a slight fishhook toward the left (Diagram 2-2), raising the hand and forearm into position to give the basic pulse.

Diagram 2–2

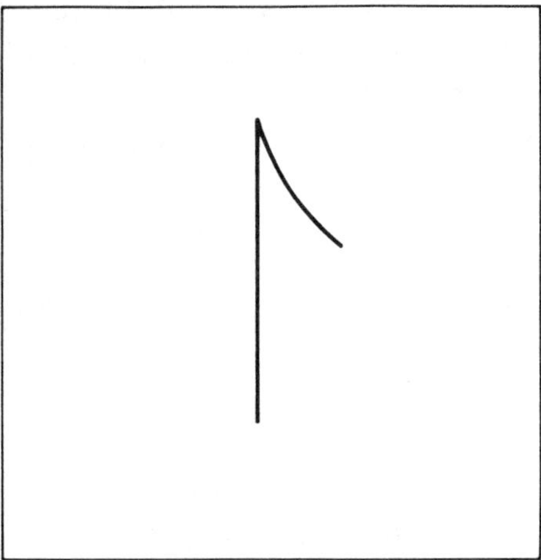

The right hand should now be in position in front of the right shoulder to move straight down toward the toes of the right foot. Do not allow the preparatory gesture to move too far toward the center of the body. If the hand moves beyond this shoulder line, the hand and arm cannot descend straight down toward the toes, but must travel at an angle to the point of ictus. This is not recommended.

Preparatory variation. Some conductors place the hand directly on the basic pulse line before the preparatory gesture is given. The preparatory gesture is then straight up, followed by the basic pulse, which is straight down along the same line.

• Nota Bene

The elbow stays approximately six to eight inches away from the body during the entire preparatory gesture. Do not pull the elbow toward the body during the preparation of the ensuing downbeat. Let the movement of the hand, forearm, and shoulder keep the elbow at an adequate distance from the body.

Exercise 2–2 Practice the preparation, the basic pulse gesture, and its rebound many times. Raise your hand to the correct height and position approximately eight inches to the right of the basic pulse line. Come to a complete stop. Move your eyes over an imaginary ensemble to be sure everyone is watching you. Then take a deep breath and give the preparation at the same time. The gesture should be of medium size. It should be made with a smooth, legato articulation. The hand and arm should flow smoothly through the air. Do not lock your wrist. The gesture should appear to be continuously in motion. Note that as your fingers reach the top of the preparation, the wrist has already begun to descend, thus giving the gesture an appearance of continuously fluid motion. Check your posture. Make the motion with eloquence. Watch your hand make the gesture, then watch yourself in a mirror. Do you like what you see? Does your gesture speak with self-confidence and control? Perform the gesture series slowly many times and concentrate on making an eloquent motion.

• Nota Bene

Dynamics. The size of the conducting gesture is regulated by the dynamics of the music that follows. Just as dynamics is a matter of degree, so is the size of the gesture. Controlling the size is a discipline. A good rule to follow is: "Conduct no more than you have to and only as much as you must." Be certain you do not give large gestures for pianissimo passages. Otherwise, your ensemble will expect gigantic motions for fortissimo passages.

Train your ensemble in the meaning of *your* gestures. Train the group to read your nonverbal gestures accurately and to respond to them in appropriate ways.

Exercise 2-3 Now conduct the above preparatory gesture and basic pulse using various dynamic levels: *p, mp, mf, f*. Continue to evaluate your gestures critically. Be sure the motion is smooth and legato. Consider the size of the gestures you make to indicate the various dynamic levels.

• To the Student

Make these gestures (preparation, downbeat, rebound) in front of a mirror at least three times a day for five minutes each time. Make them slowly and carefully. Watch your hand. Critically evaluate the gestures and what they communicate. Make adjustments where necessary. Discipline yourself to concentrate on making eloquent movements. Check your posture.

Exercise 2-4 You stand before the one thousand-member National Choir at the National Thanksgiving Rally. The lights dim and all eyes are on you. The audience rises. You raise your hand, sweep the ensemble with your eyes, and take a deep breath as you give the preparatory gesture. The downbeat falls, beginning the performance of "Faith of Our Fathers." Reflect on your posture, the grandeur and eloquence of your preparatory gesture, and the sweeping assurance and precision of your downbeat and rebound. How did it feel to have a thousand singers respond to your conducting gesture?

3 Basic Hand Motion/the Four Pattern

The Hand in Motion

Standardized conducting patterns are used to inform the ensemble of its whereabouts in any one given measure. A member of the ensemble should be able to look up and see immediately where he or she should be in that measure on the basis of the pattern given by the conductor. The following is a basic rule of conducting: The gesture for the first pulse of the measure is always down; the gesture for the last pulse of the measure is always up; and, as you will discover in time, what happens between these two gestures is experience.

The structure of the conducting pattern also helps the conductor communicate through the motions she or he makes. The hand in motion can change the music's character, alter articulations, and change dynamics and intensity, as well as maintain or change the tempo of the pulses. Conducting convention defines four different directions for the hand: down, up, to the inside, and to the outside (Diagrams 3-1a and 3-1b).

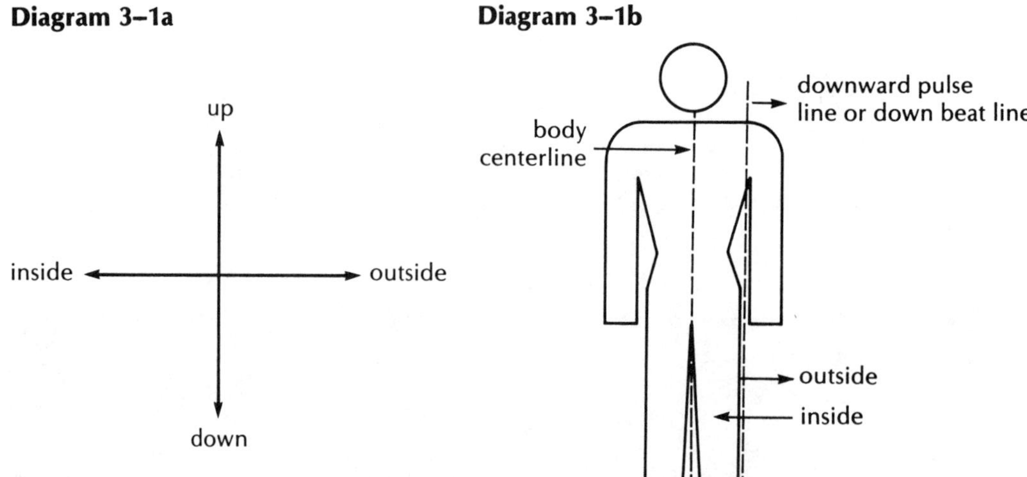

Each pulse has three components: preparation, ictus, and rebound. As noted in Chapter 2, the basic pulse gesture consists of these three components (Diagram 3-2). The hand, after completing the rebound of the downbeat, will then move in one of the four directions, depending on the metric structure of the music. Whichever direction it moves, it is at this point that rebound turns to preparation for the next pulse (Diagram 3-3). This turning point may be angular or rounded, depending on the character of the music to be expressed.

Diagram 3–2

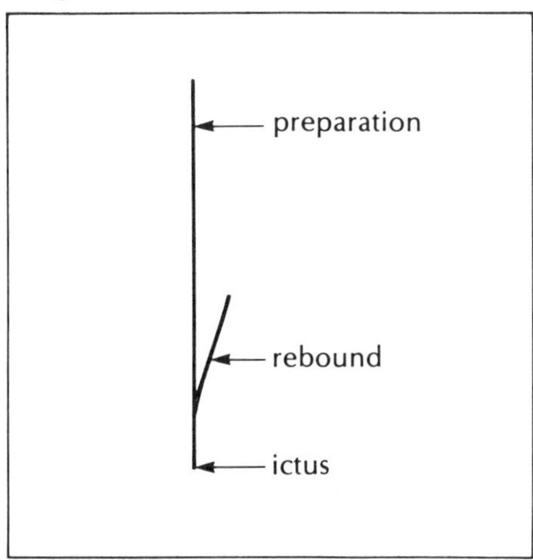

Diagram 3–3

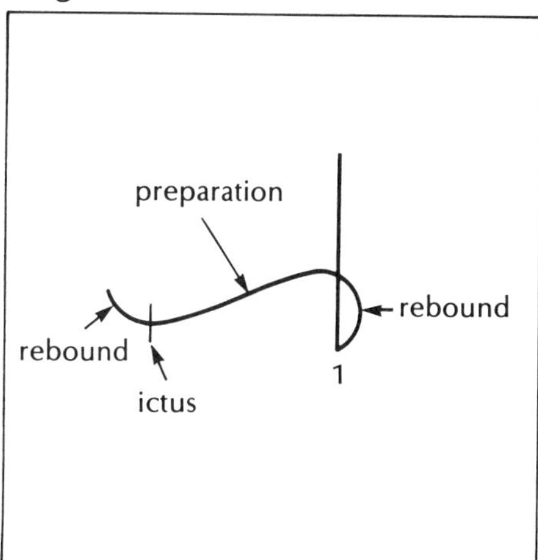

If the pulse moves to the outside, that portion of the gesture which moves the hand in that direction is preparation for the ictus. This motion tells how the pulse will be performed. At the beginning of each preparation the conductor must decide how the next pulse will be attacked (Diagram 3-4).

Diagram 3–4

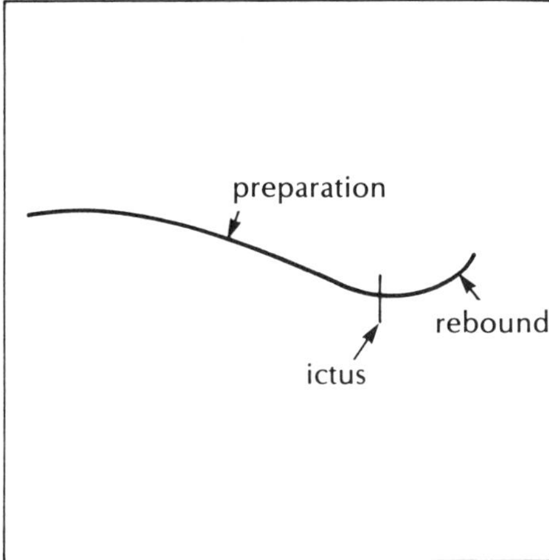

When the hand passes through the ictus it changes directions for the rebound. The rebound usually moves up and away from the preparation for the ictus. This rebound is usually in the character of the pulse it follows. If the pulse is attacked angularly, the rebound will move angularly away from the ictus. If the pulse is approached forcefully but smoothly, the rebound will leave the ictus in the same manner.

When the last pulse of the measure is executed, the preparation of the pulse moves toward the basic pulse line and the rebound carries the hand upward so that it is in position to execute the next downbeat (Diagram 3–5).

Diagram 3–5

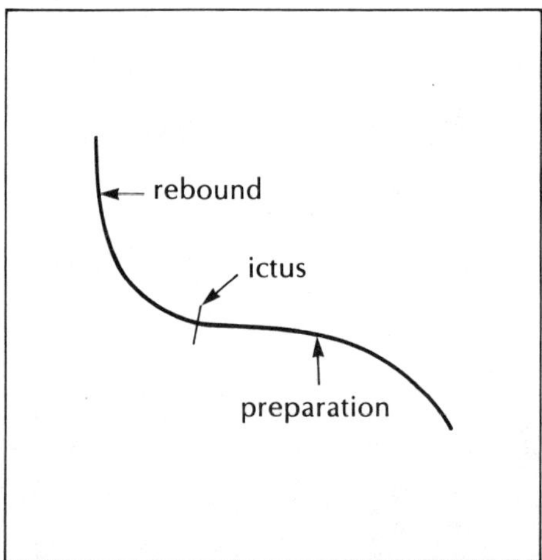

The hand in motion must be flexible and expressive. It must not make extraneous movements which mean nothing. As it moves through the standard conducting patterns, the hand, along with facial expressions and body attitude, must convey the essence of the music to the performers and inspire them to express this essence in an aesthetic manner to an audience.

The Four Pattern

The four pattern begins with the gestures you have already practiced. Following the basic pulse gesture and the rebound, the hand moves toward the inside for pulse 2, then to the outside for pulse 3, and then up for pulse 4 (Diagram 3–6).

Diagram 3–6

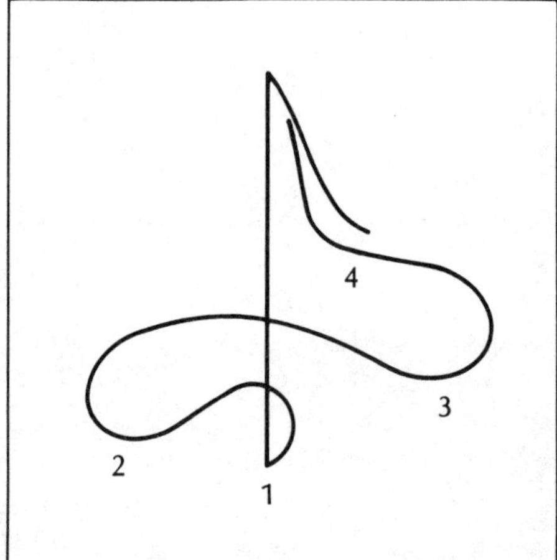

When giving the initial preparatory gesture for the four pattern, place the hand at exactly that point where the ictus of pulse 4 would be. The hand then rises sharply to a position directly in front of the right shoulder, ready to give the downbeat (Diagram 3–7a). Some conductors prefer to place the hand directly in front of the shoulder and raise the hand straight up as a preparatory gesture (Diagram 3–7b).

Diagram 3–7a

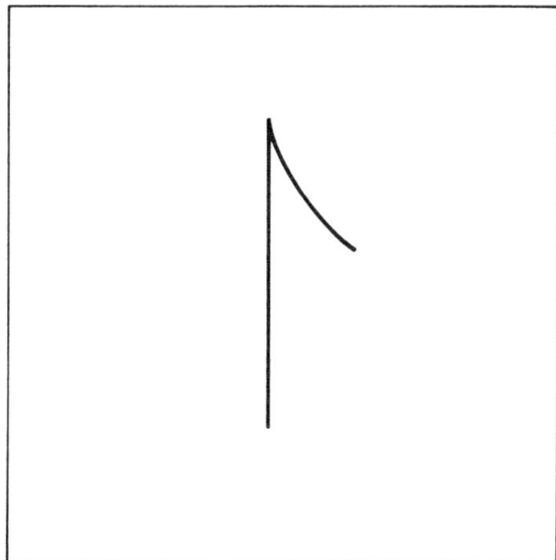

Diagram 3–7b

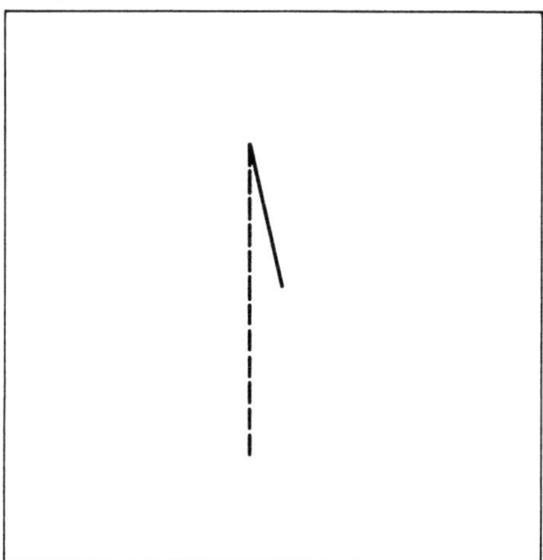

As you practice a legato four pattern, it is important to keep the hand, wrist, and forearm in the same relative position to the body throughout the pattern. The palm of the hand should either be slightly open to the side or down throughout the entire pattern. Do not roll the wrist and/or forearm as you move through the preparatory gestures into pulses 2 and 3. If the palm is open, leave it open; if down, leave it down. Excessive rolling of the wrist and forearm tends to throw the elbow out away from the body. This makes the conductor look like a giant condor ready for flight. Do not flap your arms to the side.

Throughout most of each preparatory gesture the wrist precedes the hand (Figure 3–1). The wrist must remain supple, yet controlled. The sequence of motion follows the wrist as the hand travels to catch up with it, passes it by, and then indicates the ictus with the tip of the fingers. As the fingers define the ictus, the

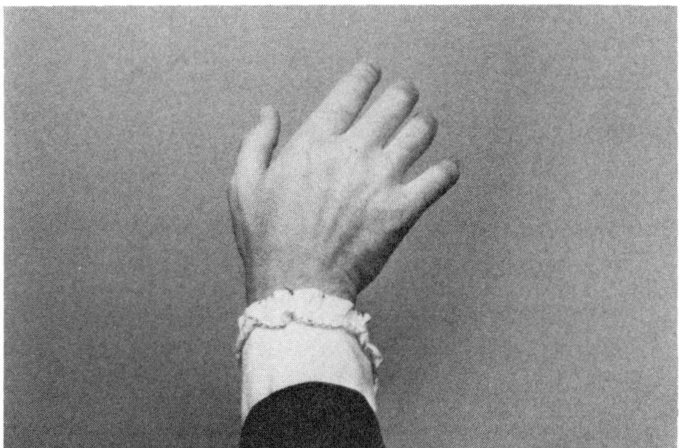

Figure 3–1. Wrist precedes the hand.

wrist moves away in a different direction (rebound), so that the appearance of continuous motion is maintained. During pulses 2, 3, and 4 of this pattern the hand should not drop below the wrist, but should be slightly above it. The hand should not be carried so high, however, that the palm shows fully to the front.

The rebound of each of these pulses tends to be up and away from the direction in which the ictus was approached. The rebound is also in a direction different from the preparation and ictus of the next pulse. For pulse 2 the rebound looks like Diagram 3-8; for pulse 3, like Diagram 3-9; and for pulse 4, like Diagram 3-10. This last rebound brings your hand into position to give the next downbeat.

Diagram 3–8

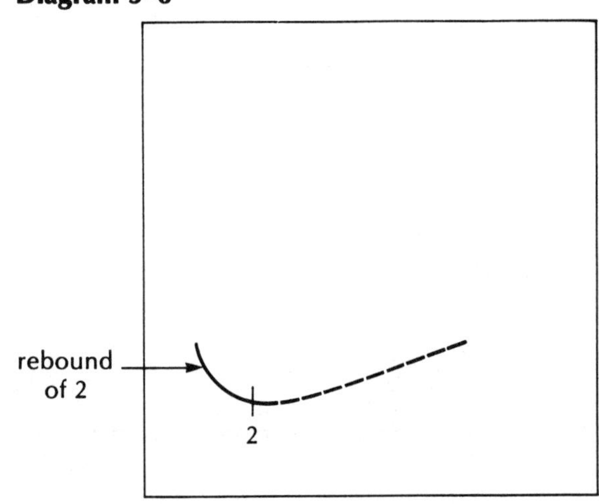

Diagram 3–9

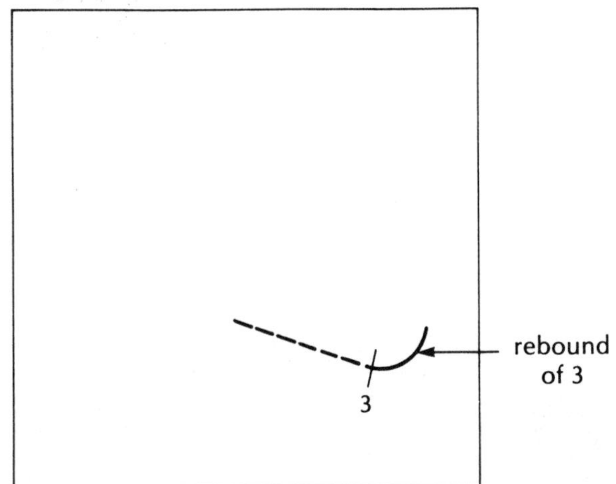

Diagram 3–10

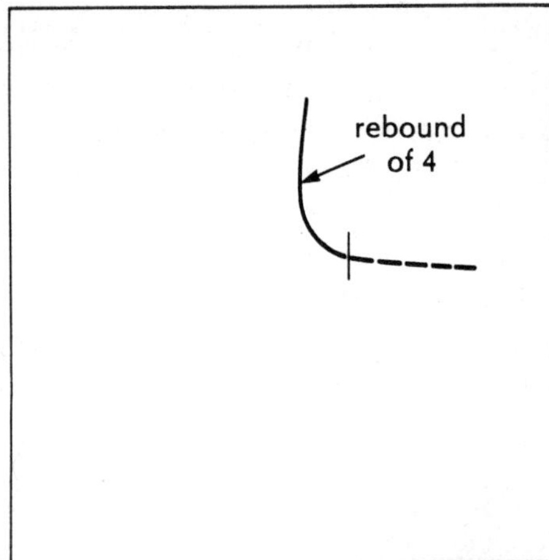

- **To the Student**

Figures 3-2a through 3-2i, showing the entire lateral sequence from the beginning of the preparation for pulse 2 through the rebound of 3, are paired. The figures on the left show the right hand making the gesture. The figures on the right show the same gesture simulated in mirror form. Use these mirror images by propping the book up in front of a mirror, assuming the conducting position being shown in the figure, and then comparing what you see in the mirror with the right-hand mirror image in the book.

Figure 3–2a. Hand position following rebound of pulse 1.

Figure 3–2b. Hand moves to inside; wrist leads hand.

Figure 3–2c. Wrist continues to lead hand.

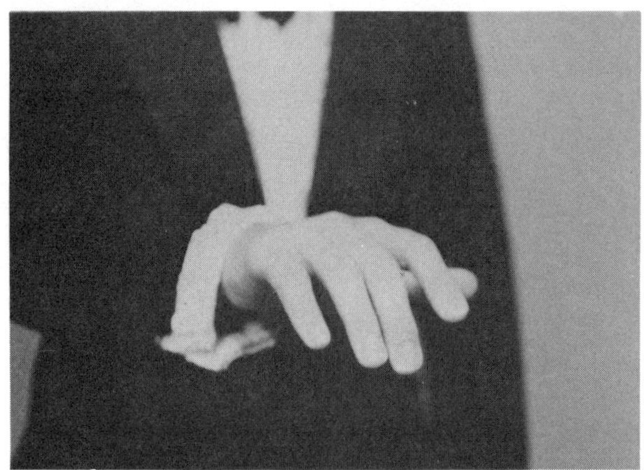

Figure 3–2d. Hand moves parallel with wrist; wrist breaks, fingers define ictus.

Figure 3–2e. Rebound of pulse 2.

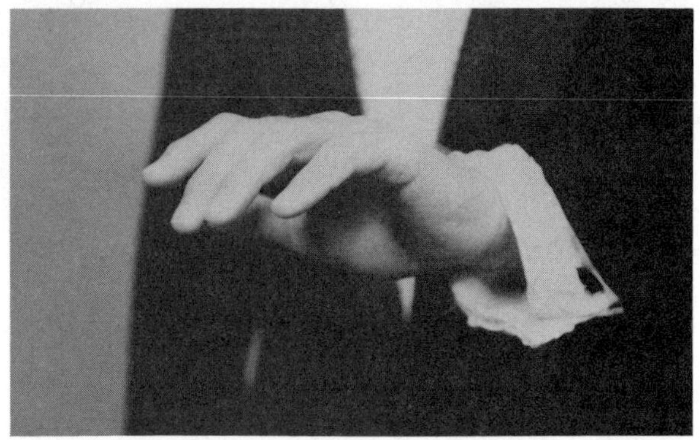

Figure 3–2f. Hand moves to outside; wrist leads hand.

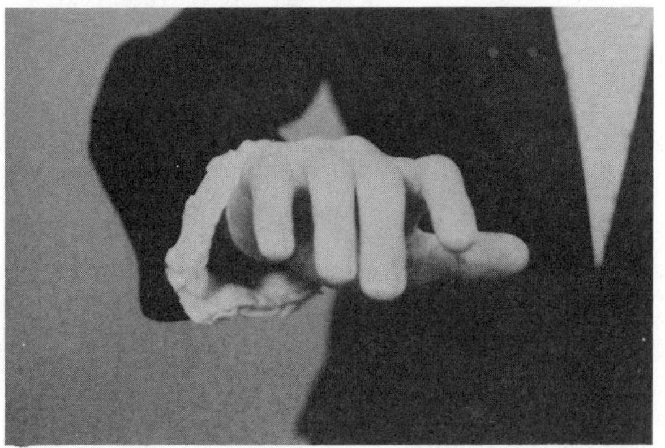

Figure 3–2g. Hand begins to catch up with wrist.

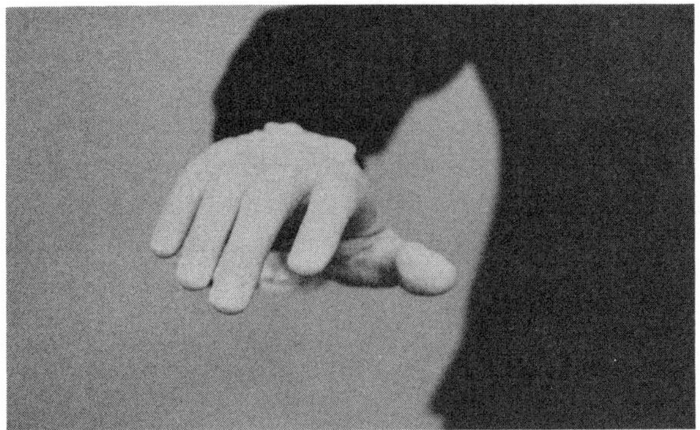
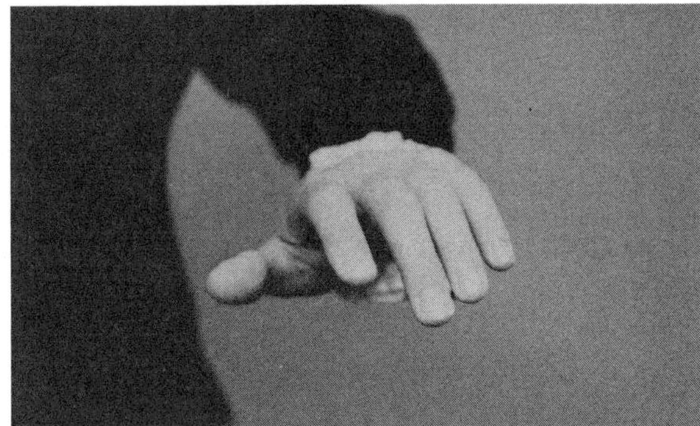

Figure 3–2h. Hand moves parallel to wrist; wrist breaks, fingers define ictus.

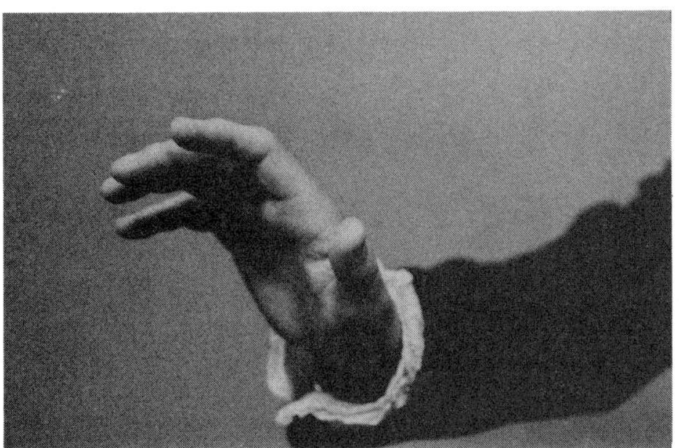

Figure 3–2i. Rebound of pulse 3.

The Planes of Conducting

The planes of conducting may best be illustrated by taping two pieces of string, each approximately two feet long, on a wall as shown in Diagram 3–11. The horizontal string should be approximately mid-waist high. Now stand facing the wall so that the vertical string is opposite your right shoulder. Assume a proper

Diagram 3–11

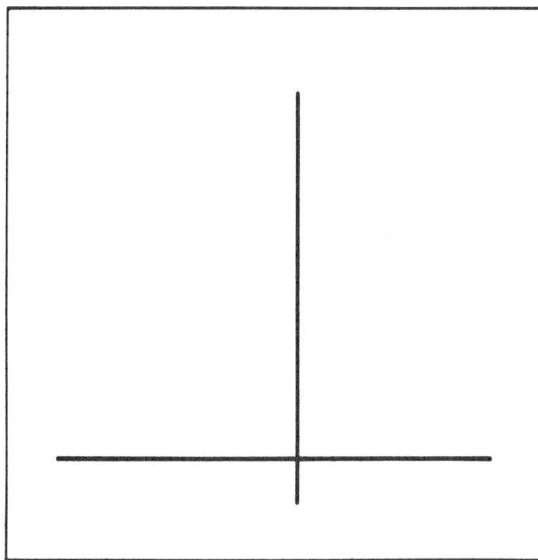

conducting stance so that the tips of your fingers are approximately half an inch from the wall. Conduct a four pattern. Pulse 1 should travel down the vertical line. The ictus for pulses 2 and 3 should be on the horizontal line. Pulse 4 should be executed so that the rebound of 4 travels back up the vertical line. The hand is now in position to execute the next downbeat (Diagram 3-12).

Diagram 3–12

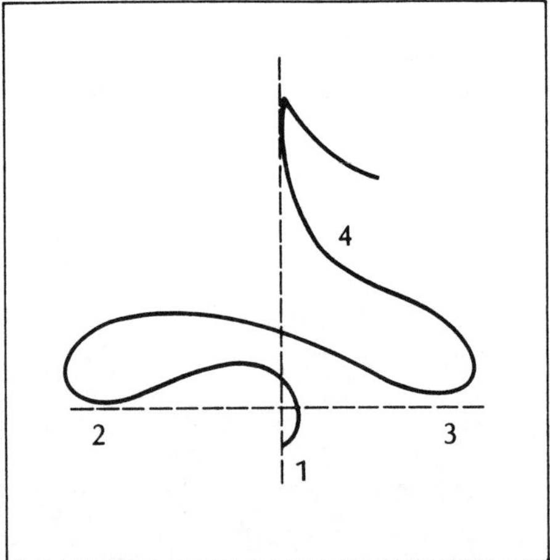

Throughout the entire pattern your fingertips should remain approximately half an inch from the wall. It appears to be natural to pull the hand and fingers away from the wall-plane on pulse 2. This pulling away is *not* recommended. Instead, you should *reach* to keep the hand and fingers along the vertical plane of conducting. As you perform this gesture, note the pull of the muscles in the arm and shoulder. This increased muscle activity conveys strength and sustaining power in the pulse 2 gesture. Pulling pulse 2 toward the body (the easy way to do it) weakens the gesture considerably.

Note that the larger the gesture, the more your body rotates at the hips and the more your right shoulder comes forward for pulse 2. This will allow you to keep the hand within the plane of conducting. However, try to keep the shoulders level. Do not dip the shoulder into pulse 2.

Now step away from the wall. Continue to imagine the wall and the lines of string in front of you. Conduct the pattern along these imaginary lines with the same feeling you had before in the arm, shoulder, and wrist.

• To the Student

If you conduct all pulses along these imaginary planes, you will avoid the in-out conducting danger which results from pulling your elbow toward your body on each rebound. Remember, the elbow stays in front of the body. It is not fixed to a point, but instead moves when necessary along an imaginary line approximately parallel to the diaphragm.

• Nota Bene

There will be times when your gestures will leave the conducting planes. There will be other times when your planes will shift to positions higher or lower, closer or farther away in relation to your body. For the present, leave the planes out and away from the body so that the arm, elbow, and shoulder can move freely. Remember to *reach* for pulse 2 so that the hand stays within the conducting plane. Discipline yourself to keep your gestures within these planes.

The Conducting Focal Point

Some conductors like to focus all motion through a point in the center of the pattern. Their pattern might be represented by Diagram 3-13.

Using this concept forces the conductor to concentrate the gesture in a small area. This tends to cut down on overly flowery gestures. The focal point also helps the ensemble focus its attention in the same small area. There are times, however, when the hand must leave the focal point, and slavish use of this concept may then be detrimental.

Some conductors may execute a pattern in which all pulses are delineated on the downbeat line (Diagram 3-14). This is extremely confusing to musicians who need your help in knowing exactly where they are in each measure.

Diagram 3–13

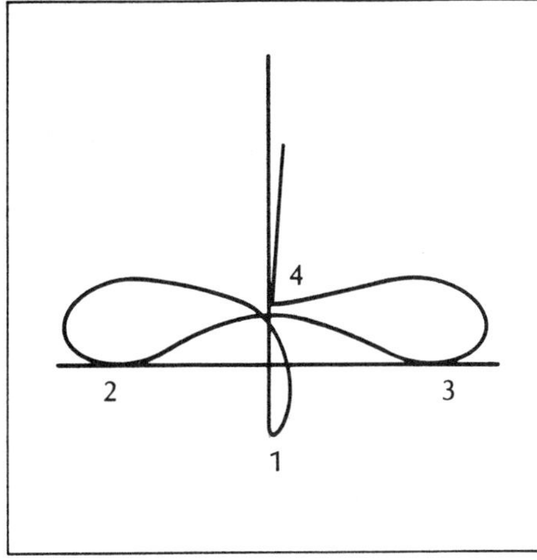

Diagram 3–14

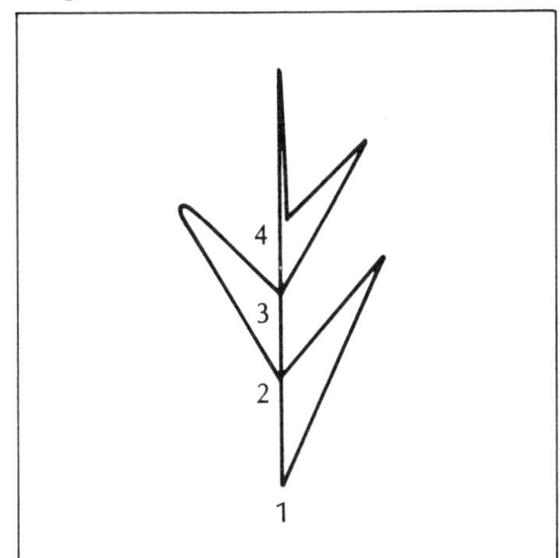

In this pattern the rebound of 1, which is generally too high and not straight up, puts the hand in a position where the ictus for 2 could occur on the vertical downbeat line. If the rebound is too high and the gesture into 2 is basically more down than along the horizontal plane, the gesture could be mistaken for another downbeat. Following this pattern of conducting, it is possible to give four downbeats in a measure of four.

This writer once observed a very famous choral conductor rehearsing a group of high school students in a very difficult work. The rehearsal collapsed several times until, in utter frustration and exasperation, the conductor shouted, "What's the matter with you? Can't you follow me?" Although the students sat with downcast eyes, not daring to oppose this conductor, the answer was plainly "No." In his growing frustration the conductor flailed away, his beat pattern getting larger and larger and the rebounds bounding higher and higher until every beat in the measure was virtually a downbeat. It was no wonder the students could not follow him. They needed a very clear, carefully delineated pulse pattern and nothing more.

REMEMBER: EACH MEASURE SHOULD HAVE ONE DOWNWARD MOTION AND ONE UPWARD MOTION ALONG THE VERTICAL PLANE. ALL OTHER GESTURES SHOULD CLEARLY TAKE PLACE ELSEWHERE.

Exercise 3-1 Tape a string on a wall parallel to the ground approximately mid-waist high. Tape another string perpendicular to the ground so that it crosses the horizontal string. Now raise your conducting hand into a comfortable position for the preparatory pulse and then move your body so that your fingertips are just barely off the wall and your right shoulder is opposite the vertical string. Conduct the four pattern so that your fingers remain very close to the wall. Pulses 1 and 4 follow the vertical string; pulses 2 and 3, the horizontal string. Use your shoulder and wrist to keep pulse 2 close to the wall along the string.

Exercise 3-2 Step away from the wall. Conduct the four pattern. Imagine the position of the strings on the wall. Be sure pulses 2 and 3 are parallel to and out in front of the body along the line in the horizontal plane.

Exercise 3-3 Practice moving the hand laterally and vertically from the wrist. Leaving the forearm still, move the hand from side to side, then up and down. During these exercises keep the palm down so that you experience both the vertical and lateral movement of the wrist.

• To the Student

As you practice these gestures, check yourself on the following points:

1. When moving the hand toward the ictus of 2, leave the elbow in front of the body. Don't pull the elbow, forearm, and hand toward the body. This pulling tends to shorten the 2 gesture, thereby weakening the gesture considerably. It also pulls the ictus of 2 "off the line" in the horizontal plane of conducting. Leave the elbow on a line parallel to the ground out in front of the body.

2. Rolling the wrist and forearm toward the body weakens the gesture considerably. If you conduct with the palm slightly open, rolling the forearm on pulse 2 leaves the palm facing the body, so that only the back of the hand is visible to the ensemble. The back of the hand is nonexpressive. If you conduct with palm down, pulling the forearm pulls the thumb toward the body, leaving only the exposed side of the forearm and the little-finger side of the hand visible to the ensemble. You cannot be very expressive with the side of your hand. If you try to be expressive in this position by using your fingers to shade a phrase or express a

nuance or even to give a release, you will discover that approximately half your ensemble cannot see the gesture. Your hand must remain out in front of the body in full view of the entire ensemble at all times.

• Nota Bene

The gestures you are practicing now are not particularly expressive; in fact, they are neutral. Your motions should be neither too large nor too small, but should be moderate in size. You should practice at a moderate tempo or a bit slower so that you have a chance to study what you are doing. Look at yourself in the mirror. Do you like what you see? If you are worried about being uncomfortable, remember that you may not be comfortable until your shoulder, arm, and back muscles are conditioned and strengthened enough to make these gestures over and over again. Some of the gestures will feel awkward. You must make them repeatedly until they become second nature. Just picking up your arm and hand and putting it into a good conducting position to begin your first preparatory movement may feel awkward until you have done it perhaps several hundred times.

It should be noted again that later on there will be times when you leave the planes of conducting to make certain gestures. You will also move your fingers, hand, and arm differently than is now being prescribed in order to be musically expressive. What you are learning now is fundamental: a clean, clear conducting gesture that will provide you forever with a point of return when absolute clarity is demanded in either rehearsal or performance. You cannot go wrong if you discipline yourself to give a basic, clean conducting gesture.

4 Releases and Cues

The Release Gesture I (on Pulse 4)

The purpose of the release gesture is to inform the ensemble to stop producing sound at designated places, either within the music or at the end of the work. Because of the importance of the release, it should have a specific motion all its own, i.e., no other gesture should resemble it.

A number of releases are effective, and all should be within the vocabulary of the conductor. The particular gesture to be discussed here is unique and corresponds to the release conductors use with a baton. It is a clean, clear, well-prepared gesture that will look like no other motion in your conducting vocabulary. Other types of releases are discussed in Chapter 11.

Release on Pulse 4

A release is executed on pulse 4 when a rest occurs on that pulse or when there is a marked breath (') or an implied breath (because of the text) on the pulse (Example 4-1). If the music continues after the breath, the hand must be in position after the release on pulse 4 to continue with the downbeat on 1.

Example 4-1:

The pattern indicating the release (R) on pulse 4 is given in Diagram 4-1. Note that after pulse 3 the rebound is higher than usual. The hand moves to approximately eye level for the ictus of pulse 4. The fact that you are doing something different tells the ensemble to watch and be alert. The release gesture is marked with a preparatory curl or loop. It is the loop that makes this particular release gesture unique. The loop moves slightly to the left of the basic pulse line so that when the release is made on 4, the hand is in exact position to drop straight down for the downbeat along the vertical pulse line.

Diagram 4–1

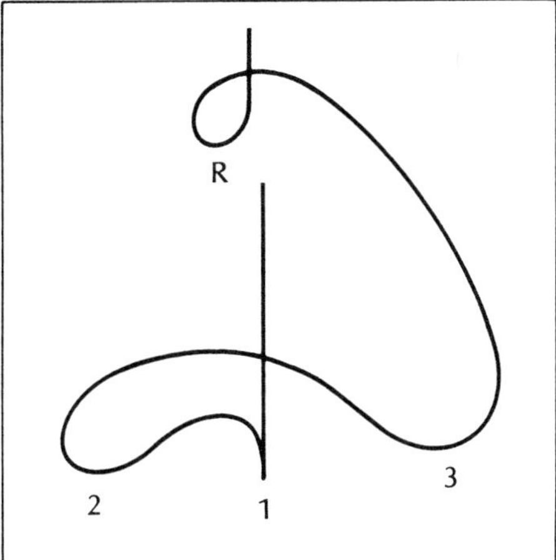

A common error is executing the release too far to the outside (Diagram 4-2). This release puts the hand completely out of position to execute the downbeat for the next measure. Care must thus be taken to ensure that the hand is in an appropriate position for the downbeat following a release on pulse 4.

Diagram 4–2

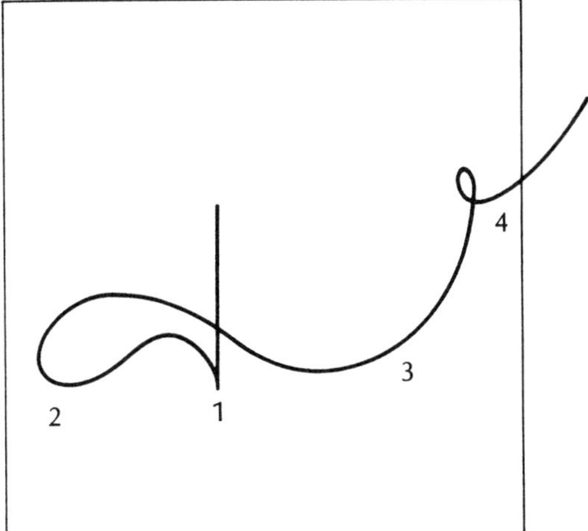

Many conductors like to touch their thumb and forefinger lightly together to show the moment of release explicitly. The thumb and middle finger may also be used. This thumb-forefinger release can be done easily within the loop release gesture shown in Diagram 4–1, thus adding another visual element to the release. The use of this thumb-forefinger release gesture is recommended in conjunction with the loop.

It should be noted, however, that when using a baton, this thumb-forefinger release is impossible. Practice making releases with a baton utilizing the loop as the preparatory gesture.

Exercise 4–1 Coordinate the loop and the thumb-forefinger release. Hold the forearm still and execute the loop with just the wrist. At the moment of release, gently squeeze the thumb and either the forefinger or middle finger together. For now, separate the finger and thumb immediately after the release.

Exercise 4–2 Make a larger motion into the release gesture on 4, using elbow and forearm to move the wrist and hand into place just to the left of the basic pulse line in preparation for the release (Diagram 4–3). As the release is given, be sure the hand travels straight up into position in front of the right shoulder in preparation for the downbeat.

Diagram 4–3

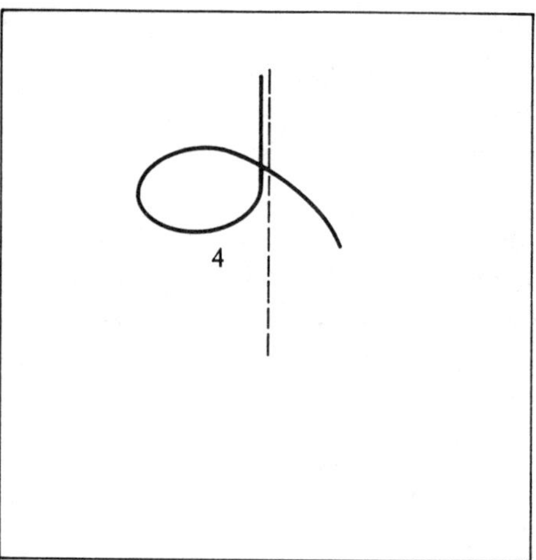

The Release Gesture II (The Final Whole Note)

Two basic techniques can be used for the release if the final note of the work is a whole note. The first, and perhaps the most common, is the melded pulse gesture. The conducting hand gives the downbeat, then melds—or combines—all other pulses of the measure into a single movement until the preparation for the release (Diagram 4–4).

After the downbeat and rebound, the hand and forearm begin a diagonal movement upward slightly to the right. To signify that the music is to continue and that the performers are to continue pouring energy into the sound, the hand and forearm must continue to move throughout the gesture.

DO NOT STOP THE HAND AND ARM UNTIL AFTER THE RELEASE.

Diagram 4–4

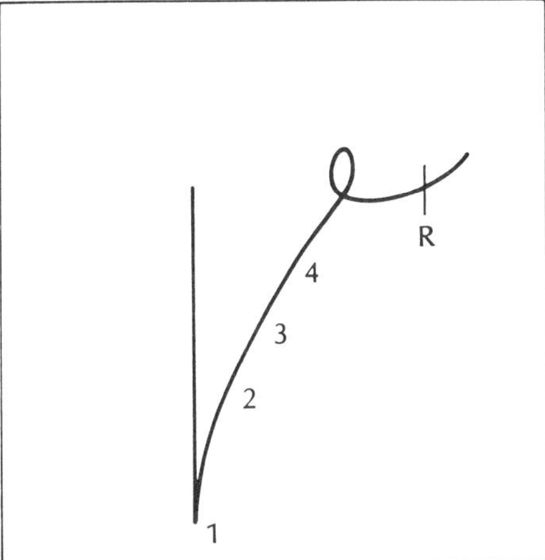

Count the melded pulses in your head. Count "two, three, four" in the regular tempo and then give the release on the next pulse. The actual release should occur at approximately eye level.

The danger in this melded beat gesture is moving the hand too far to the right. Again you must consider what it looks like to the audience to be overextended to the side. Timing the gesture so your hand is in the correct position at the moment of release is absolutely essential.

Some conductors, instead of moving the hand diagonally, move the hand straight up for the melded release gesture. An advantage of this variation is that it ensures that the hand will not be extended too far to the right at the moment of release. However, timing is again important to be sure the release is not given too high. The release should be given at approximately eye level.

Some conductors end a piece by continuing the four pattern, then giving a release to the outside (Diagram 4-5). Note that as pulse 4 is given, the hand begins the preparation of the loop by moving slightly away from the basic pulse line, and the release is made slightly to the right of this line. Overextension to the right is also the primary danger in this release gesture. The release should, again, be given at approximately eye level.

Diagram 4–5

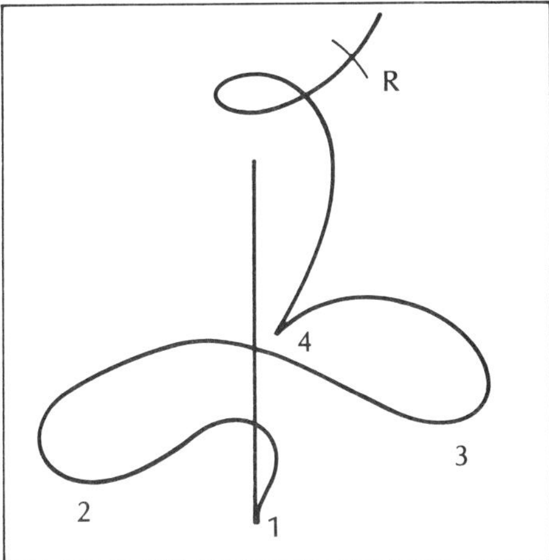

• Nota Bene

Because the hand has farther to travel within the preparatory loop, it speeds up. The loop and the speeding up warn the ensemble that a release is coming. The fingers mark the exact moment of the release pulse, and the hand comes to a complete stop after a small rebound. For the final release gesture the thumb and forefinger will often stay together until after the rebound.

All releases must be in the character of the music. A soft, gentle ending to a work demands a soft, gentle release.

Release Variations

Many conductors conduct with thumb and forefinger together throughout portions of a work (Figure 4-1). Thus, it is impossible to put the thumb and forefinger together to indicate the release. In this instance the release may be indicated by separating the thumb and forefinger at its exact moment and opening the palm to the ensemble. The gesture must be made in front of the body so that it is visible to the entire ensemble.

Figure 4–1. Thumb and forefinger together.

Another release gesture, often used by conductors of instrumental ensembles, is the inside loop release. Instead of the hand moving to the outside following the release gesture, the direction of the release loop moves the hand toward the inside (Diagram 4-6). This gesture prohibits the release from being given too far to the outside.

Diagram 4–6

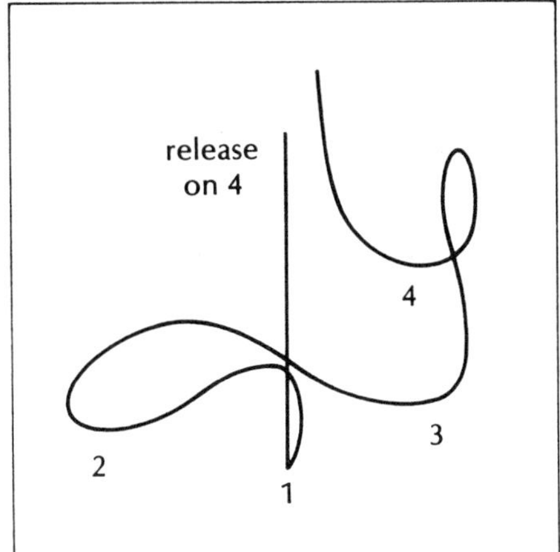

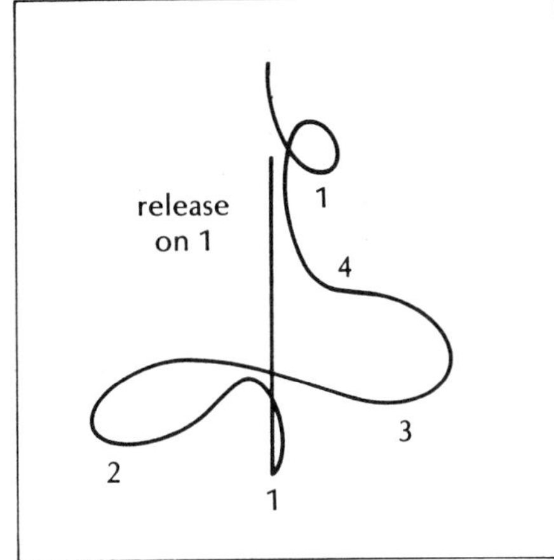

• To the Student

The musical exercises in this book have been melodically conceived. They are diatonic and uncomplicated. These exercises provide you with basic conducting materials that you can immediately grasp. Instead of spending hours learning complicated music, spend your time practicing the conducting motions. Learn the melodies as quickly as possible so that you can concentrate on the conducting gestures involved. Each exercise is designed to help you solve a conducting problem. Tempo and dynamic markings are not given. Practice each exercise at various tempos and dynamic levels. Sing and conduct each line musically; concentrate on getting the physical gesture to express your innate musicality.

Conduct Exercises 4-3 and 4-4. Sing them on a neutral syllable of your choosing. Conduct and sing each melody smoothly and eloquently. Give a release for each rest and breath mark in the examples. Check your posture before beginning each exercise. Transpose the melodies to a comfortable range if necessary.

Exercise 4-3

Exercise 4-4

Supplementary Conducting Exercises: Release on 4

HAYDN: Gloria in Excelsis (*Harmoniemesse*)

MOZART: Ave Verum Corpus

Cor - pus na - tum de Ma - ri - a Vir - gi - ne:
bless - ing, Tune my heart to grate - ful, grate - ful lays;
Cor - pus na - tum de Ma - ri - a Vir - gi - ne:
bless - ing, Tune my heart to grate - ful, grate - ful lays;

Cueing I (Basic Gesture)

The cue is an invitation for the ensemble, or a portion of it, to perform. Many different gestures may indicate this invitation, from a secretive glance to an emphatically raised fist. Whatever gesture is used, it must always be in the character of the music.

The cue gesture discussed here is executed within the basic conducting pattern with the conducting hand. The hand position which you have carefully practiced will remain basically the same. Only the relative height of the pattern will change.

As with all gestures, the cueing gesture must be prepared. If you cue the entire ensemble, your eyes should sweep the ensemble before the cue is given. If you cue a particular section, your eyes should move to that section at least one full pulse before the gesture is given. The importance of this eye contact cannot be stressed strongly enough. Pre-preparation warns the performers in advance that something important is about to happen. When an ensemble misses an important entrance because you fail to look up in advance and prepare it for the entrance, you will know what is meant by the importance of good eye contact. To look up late and scowl at the errant section after it has missed its entrance is to blame the victim.

• Nota Bene

It is possible to cue with just the eyes and head by looking in advance at the section and then giving an invitational nod with the head on the desired pulse of entrance. It is recommended, however, that you immediately develop hand gestures for cueing, since head nodding will be of limited use. The hand cue can be much stronger than the head cue.

The Cue Gesture

When you are making a cue on any pulse, your hand will leave the horizontal plane and move to approximately eye level. The ensemble thus has the benefit of both hand and eye in the cueing gesture. Your hand should not necessarily cover your face or eyes when you are executing the cue; it is better to look directly and without obstruction at the section of the ensemble being cued.

Cue on 1: Four Pattern

If the cue occurs on pulse 1 of the four pattern, the downbeat will be shortened so that the ictus comes at eye level (Diagram 4-7). The eyes and ictus are thus focused on the section receiving the cue.

As soon as the shortened rebound is completed, the hand moves back toward the planes of conducting, so that pulses 2, 3, and 4 occur in normal position within the planes.

Diagram 4–7

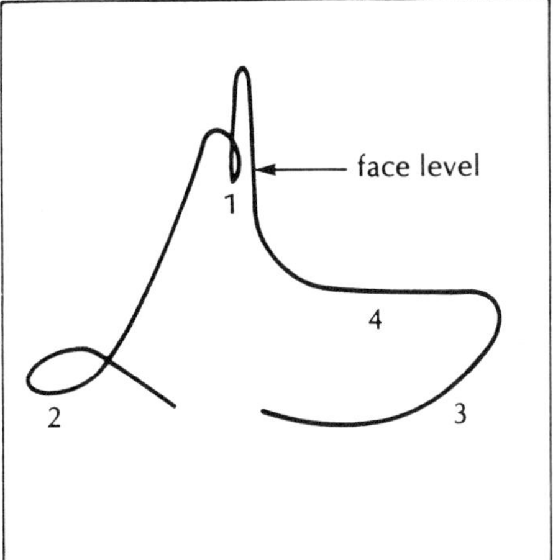

Exercise 4–5 Conduct the following melody, executing a cue after each rest.

Cue on 2: Four Pattern

When cueing on pulse 2, the ictus of 2 is raised to eye level. The rebound of pulse 1 must be higher so that the hand does not travel diagonally to execute the ictus of pulse 2. The hand moves laterally to the ictus of the cue (Diagram 4–8). Remember that eye contact with the ensemble should precede the cue itself. The hand returns to the netural pattern as soon as the cue is delivered.

Diagram 4–8

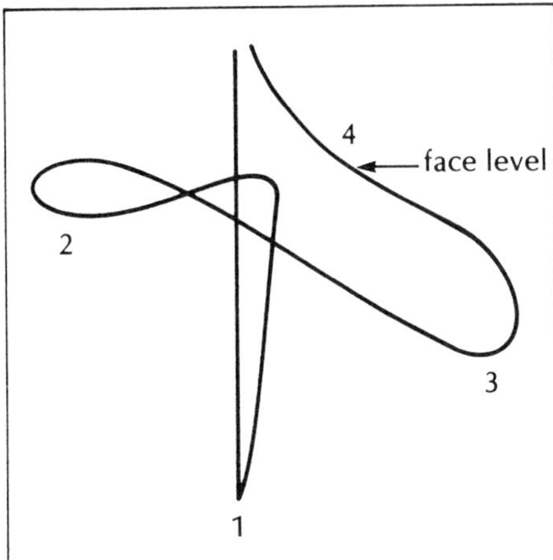

Exercise 4-6 Conduct the following melody, executing a cue after each rest. Disregard the release on 1. Concentrate on moving your eyes to an imaginary section of an ensemble before the cue is given.

Cue on 3: Four Pattern

When cueing on pulse 3, the rebound of 2 will be higher so that the hand moves laterally into pulse 3 (Diagram 4-9a). The rebound of pulse 3 should be short. The ictus of 4 may either drop below the preparation for 3 (Diagram 4-9a) or, by shortening of the preparation into 4, remain above the entire preparation of pulse 3 (Diagram 4-9b).

Diagram 4–9a

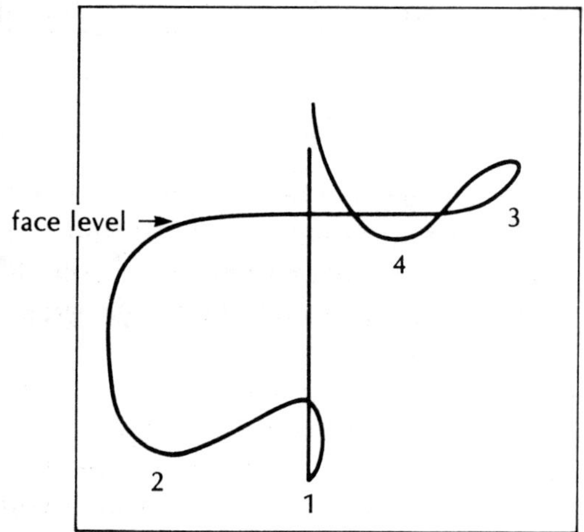

Diagram 4–9b

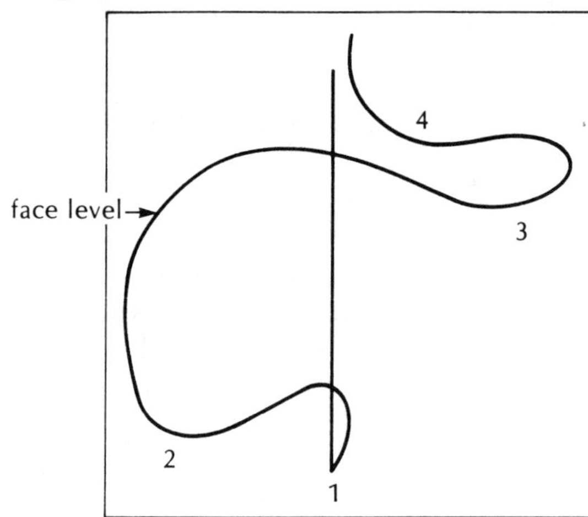

Exercise 4-7 Conduct the following melody, executing a cue after each rest. Disregard the release on 2. Concentrate on moving your hand laterally into the cue at eye level.

Cue on 4: Four Pattern

When cueing on pulse 4, the rebound for 3 moves upward. The ictus for the cue on pulse 4 is approximately at eye level, followed by a short rebound (Diagram 4-10). This short rebound places the hand in position to execute the following downbeat.

Diagram 4–10

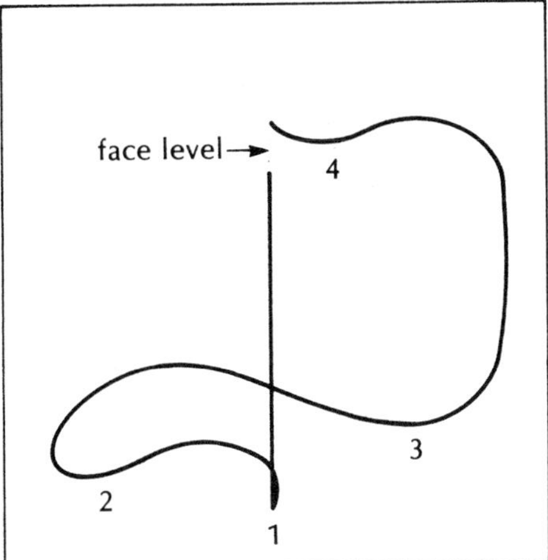

Exercise 4-8 Conduct the following melody, executing a cue after each rest. Disregard the release on pulse 3. Concentrate on giving a clear, precise cue to each imaginary section.

• Nota Bene

The cue must always be in the character of the music. If the ensemble is to enter vigorously, the cue must be executed vigorously and pointedly. If the entrance is soft and legato, the cue must portray this softness and smoothness, yet be unmistakably precise. Note that the rebound immediately preceding the cue moves in an *upward* direction.

A diagonally moving cue is weak and ineffective. If the preparation for a cue on pulse 3 begins too low and moves diagonally across the body rather than laterally, the cue will look awkward and lack strength and positiveness (Diagram 4-11).

It is permissible to tap the cue ictus slightly with the finger(s) in which you place the responsibility for showing the ictus. The finger(s) may thus move slightly to show the exact point of the ictus.

Diagram 4–11

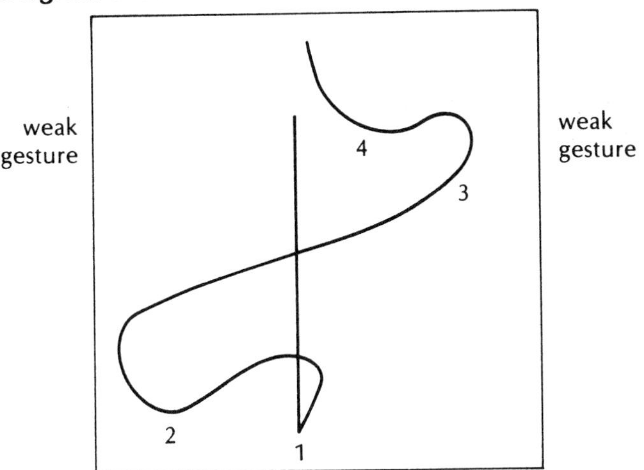

Developing Right-Hand Independence

Although there are times when the left hand will mirror the right hand,* the left hand often indicates something totally different. Each hand must become completely independent of the other. Gestures in the right hand should not affect certain motions in the left hand. Patterns which you "teach" your right hand must become automatic, secure against all interruptions, shifts of concentration, and impeding physical movement. Your right hand must be able to conduct a correct, steady pattern while your mind concentrates on something else.

Exercises 4-9 through 4-11 will help you develop an "automatic" right hand. The physical gestures must be well learned and secure before you begin these exercises. If the patterns are not secure, precision, visual effectiveness, and direction will quickly deteriorate when the motion is challenged by a countermotion. New patterns learned later should also be subjected to these same exercises.

Exercise 4-9 Begin conducting the four pattern. Concentrate on the coordination of your body, arm, wrist, and hand. For ten seconds, while continuing to conduct, think of anything that will take your mind totally off the conducting gesture. After approximately ten seconds, again concentrate on the conducting pattern. Is the gesture the same as when you mentally left it? Try this exercise several times. When you feel quite successful at keeping the pattern intact, gradually increase the length of time you concentrate on other matters from ten seconds to thirty seconds.

Exercise 4-10 Begin conducting the four pattern. Concentrate on the coordination of your body, arm, wrist, and hand. Then, while continuing to conduct, expressively read aloud a paragraph from a book. Do not read metrically in coordination with your hand movement. Upon completion of the paragraph, concentrate again on the conducting pattern. Is the gesture the same as when you began reading? Try this exercise several times. As you become more secure, increase the length of the selection you read.

Exercise 4-11 Conduct the four pattern as you walk. Keep the pulse constant. Now vary the speed of your walking by small amounts. Be sure these slight speed changes do not coincide with the subdivisions of the pulse pattern you are conducting. Speed up, then slow down. Concentrate on your walking, not on your conducting. Remember to keep the tempo of the pulse pattern in your hand constant throughout the exercise.

Left-Hand Cues

The left hand can be helpful in giving releases and cues. Often the left hand will give the release or cue while the right hand continues to conduct the pattern. At

* Most conducting texts assail the use of the mirror gesture in which left and right hands do exactly the same thing. Many conductors, however, use mirroring extensively. A two-handed gesture may add power, grandeur, and stature to the movement, as well as contribute to better ensemble precision, eye contact, and control. Excessive mirroring, however, loses its effectiveness and is simply a waste of the conductor's energy.

other times the left hand mirrors what the right hand does, with both hands giving the release or cue simultaneously.

Once the left hand becomes independent, the problem is not how to make the gesture but what to do with the hand once the gesture is completed. Should the hand stay in the pattern? If it does, for how long? What happens when it leaves the pattern?

There are two places of neutrality for the inactive left hand, either down at your side or folded unobtrusively across the abdomen. The hand should *not* be left bobbing in midair if it no longer serves an active musical function. After the left hand has participated in the gesture and is no longer needed, it should be dropped to the side or folded across the abdomen at the most convenient time.

As mentioned above, the left hand can be used effectively for cueing as the right hand continues to conduct the pulse pattern. Cues by the left hand may consist of pointing emphatically at a particular section or even raising a fist when the most bombastic of entrances is desired.

More subtly, the left hand should rise from its position of neutrality to approximately eye level. The wrist and hand are then used to indicate the exact moment of pulse-entrance by tapping the pulse (Diagram 4-12). This type of cue gesture should be executed with the palm down. It should be precisely directed at the section intended. Eye contact should precede the left-hand cue gesture. Following the cue the left hand should be moved to a neutral position as unobtrusively as possible.

Diagram 4–12

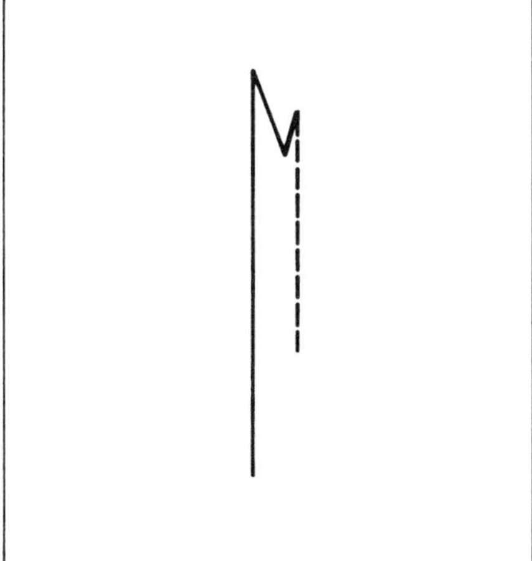

Exercise 4-12 Raise the left hand and execute a cue gesture several times. Be sure the motion is smooth, precise, and eloquent. Eye contact with an imaginary section should precede the actual gesture. Then count aloud a pulse pattern and give cues on various pulses.

Exercise 4-13 Conduct the four pattern with the right hand. With the left hand execute cues on various pulses of the pattern.

• To the Student

Remember: The cue is an invitation to perform. As you study your cue gesture in the mirror, ask yourself the following questions:

1. Is the gesture truly an invitation to perform?
2. Does the cue command authority and respect, even if it is soft and delicate?
3. Is the cue precisely executed?
4. Is there ample preparation for the cue?
5. Does eye contact precede the cue? The importance of eye contact with the section to be cued cannot be stressed strongly enough.

Mirror Cues

There are times when both the left and right hands will give a cue to the same section on the same pulse. The mirror cue, in which both hands give identical cues, can be effective when added eye contact, attention, and precision are demanded of the performers.

On the pulse before the cue, raise the left hand to a position of approximately eye level. The left hand will then execute exactly the same cue as the right hand. For a cue on pulse 1, the left hand portion of the cue will look like Diagram 4–12. For a cue on pulse 2 or 4 of the four pattern, the cue will move to the inside (Diagram 4–13). Care must be taken that the hands do not come together or overlap when giving mirror cues on pulse 2 or 4. Again, eye contact is extremely important. Look directly at the section to be cued.

Diagram 4–13

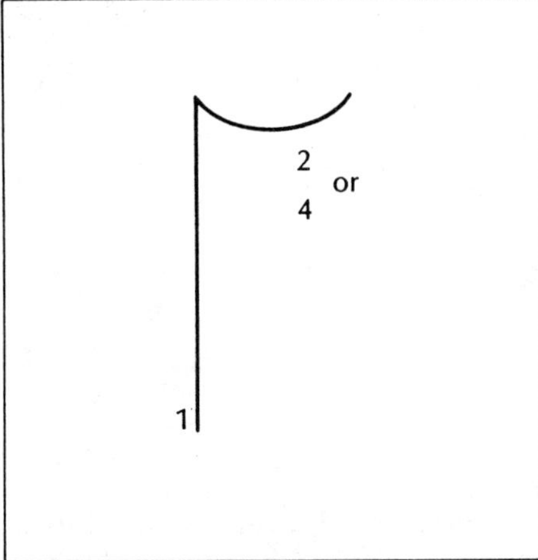

For a cue on pulse 3, the mirror cue by the left hand will move to the outside (Diagram 4-14).

Diagram 4–14

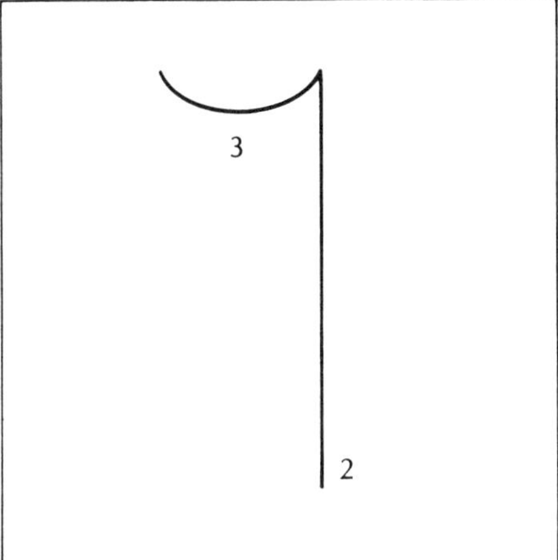

The mirror cue may also be used effectively when two sections enter at the same time. If the sections are separated spatially, the left hand may be directed at the section to the left and the right hand at the section to the right. Just before the cue, sweep both sections, establishing eye contact, even for a brief moment. The ictus of the cues should occur at eye level.

• Nota Bene

Following mirror cues on pulse 1, 2, or 4, the left hand is in position to move immediately to a neutral location. Because the cue on pulse 3 moves to the outside, many conductors will continue moving the left hand in the conducting pattern through pulse 4 into the downbeat. At this point the hand can be moved unobtrusively to a neutral position.

Exercise 4-14 Alternate cues and releases on pulses 1 and 3, then 2 and 4 of the four pattern. Use the left hand both independently and in mirror fashion. Include cues to the left and right sides of the ensemble.

Exercise 4-15 Conduct Exercises 4-5 to 4-8 using left-hand cues when appropriate.

Supplementary Conducting Exercises: Cueing

BRAHMS: Wondrous cool, thou woodland quiet

SOPRANO
dim.
thee, He will quick - en thee,
ALTO
dim.
thee, He will quick - en thee,
TENOR
dim.
p
thee, He will quick - en thee, Shouldst thou,
BASS
dim.
He will quick - en thee,
dim.
dim.
p
p
He, watch - ing o - ver Is - ra - el,
p
He, watch - ing o - ver Is - ra -
walk - ing in grief, lan - guish;
p
He, watch - ing

HANDEL: Hallelujah, Amen (*Judas Maccabaeus*)

VICTORIA: Ave Maria

PRAETORIUS/KURT STONE: Psallite

5 Score Preparation/ Left-Hand Releases

Studying the Score

To know a musical score means to know what the composition will sound like as a finished product. The conductor must know the music thoroughly *before* rehearsing it with an ensemble. Some conductors have the capacity to hear the entire score mentally. Others may play the score at the keyboard. Once the pitches are securely learned, these conductors develop a mental image of the music, combining pitches, ensemble timbre, text, texture, and appropriate style characteristics.

As you study the score you must determine where performance problems will occur. These problems normally take two forms. Problems in the technique of conducting, i.e., the technical aspect of the nonverbal communicative gesture, must be solved *before* rehearsals even begin. If there are meter changes, tempo changes, or complex cueing and release sequences in the music, you must practice the appropriate gestures until they can be made instinctively. You must be able to give the appropriate conducting gesture automatically when rehearsals begin. The rehearsal is not the place to decide which gesture you should use.

The second set of problems which you must anticipate are those the ensemble may experience. These problems may involve difficult intervals in various voice parts, intonation dangers, diction problems, and articulation and interpretation of the text. You must be prepared to deal with any problems which the ensemble may have in performing the score. Rehearsal efficiency will be greatly enhanced if you can anticipate and solve problems before they occur.

Because music is created within a historical-political-economic context, you should also research the composer and the historical times which spawned the music. Knowing when and why a particular work came into existence within a historical framework helps you understand the music. Biographical dictionaries, biographies, autobiographies, and history books should be consulted to find information about the composer, the particular work in question, and the historical climate in which the work was composed.

Marking the Score

Each conductor develops his or her own techniques for preparing the score. The marks which are already in the score and those which you place there are much like traffic signs. These signs should be highlighted so that you can see them at a glance. There are stop signs (𝄐, ||, |▌), regulatory signs (staccato, accents), speed signs (*andante, rit., accel.*), and warning signs which you may place at difficult passages or at page turns. As a matter of personal preference some conductors like to color-code these signs.

The following discussion on score marking is by no means exhaustive. It is the bare minimum of what should be done with each score you conduct. As you gain experience as a conductor and musician, your score marking will become more precise. Marking the score as you study it provides you with an instant reminder of the decisions you have made about how the music is to be performed. If you own the score, mark these reminders in red or some other color so that they stand out boldly. If the score is borrowed, markings should be *in pencil.* All marks should be erasable, since you will sometimes change your mind in the course of rehearsing a piece of music.

Meter

Highlight the beginning meter sign. It is appropriate to write "IN 4" boldly above the first measure to ensure that you begin the work with the proper conducting pattern. Any meter changes in the work should be highlighted by underlining the meter, copying over the meter in red, enlarging the meter sign, or writing "3" or "4," etc., above or even within the actual measure where the meter change occurs. Because of the importance of meter changes, it is imperative that any meter designation stand out boldly so that you can see it at a glance.

Tempo

More music may be improperly performed because of incorrect tempo than any other factor. All unknown foreign tempo designations in the music should be translated to familiar terms. They should be underlined. A metronome should be used to establish an appropriate tempo. Write the metronome marking you choose at the beginning of the score. When learning the score the beginning conductor should practice with the metronome to ensure steady, even pulses at a proper speed. All tempo changes throughout the work should be highlighted as they occur in the score.

• To the Student

In certain works the editor of the music, not the composer, has inserted tempo designations or metronomic markings. Your historical studies will help you determine whether the tempo markings are the composer's or the editor's. An editorial marking is only a suggestion. As the conductor, *you* will have to decide an appropriate tempo.

The acoustics of rehearsal and performance rooms often suggest slight modifications in tempo. Fast music may have to be performed somewhat slower in rooms with considerable reverberation. Slow music may have to be performed more quickly in rooms with little reverberation. Slavish adherence to tempo markings may be detrimental to the music in performance. However, the conductor should not totally disregard tempo markings, and any changes from what is given or suggested should be given considerable thought and study.

Markings

Attacks. Attacks demand a cue gesture. The main entrance of each section within the work should be marked by a large, bold arrow (↘) in the score. It is not possible to cue every section for every entrance it makes, but certainly prominent entrances should be marked. Entrances where problems may result should also be marked. If the bass section has not performed for fifteen measures, it would be wise to mark its next entrance so you can be sure it enters on time.

Releases. Releases should also be marked when appropriate. All releases cannot be given to all sections, so you will have to decide on those releases that are absolutely essential. The release on a rest may be indicated by a vertical line drawn through the staff and rest. Some conductors will also write below the vertical line the pulse on which the release occurs. A release indicating a breath may also be designated by a large apostrophe (**,**) (Example 5-1).

Example 5-1:

Dynamics. Dynamics are either designated (*mf, f, cresc.,* ——) or implied because of text, style considerations, or direction of melodic movement. When you are preparing the score the designated dynamic markings should be highlighted, underlined, or enlarged for easy observation. As the music is learned, add subtle, implied changes in dynamics to the score as you make performance decisions.

Phrasing. The text may suggest a *Luftpause:* a slight break in the musical line, yet not a breath. Designate such a place in the score by a bold, short vertical line (|). If there is the potential that the ensemble will break the musical line when no break is desired, a curved, dotted line should connect the notes on either side of the potential problem (Example 5-2).

Example 5-2:

The above discussion of score marking is a suggested, minimum format. As other problems occur, you must decide how these are to be indicated.

MARK THE SCORE SO IT IS OF USE TO YOU.

Cluttering up the score with so many marks that none of them stand out is a primary danger. The result of so many markings is a blur. As you commit the score to memory and certain gestures become automatic, simply erase those markings which are no longer absolutely essential.

Conduct the melodies in Exercises 5-1 through 5-3. Mark each score. Following each melody is a mini-conducting analysis which will help you. Indicate a dynamic marking and a metronomic marking for each melody. Mark all breaths, phrasing, and releases. Be able to conduct each of the melodies from memory.

Exercise 5-1

Johnny Has Gone for a Soldier *American Folk Song*

Analysis

"Johnny Has Gone for a Soldier" should be conducted with a smooth, legato gesture, m.m. ♩ = 84. At measures 2, 4, and 6 give a release on pulse 4. In measure 8 use one of the final releases discussed in Chapter 4.

Exercise 5–2

Holy, Holy, Holy *Traditional Hymn "Nicaea"*

Ho - ly Ho - ly, Ho - ly! Lord God Al - migh - ty! Ear - ly in the
morn - ing our song shall rise to Thee; Ho - ly, Ho - ly, Ho - ly!
mer - ci-ful and migh - ty! God in Three Per - sons, bless - ed Tri - ni - ty!

Analysis

"Holy, Holy, Holy" should be conducted with a more vigorous, more animated gesture. Each pulse should be clearly defined by a slight bounce of the hand at the time of ictus. Because of the grandeur expressed in the melody, your physical posture must be *magnifique*. Keep the words "flowing majesty" in mind as you prepare the score. At measures 2, 4, 8, 10, and 12 give a release on pulse 4. At measure 6 you will wish to keep the ensemble from breathing after "morning." Increase the size of the pattern slightly, lean slightly forward, and be sure to look directly at the ensemble at this point. At measure 14 the ensemble should not breathe. At measure 16 use one of the final releases described above.

Exercise 5–3

All Through the Night *Welsh Song*

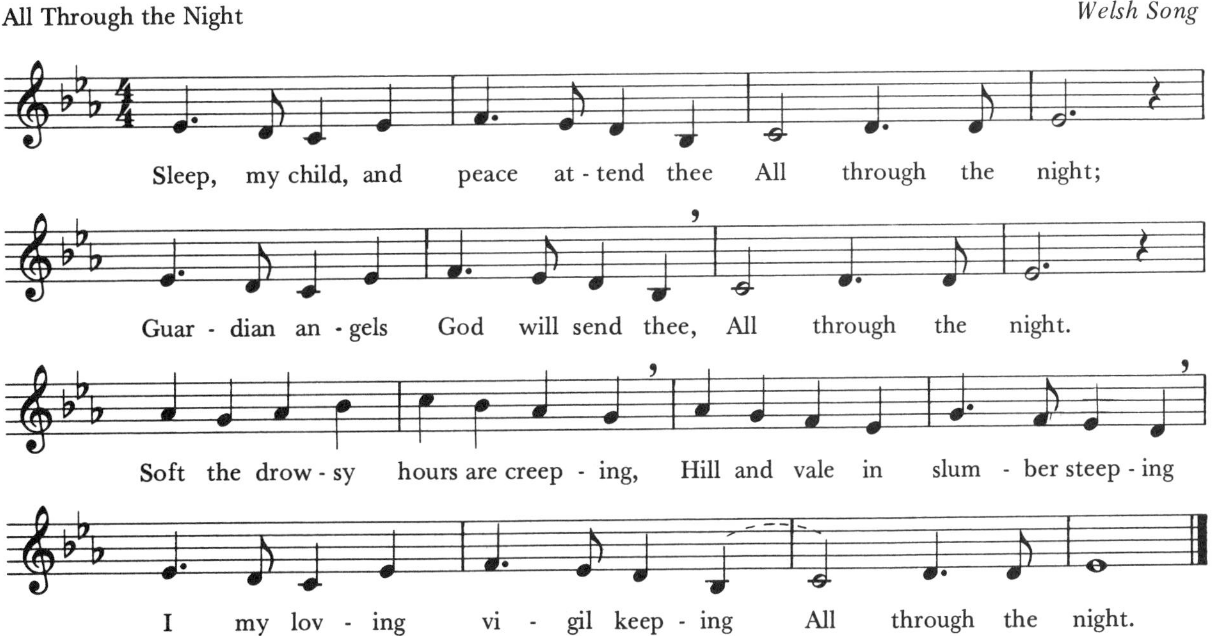
Sleep, my child, and peace at - tend thee All through the night;
Guar - dian an - gels God will send thee, All through the night.
Soft the drow - sy hours are creep - ing, Hill and vale in slum - ber steep - ing
I my lov - ing vi - gil keep - ing All through the night.

Analysis

"All Through the Night" should be conducted with a smooth, legato gesture. The quarter note equals approximately m.m. 76. Because the first phrase is a full four measures long, be sure you take a big breath as you give the initial preparatory gesture. Although the singers will want to breathe between measures 2 and 3, signal them not to do so by increasing the size of the pattern slightly on pulse 4 of measure 2 and by looking directly at the ensemble as if to say, "Don't you dare breathe here." You may even lean slightly toward the singers at this point to emphasize physically that they are not be breathe. In measure 4, give the release on pulse 4, being sure that following the release your hand is in position to execute the downbeat of measure 5.

The ensemble should breathe at the end of measure 6. Execute a gentle release directly on pulse 4. You will thus be giving the release at the same time the ensemble sings the word "thee." Because of the release, the ensemble will shorten the word "thee," take a breath, and then sing the word "All" on the first pulse of measure 7. Do not, however, allow the ensemble to clip "thee" too short. The more energy you give the release, the shorter and more clipped will be the execution of "thee" by the ensemble. Give a release on pulse 4 of measure 8. Release directly on pulse 4 in measure 12 while the ensemble sings ". . . ing." Because ". . . ing" can be sustained, the singing of this liquid consonant will occupy approximately half the pulse, with the remainder of the pulse being used by the ensemble for breathing. Again, do not allow the ensemble to clip this syllable too short. At measure 16 use one of the final releases shown in Chapter 4. Throughout the entire work, keep the gesture flowing and relatively small.

The Release Gesture III (Internal Pulses)

Releases must also be given in the middle of measures as demanded by the phrasing of the music. Because the pulse pattern continues, the releases must be given within the context of the pattern. The release must still be clear and distinctive. The circular gesture recommended for releases in this text can still be used.

Release on Pulse 2

When the release occurs on pulse 2 (Example 5-3), the rebound of pulse 1 is higher, bringing the hand closer to eye level. Unlike the final release, when a complete loop is made, the loop is only partially completed. The rebound motion is angular, carefully defining where the ictus of the release is by its movement in the opposite direction. Following the rebound of pulse 2, the hand moves across the downward pulse line into position for 3 (Diagram 5-1).

Example 5-3:

Diagram 5–1

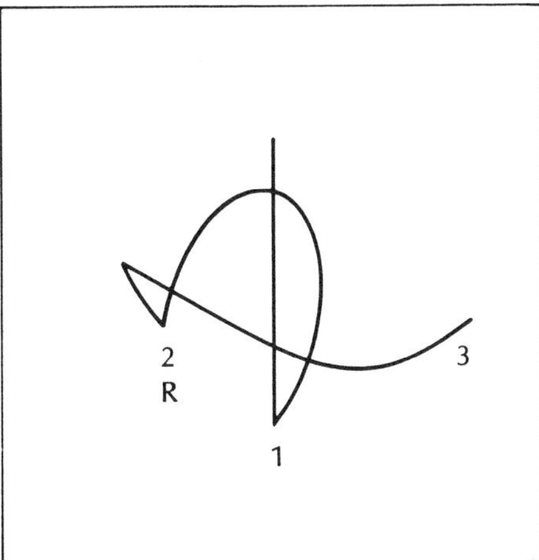

The wrist is very important in controlling the release and rebound gestures, but you must make skillful use of the arm and hand as well to make fluid releases in legato music, more vigorous releases in staccato and marcato music. The entire pattern is given in Diagram 5–2.

Diagram 5–2

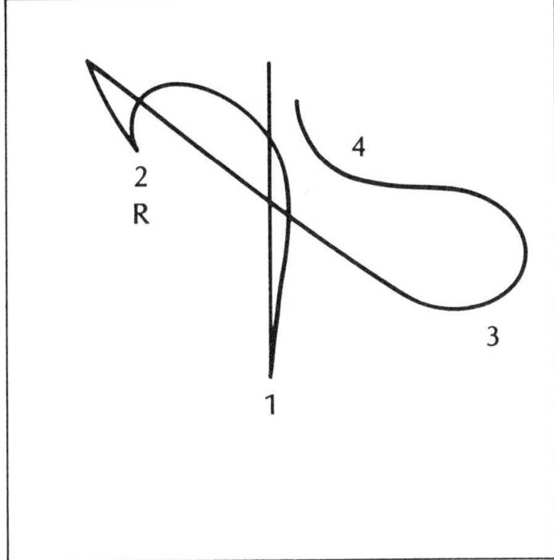

Exercise 5–4 Conduct the following melody. Execute a release for each rest.

Release on Pulse 3

When the release occurs on pulse 3, the rebound of 2 moves at a diagonal back along the preparatory gesture for 2 (Diagram 5-3). On approximately the "and" of 2, the preparatory loop for the release begins. Note that the diagonal rebound of 2 brings the hand to approximately eye level.

Diagram 5–3

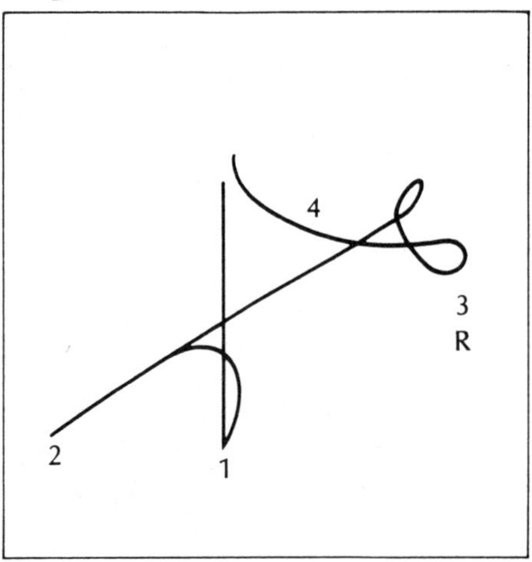

• Nota Bene

The preparatory loop for the release should not start too far out to the side of the body. The release loop should begin approximately opposite the right shoulder. The loop does not have to be large, but it must be well defined and the ictus of the release clearly given, usually by a light tapping motion with the fingertips as the ictus occurs or by lightly touching the thumb and forefinger together at the exact moment of release.

Exercise 5–5 Conduct the following melody. Execute a release at each rest.

Release on Pulse 1

Because the release on pulse 1 is so common it must be practiced very carefully. Note in Diagram 5-4 that the release loop begins immediately after pulse 4. The rebound of 4 is part of the loop. This gesture should be practiced several times to acquire the feeling of tapping pulse 4 and then pulling away to begin the loop. The loop travels beyond the vertical downbeat line so that when the release is made on pulse 1, the hand is in proper position to give a short rebound straight up, then move into pulse 2 (Diagram 5-5).

Diagram 5–4

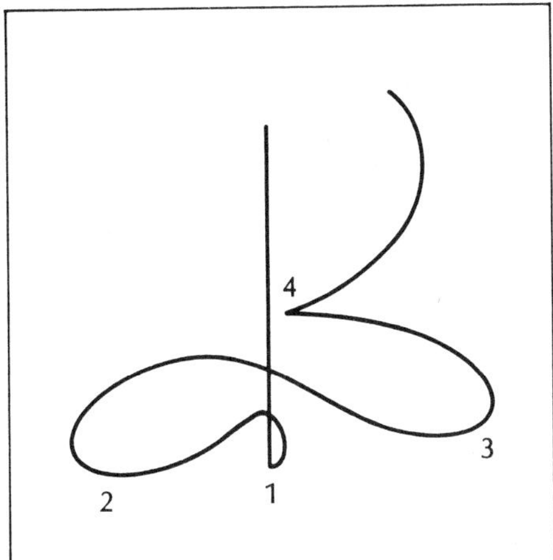

Diagram 5–5

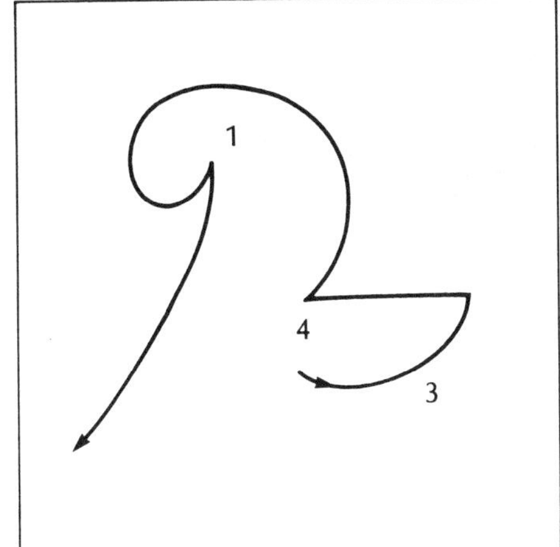

Note that the release is at face level. The rebound must thus be very short so that the hand is not over the head. The release gesture and ensuing rebound should not bring the hand higher than forehead level.

Exercise 5–6 Conduct the following melody. Execute a release at each rest.

Some conductors *always* give pulse four as a loop (Diagram 5–6). In this case the release gesture recommended above will obviously be relatively confusing. These conductors must develop a different release gesture that says "release" and nothing else. As said before, the gesture for a release should be used only for that purpose. The gesture must be unique.

Diagram 5–6

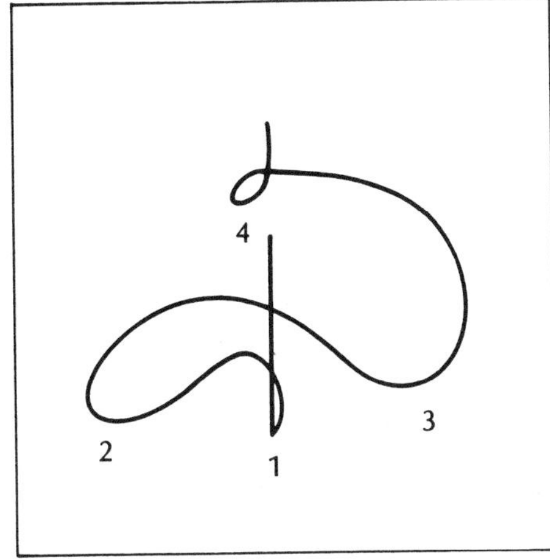

Conduct Exercises 5-7 and 5-8, emphasizing internal releases.

Exercise 5-7

Exercise 5-8

- **Nota Bene**

If your patterns are generally large loops (Diagram 5-7), the recommended release gesture may cause some problems. Because of the general "loopiness" of the pattern, the hand and arm will occasionally be out of position for executing the release gesture. It is imperative that the conducting gesture maintain clarity within the need to be expressive.

Diagram 5-7

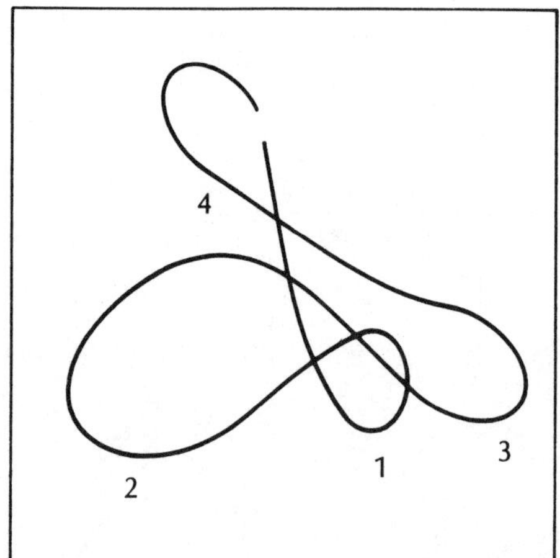

Left-Hand Releases

The left hand can be very effective in giving releases as the right hand continues to conduct the pulse pattern. The left hand should begin to rise from its neutral position on the pulse before the release is to be given. The release gesture is given approximately at eye level. The circular preparatory loop, as used previously by the right hand, can also be used by the left hand. The release loop should be made to the outside (Diagram 5-8). Care must be taken that the release is given exactly at the correct moment. This demands fine motor coordination, since each hand is doing something different.

Diagram 5–8

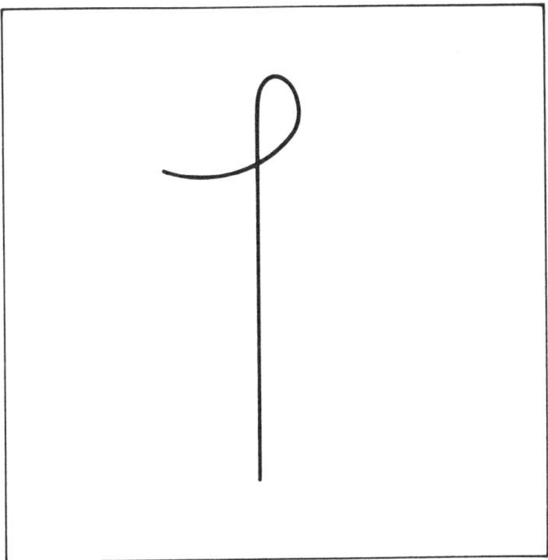

Exercise 5-9 Practice raising the left hand and executing the release loop several times. Count a pulse pattern out loud and make releases on various pulses.

Exercise 5-10 Conduct the four pattern with the right hand. With the left hand execute releases on various pulses of the pattern. Be sure the release and the pulse are exactly together.

• To the Student

As you watch yourself in the mirror, be sure the transition of the left hand from a position of inactivity to one of activity is smooth and continuous. The release should always be in the character of the music. The performers must have ample preparation from the left hand. Thus the left hand cannot be brought into the release position too quickly. Following the release, the left hand should be dropped to a neutral position as unobtrusively as possible.

Mirror Releases

There are times when both left and right hands will give a release on the same pulse. The mirror release, in which both hands give identical releases, can be effective when added eye contact, attention, and precision are demanded of the performers. Final releases are often mirror releases.

On the pulse before the release, the left hand should enter a mirror of the pattern being executed by the right hand. If the release is on pulse 3, the left hand will participate in a mirror of the diagonal rebound of pulse 2, with the release being given to the outside (Diagram 5-9).

Diagram 5–9

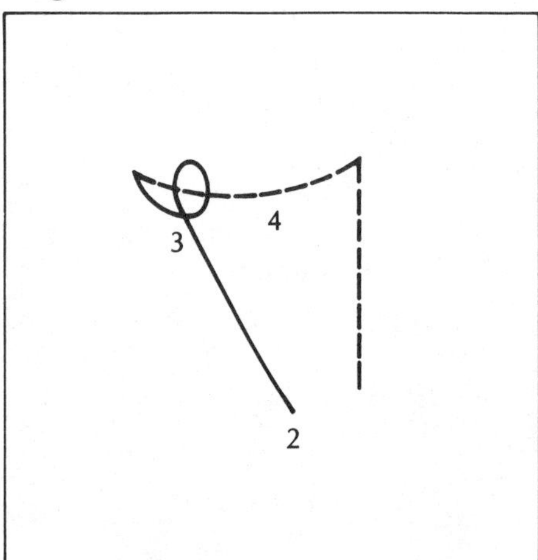

However, the release should not be executed too far to the outside. With the left hand extended in this position following the release, dropping the hand to a neutral position at this point may seem awkward. Some conductors continue the left hand in the pattern through pulse 4 into the downbeat, when it is most convenient to drop the hand into a neutral position. Others will gradually lower the left hand, being careful not to show any additional pulses while the hand is being lowered.

When a mirror release occurs on pulse 2, care must be taken that the hands do not execute the release too close together at the center of the body. The left hand should rise vertically, execute the release on pulse 2, and then move unobtrusively to a neutral position.

- **Nota Bene**

If you use the thumb-forefinger release with the release loop in the right hand, the left hand should mirror that exact motion.

Supplementary Conducting Exercises: Releases

MENDELSSOHN: Help, Lord (*Elijah*)

Used by courtesy of G. Schirmer, Inc.

SCHUBERT: Kyrie (*Mass in A flat*)

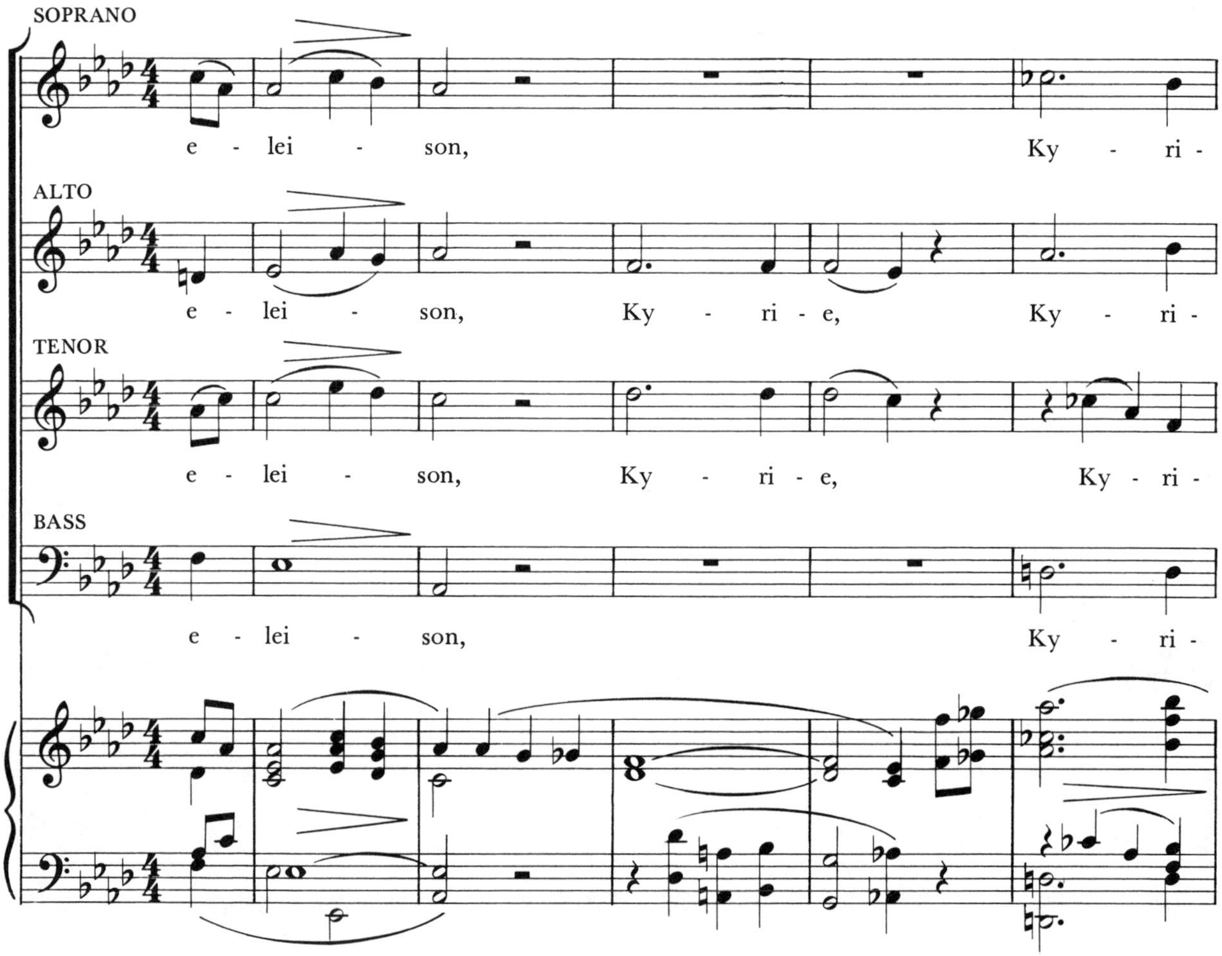

SOPRANO
e - lei - son, Ky - ri -
ALTO
e - lei - son, Ky - ri - e, Ky - ri -
TENOR
e - lei - son, Ky - ri - e, Ky - ri -
BASS
e - lei - son, Ky - ri -

DIETRICH: Kyrie Eleison

SOPRANO
p
Ky - - - ri - e, e - le - i - son, e -
le - i - son,

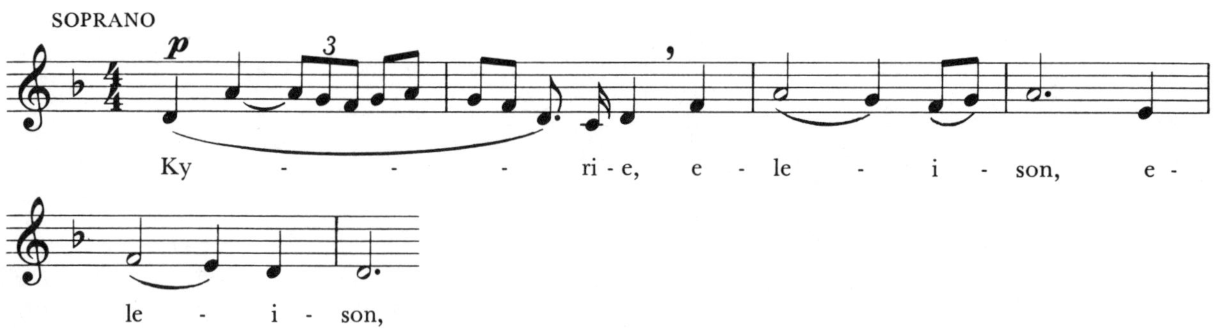

FAST: Let Me Grow Lovely, Growing Old

SOPRANO
p
A - do - ra - mus te.
ALTO
p
A - do - ra - mus te.
TENOR
p
A - do - ra - mus te.
BASS
p
A - do - ra - mus te.
50
f
Glo - ri - fi - ca - mus te,
f
Glo - ri - fi - ca - mus te,
f
Glo - ri - fi - ca - mus te,
f
Glo - ri - fi - ca - mus te,
f

Additional Suggested Choral Repertoire

Because many teachers of conducting wish their students to "get to the music" as quickly as possible, the following works are recommended as appropriate to the beginning level of conducting. Each of these works may be conducted with the gestures learned thus far.

• For Beginning Levels of Conducting

Britten, Benjamin, arr. *The Sally Gardens.* Unison. Boosey and Hawkes, #5448.
Butler, Eugene. *Hallelujah.* Unison. Broadman Press, #4550-61.
Eilers, Joyce Elaine. *Tiny King.* SSA. Schmidt Music Center, #240.
Nelson, Ron. "Cause Us, O Lord," from *Four Anthems for Young Choirs.* Three equal voices. Boosey and Hawkes, #5576.
Seiber, Matyas, arr. "Apple, apple," from *Three Hungarian Folk-Songs.* Two-part. G. Schirmer, #10826.

Since this book may also be used as review material for intermediate and advanced levels of conducting, some works have been chosen from the following two anthologies of choral music, which exhibit a wide diversity of literature and style. Each anthology has been widely used, and thus the materials are well known to many choral conductors. Each work suggested here contains conducting problems appropriate to the material studied thus far in this book. The list of appropriate works is by no means exhaustive, and other works may be substituted where necessary.

For Advancing Levels of Conducting

From: Kjelson, Lee, and James McCray. *The Conductor's Manual of Choral Music Literature,* SB 911. Melville, New York: Belwin Mills, 1973.
Croce, Giovanni. *O Vos Omnes.* SATB, pp. 21-23.
Handel, George F. *Glory to God.* SATB, pp. 90-94.
From: *Five Centuries of Choral Music for Mixed Voices,* ED2529. New York: G. Schirmer, 1963.
Brahms/Wasner. *Wondrous cool, thou woodland quiet.* SATB, pp. 49-51.
Mendelssohn, Felix. *He, watching over Israel.* SATB, pp. 25-31.
Mozart/Mueller. *Ave Verum Corpus.* SATB, pp. 9-12.
Victoria/Parker-Shaw. *O Magnum Mysterium.* SATB, pp. 135-151, ending at the Alleluia section.

6 The Three Pattern/ Basic Gestures of Interpretation

The Three Pattern

The initial preparation for the three pattern is given exactly as the preparation for the four pattern. After the basic pulse gesture is executed, however, the hand and arm move to the outside of the body to give the ictus for pulse 2 (Diagram 6–1). Care should be taken to place the second pulse along the line in the horizontal plane of conducting. Pulse 3 moves the hand into position to execute the next downbeat. If pulse 3 moves into the focal point it is executed close to the basic pulse line, as shown in Diagram 6–2.

Diagram 6–1

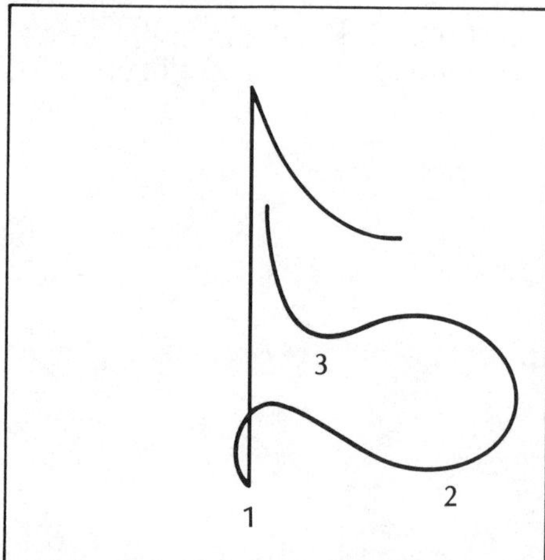

Diagram 6–2

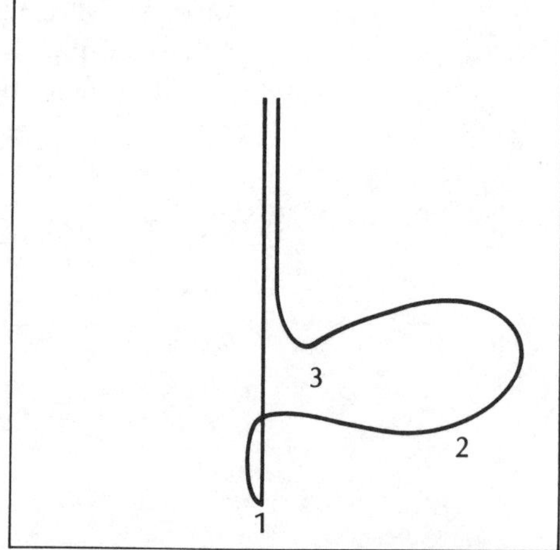

• To the Student

The basic rules established for the four pattern are also appropriate for the three pattern. As you practice in front of the mirror, critically evaluate the position of your hand and arm. Be sure that:

1. You do not roll your forearm or wrist toward your body.
2. The basic pulse gesture is straight down and the rebound straight up. A common error in the three pattern is to pull this downward pulse gesture toward the body (Diagram 6–3). Pulse 1 now looks more like a pulse 2 in a four pattern. Guard against this pulling motion.

Diagram 6–3

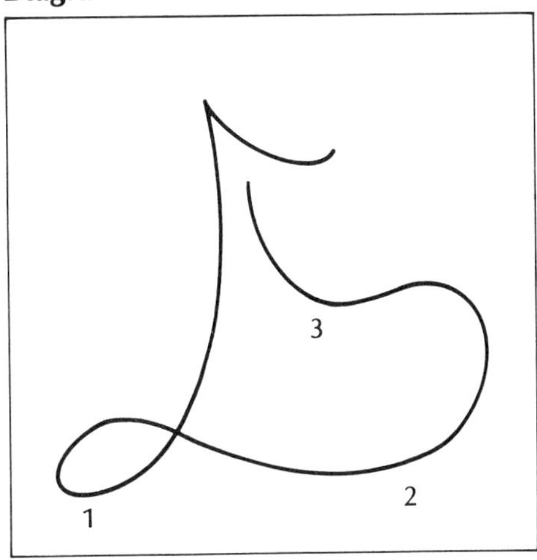

3. Your elbow remains in front of the body as you execute the basic pulse. Do not pull the elbow toward the body.
4. The hand and fingers remain in the same basic position as they were when the initial conducting position was assumed. They should not move unnecessarily.
5. The wrist leads the hand into each pulse.
6. The hand is carried above the wrist except for the execution of the ictus of the downbeat.
7. Your gestures are musical, eloquent, and graceful.

As you conduct the three pattern ask yourself the following questions:

1. Do I like what I see?
2. Is my posture correct? solid? positive? confident?
3. Is the position of my hand and arm appropriate?
4. Is my gesture unmistakably clear? If I were in the ensemble, would I understand the gesture?

Be sure to see yourself mentally conducting the "perfect" three pattern. Improvise melodies in triple meter to conduct as you practice this pattern.

The melodies in Exercises 6–1 and 6–2 are in triple meter. Analyze them and mark the score accordingly. Memorize each song so that you can conduct it without the score.

Exercise 6–1

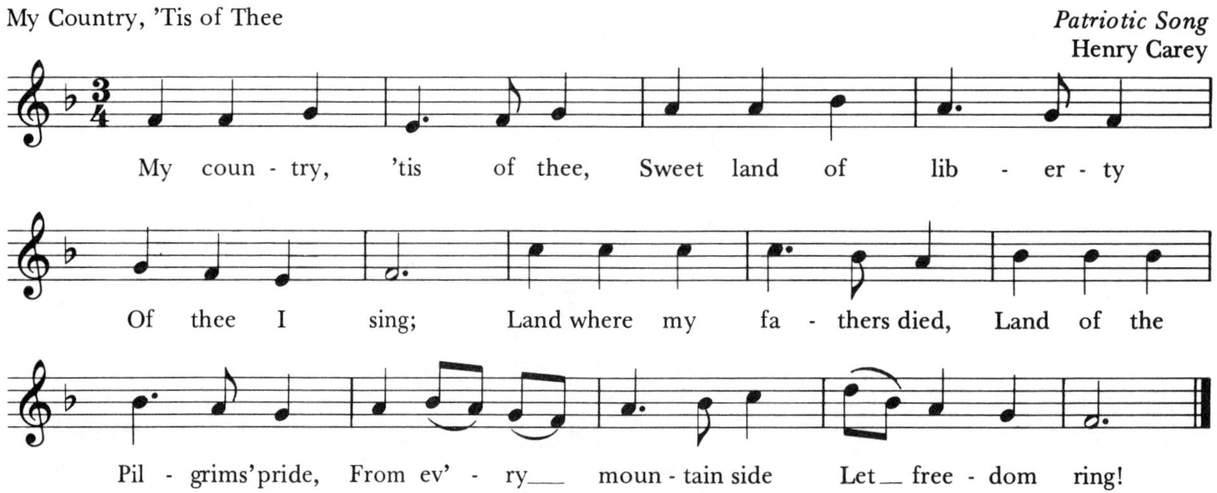

Exercise 6–2

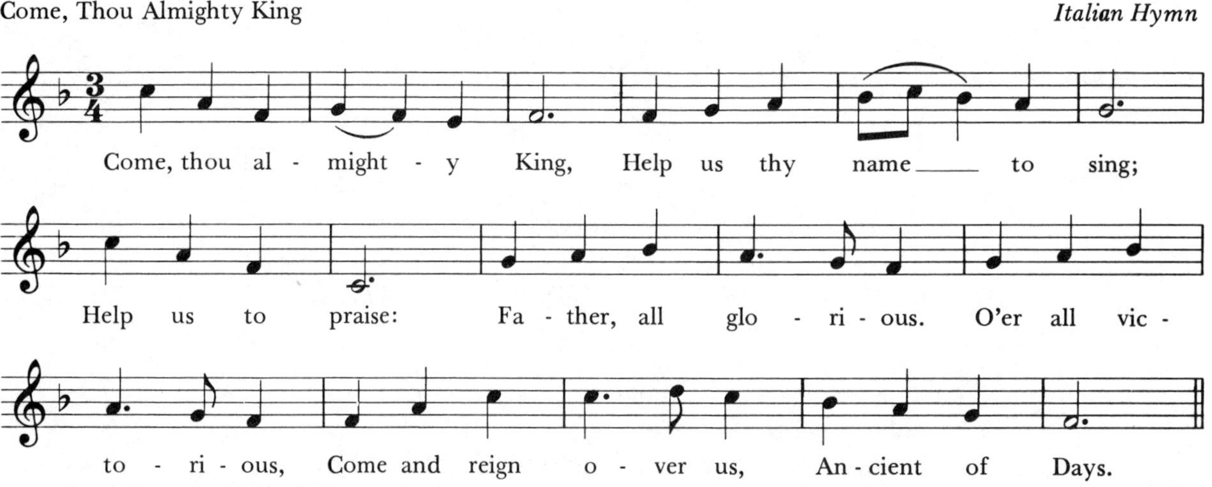

Phrasing and Climax in Music

Phrasing is based on building tension and then relaxing that tension. It gives life and emotion to music.

Phrases in music of the fifteenth and sixteenth centuries are developed melodically along the concept of *arsis and thesis,* i.e., the rise and fall of the melodic line. As the musical line rises, more energy is applied by the performer and intensity increases. As the musical line descends, the intensity relaxes (Diagram 6–4). Not all

Diagram 6–4

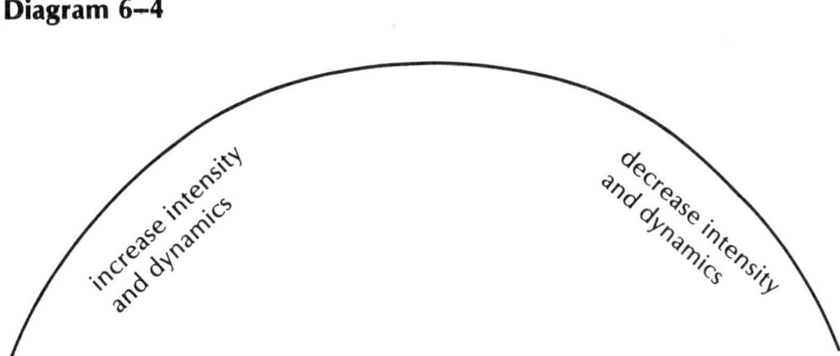

melodic phrases, of course, are symmetrical in shape. Some phrases may rise quickly to the climax and then slowly release the energy, while others may rise slowly to the climax and then release the energy more suddenly.

In music of the seventeenth, eighteenth, and nineteenth centuries, harmonic implications are used to create areas of tension and relaxation. The highest pitch of the melodic line is not always synonymous with the highest degree of tension in the phrase. Extremely unstable harmonies may shift the climax away from the highest pitch of the melodic line. Increased chromatic movement and sudden changes in dynamics may also create points of climax. Climax does not necessarily mean the loudest place in the music. Rather, it has much more to do with the degree of tension derived from the use of any number of compositional devices used by composers at various periods in the history of music.

Many means are used to create tension in twentieth-century music. The composer's manipulation of intervallic tensions, nontonal harmonies, timbre blocks, unusual and electronic musical sounds, new rhythmic and harmonic systems, and microtonal tensions, to name but a few, has resulted in new means for creating climaxes and tension.

As you become more skilled in analytic techniques through continued studies, new vistas of score analysis will open to you. The makeup of music will become more apparent, and this information will help you greatly in the preparation of the score.

Intensity and The Conductor

Many conductors seem intuitively to sense musical movement toward a climax, and they are able to supply the increased intensity through the physical gesture that such movement requires. Other conductors may sense what is required but have difficulty expressing it through the necessary nonverbal means. Conductors need to show increased intensity by increasing muscular tension. Abdominal muscles contract; back, arm, and shoulder muscles work harder. The process is very similar to isometric exercises in which certain muscles provide resistance to other muscles. The sensation of increasing intensity may best be described as pulling the hand through thick oil. The more energy you apply to the motion, the more resistance the oil provides. All gestures tend to become slightly exaggerated as muscles become more involved. In the conducting process, the hand, arm, and wrist thus tend to be pushing against an invisible resistance as intensity increases. Care must be taken that the gesture of increased intensity is not so grotesque that singers respond by constricting the muscles of the throat.

The performers must also supply more energy. Intensity is increased by singing out, yet holding back at the same time. Vibrant, soft singing is like singing a loud tone as softly as possible. This statement implies that the singer must pour out energy, yet cap it, hold it back, like potential energy in a capped oil well. The conductor must also pour energy into the gesture, yet at the same time hold back while maintaining the gesture's fluidity and clarity.

A common problem in choral singing is allowing the energy to dissipate too much at the ends of phrases, resulting in a loss of vitality, a blurring of diction, and usually a drop in pitch. The conductor must continue to pour a relatively high degree of energy into the conducting gesture at the ends of phrases. An unenergetic motion will cause the death of the phrase.

Increased musical energy is required in order to create musical accentuation. These musical accentuations are achieved by:

1. Dynamic stress
2. Highness of pitch
3. Length of tone

Dynamic accents (<, *sfz,* sudden changes of dynamics) require more energy on the part of the performer. The higher one sings, the more energy one is required to pour into the tone. If a note is given an agogic accent (held longer than the surrounding notes), the singer must poor more energy into the tone or it tends to become dull, lifeless, and unexciting. The conductor, through the intensity level of the gesture, must show the performers just how much energy they must supply to the tone.

In conducting the first phrase of "My Country, 'Tis of Thee" attention must be given to increases of energy which give prominence to certain words. The first six measures should be sung with one breath, though a slight pause may be given at the end of the second measure. Since there are no dynamic accents, accentuation will be the result of rising line, agogic accent, and harmonic implications. Although the word "of" has the highest pitch, it is a relatively unimportant word and occurs on a weak pulse of the measure. The important syllable is "lib-" in this instance. The intensity level must rise to the syllable "lib-" before beginning to relax. The implied dominant on the word "I" should be energized to heighten the final climax before the last word, "sing."

Diagrams 6-5a through 6-5g will give you some idea of how to show intensity growth and release in your conducting gesture used in the first phrase of "My County, 'Tis of Thee."

Note that as intensity increases, the pulse pattern becomes slightly larger and there is more resistance to the gesture. As the musical line deenergizes, there is less resistance and the pattern becomes somewhat smaller.

Dotted quarter-eighth figures often demand special attention, since precision in performance is essential. There are several ways to conduct this pattern which will help the performers execute the figure accurately.

The first method is to increase the energy into pulse 2, striking the second pulse slightly harder than the musical sound demands. Because the performers are holding over through the second pulse, they tend to transfer the energy which was applied to the second pulse to a clear and accurate execution of the eighth note.

Diagram 6–5a

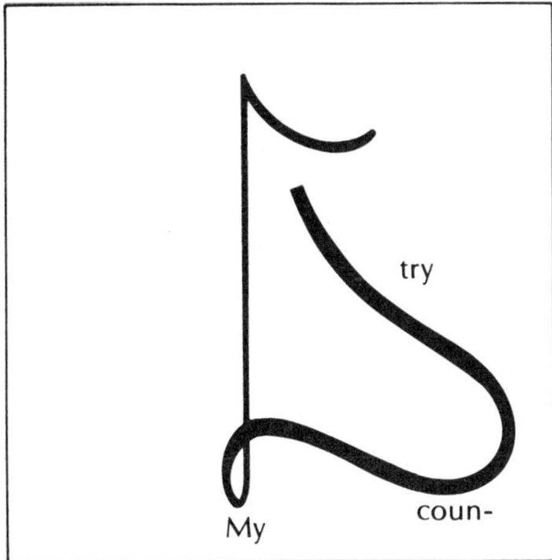

The preparation should be carefully, but strongly, given. The downbeat should be solid with an energetic rebound. The energy level should be moderate throughout measure 1.

Diagram 6–5b

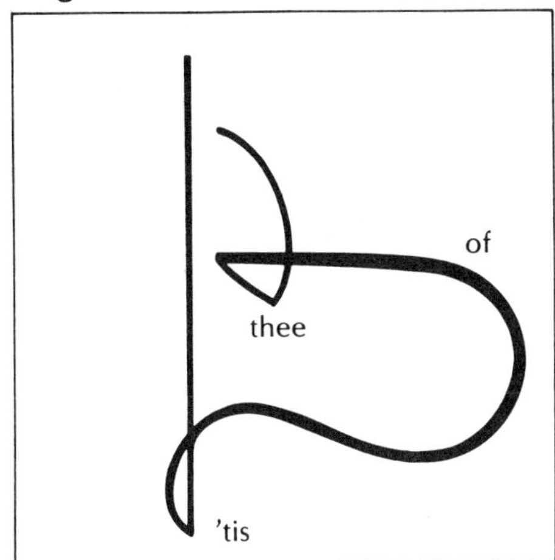

There are two ways to analyze the next measure. In both instances additional energy is needed on the word "'tis" since it is of longer duration than preceding notes. If the measure is perceived with a slight phrase at the end of the measure, then energy begins to relax somewhat on the word "of," since it is a relatively unimportant word. A phrasing break (see the next section of this chapter) is then indicated on pulse 3, softening the word "thee," singing it more in a reverent, rather than a forceful, character.

Diagram 6–5c

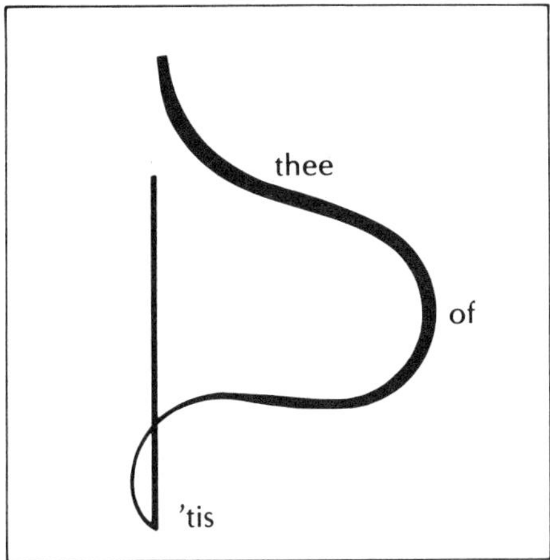

If, however, the measure is perceived as a line rising to measure 3, then energy will be increased throughout the entire measure with no stop or pause at the end of the measure. This interpretation has more power and sweep, more forward motion and drive.

Diagram 6–5d

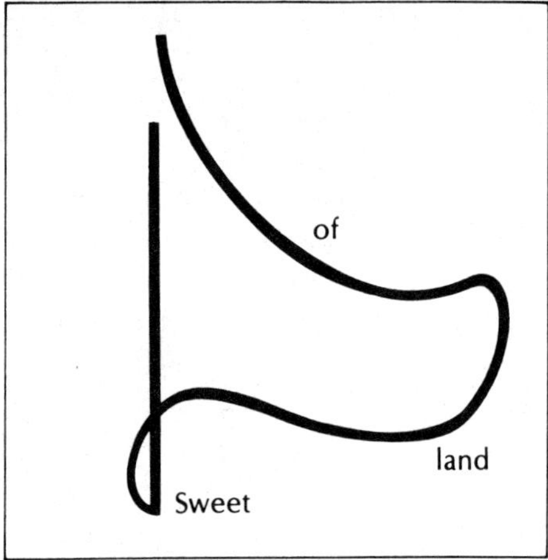

In measure 3 the line continues to rise. "Sweet" must be sung energetically. Intensity increases throughout the measure. Although the word "of" occurs on the highest pitch, the word itself is of little consequence, so the line is aimed toward "lib-," which is the highlight of the phrase.

Diagram 6–5e

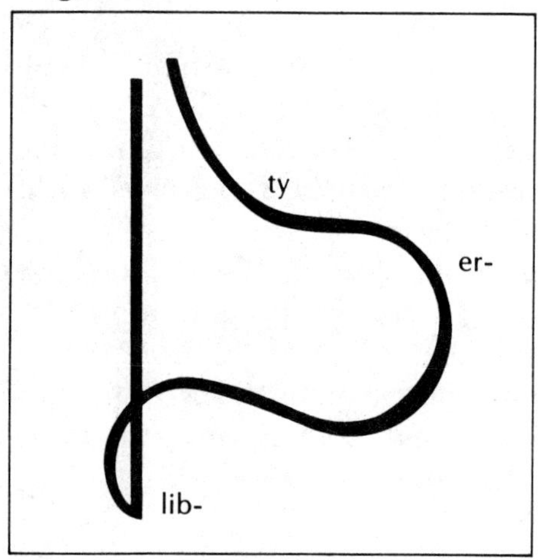

The syllable "lib-" must be well energized. Because it is a dotted quarter—and also because "liberty" is an important word of the text—the syllable receives an agogic accent. Energy must continue to grow through pulse 2. From here the line tends to descend, and intensity should be gradually released.

Diagram 6–5f

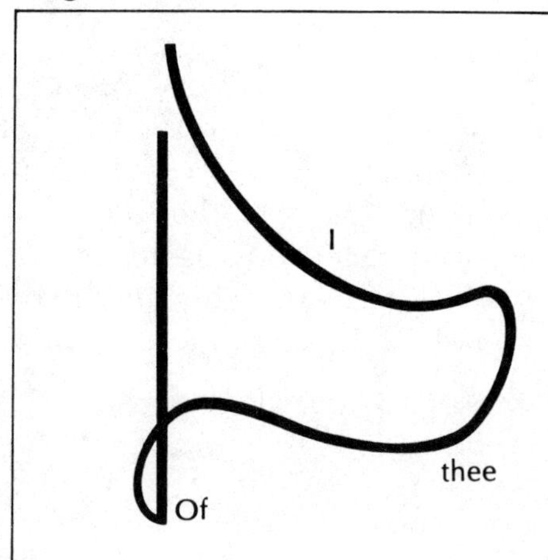

The line relaxes further. The line does not, however, become limpid. Remember that energy is a matter of degree. More energy should be placed on pulse 2 ("thee") because it is more important than the word "of." Because of the implied dominant on "I," energy must be maintained at a relatively high level.

Diagram 6–5g

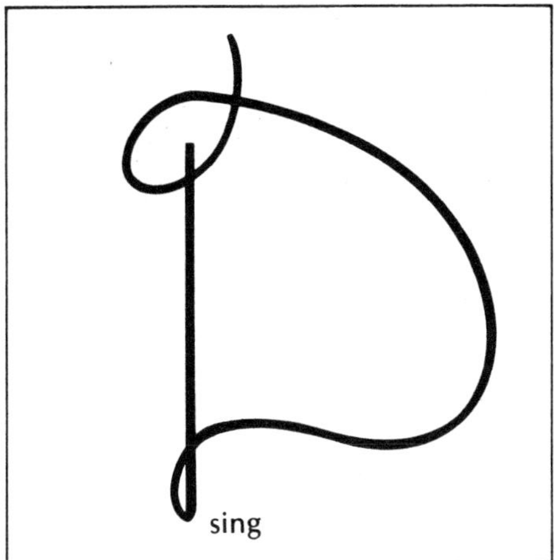

Although "sing" occurs on a dotted half, it is the end of the phrase. Duration indicates an increase in energy, but the end of the phrase and lower pitch suggest a release of intensity. However, after the tone is attacked you will have to intensify pulses 1 and 2 so the ensemble does not further relax the line. The last note should be sung solidly. Energy should be increased slightly to keep the tone vibrant and alive until the release.

Another approach is to give a very angular gesture which delineates clearly both the second pulse and the subdivision ("and") of that pulse. In conducting the phrase "'tis of thee" with this gesture, the gesture would look like Diagram 6–6. This angular gesture might be used with inexperienced ensembles to clearly delineate exactly where the eighth note is to be performed.

Diagram 6–6

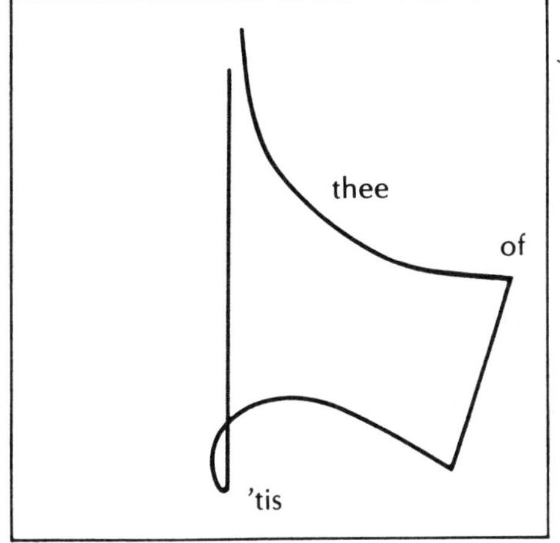

Diagram 6–7

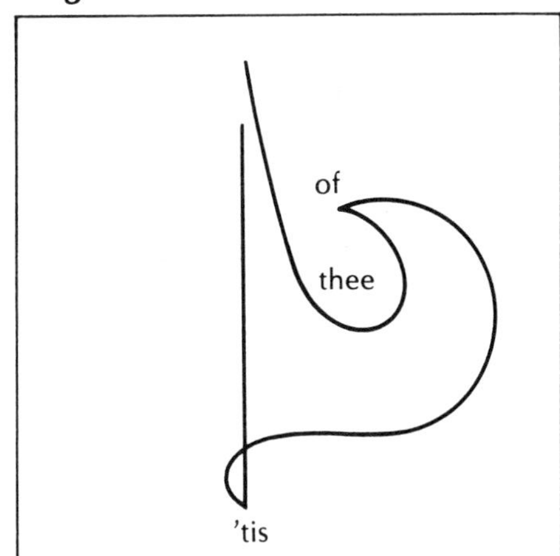

Another approach used by some conductors is to apply a "hook" at the end of the second pulse. Applied to "'tis of thee" it looks like Diagram 6–7. Both the ictus of pulse 2 and the "and" of 2 are bounced considerably to delineate pulse and subdivision clearly.

The hook, once learned, is often applied to penultimate gestures in each measure. This is *not* recommended. The hook should be used only when it is necessary to delineate clearly the "and" of the penultimate pulse of a measure. The hook also looks like the beginning of a release loop, which tends to diminish the uniqueness and effectiveness of the release gesture. It is suggested that you explore other means of conducting the dotted quarter–eighth pattern before resorting to the use of the hook gesture.

The Phrasing Break

A phrasing break, or *Luftpause,* is executed by the conductor when the ensemble is to stop the sound momentarily between words but is not to breathe. The phrasing break is analogous to the effect of a comma in a sentence. There is a slight pause after the comma, but the sentence goes on and no breath is taken. (Read the preceding sentence again for the effect of the phrasing break.)

The phrasing break may be executed in two ways. In the first method the hand is pulled back slightly toward the body about four to six inches on the rebound of the pulse where the break occurs. If the break occurs on pulse 4, execute pulse 4, then gently pull the hand back toward the body on the rebound. The hand should come to a momentary stop at the end of the rebound (Diagram 6–8). After the slight pause, reach forward to return to the plane of conducting for the downbeat.

Diagram 6–8

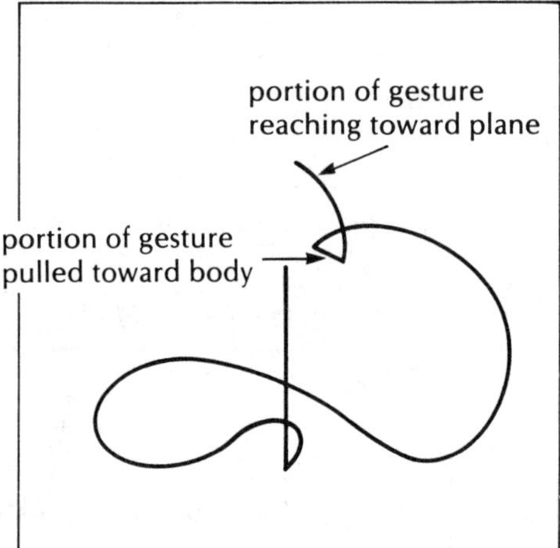

If the phrasing break occurs on pulse 2, the hand pulls back slightly toward the body on the rebound of pulse 2, stops, then reaches forward on the ensuing preparation so that pulse 3 is executed in the proper conducting plane (Diagram 6–9).

Diagram 6–9

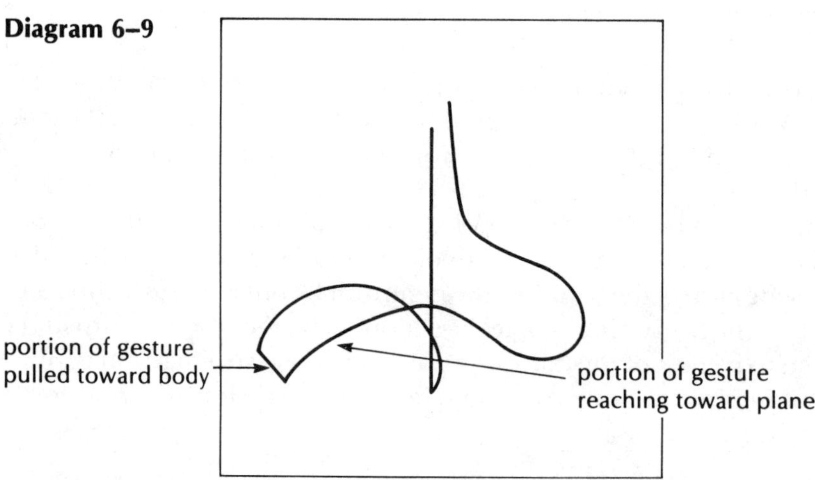

The second method of indicating a Luftpause is to stop the gesture at the top of the rebound as if momentarily suspending motion. The ensemble should soften the last sound, then stop completely. As the hand continues into the next pulse, the performers increase bodily energy in preparation to sing on that pulse. The conductor must be sure he does not breathe himself. No time gap is created for the breath. After the hand stops momentarily on the top of the rebound, the hand must move into the next pulse so that a continuous pulse is maintained (Diagram 6-10).

Diagram 6–10

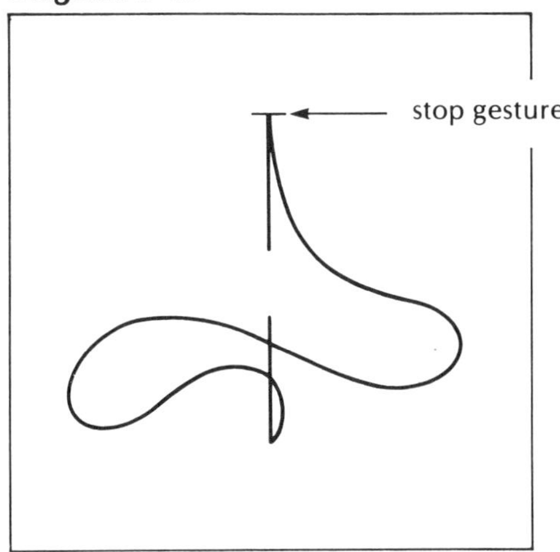

Conduct the melodies in Exercises 6-3 and 6-4, indicating phrasing breaks where the vertical phrasing mark occurs.

Exercise 6–3

Exercise 6–4

Cueing II (The Three Pattern)

Cues executed within the three pattern will follow the same basic format as those in the four pattern.

Cue on 1: The Three Pattern

When cueing on pulse 1 in the three pattern, the downbeat is shortened so that the cue gesture occurs at eye level. After the rebound the hand returns to the neutral position (Diagram 6–11).

Diagram 6–11

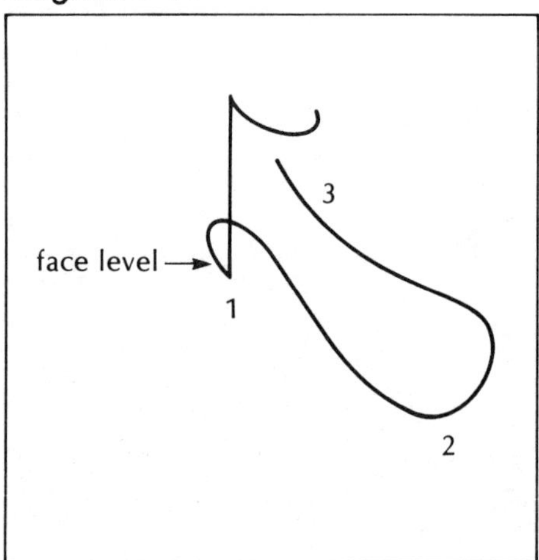

Conduct Exercises 6–5 and 6–6. Execute a cue following each rest.

Exercise 6–5

Exercise 6–6

Cue on 2: The Three Pattern

When the cue occurs on pulse 2 of the three pattern, the rebound of pulse 1 is higher to allow horizontal movement into pulse 2 at eye level (Diagram 6–12).

Diagram 6–12

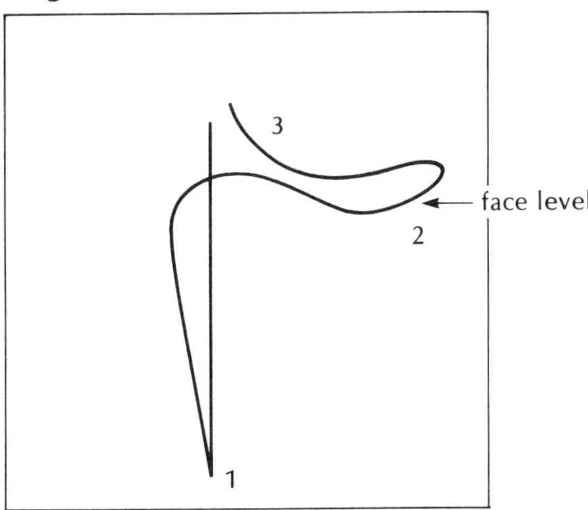

Conduct Exercises 6–7 and 6–8, executing a cue after each rest.

Exercise 6–7

Exercise 6–8

Cue on 3: The Three Pattern

When cueing on pulse 3, the rebound of 2 is more up than out, bringing the hand to eye level. The cue on pulse 3 is executed horizontally toward the basic pulse line. The rebound of 3 must be shortened so that it does not extend too high (Diagram 6–13).

Diagram 6–13

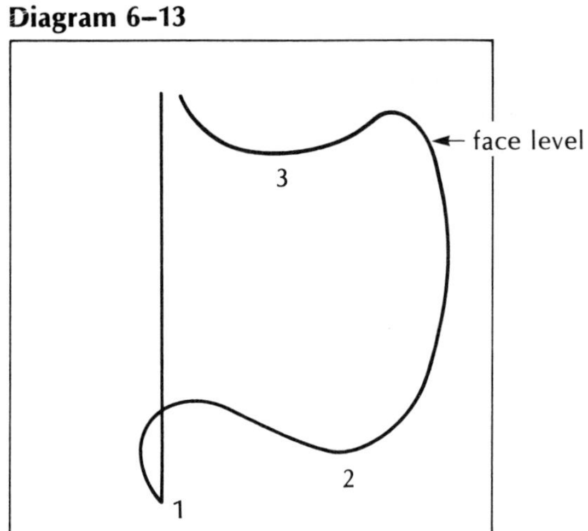

Conduct the following Exercises 6–9 and 6–10, executing a cue following each rest.

Exercise 6–9

Exercise 6–10

Exercise 6–11 The sopranos and tenors are to your left, altos and basses to your right. The tenors and basses are to the back of the ensemble and elevated on risers. Practice making cues to the sections of this ensemble, both high and low. The higher you lift your eyes, the higher you will raise the cue gesture. Make cues on all pulses of the three and four patterns until the gestures feel comfortable. When viewing yourself in the mirror, decide if your gesture for cueing is actually an invitation to perform. Is your cue decisive, precise, unmistakable, yet in the character of the music?

Exercise 6–12 In a four pattern, practice giving cues on pulses 1 and 3 in the same measure, one cue high, the other low. Do the same for pulses 2 and 4. Then reverse the high and low gestures.

Exercise 6–13 In a three pattern, give a cue on pulse 2 and then pulse 1 of the next measure. One cue should be high, the other low. Also practice giving cues on pulses 1 and 3 of the same measure.

Supplementary Conducting Exercises: Cueing

HAYDN: Gloria in excelsis (*Harmoniemesse*)

BARBER: Sure on this shining night

Kind - ness must watch for
night, Kind - ness must
shad - ows round, Kind -
night, Kind - ness must

Use of the Left Hand (Developing Left-Hand Independence)

The following exercise* begins to develop actual independence of the left hand.

Exercise 6-14 With the right hand conduct the four pattern. With the left hand touch your left ear on pulse 1, your nose on pulse 2, your right ear on pulse 3, your left ear on pulse 4, your nose on pulse 1, your right ear on pulse 2, and so forth. Your left-hand pattern is always left ear, nose, right ear. In effect your left hand is "conducting" a three pattern while your right hand conducts the four pattern. Do not allow the right-hand motion to deteriorate as you "conduct" this three pattern with your left hand.

Increase in Dynamics: The Crescendo

The left hand is traditionally used to indicate increases and decreases in dynamics. The following exercises develop the vertical movement of the left hand. As the hand ascends the palm is up with the wrist turned slightly toward the center of the body (Figure 6-1). The arm should be slightly bent at the elbow to avoid a look of stiffness. The palm remains up as the hand ascends. The angle of wrist to hand will change slightly during ascent to allow the palm position to remain constant. This angle change increases muscle use in forearm and shoulder, thereby increasing the intensity of the gesture.

Figure 6-1. The crescendo gesture.

Exercise 6-15 Starting with the left hand approximately at belt level, indicate a crescendo by raising the arm and hand slowly during four pulses to approximately eye level. By maintaining the palm at the same angle to the ground, feel the tension increase throughout the forearm and shoulder. The left hand should rise in a smooth, vertical line opposite the left shoulder.

*Contributed by Patricia Morris, former graduate assistant in conducting at the University of Miami.

• **Nota Bene**

The crescendo gesture should show only the increase in dynamics, not indications of the pulse. The ensemble must sense that the hand is "lifting" the dynamics throughout the motion. The palm should not turn fully toward the conductor with only the back of the hand showing to the ensemble. When the hand tips up so that the palm faces the conductor, the strength—lifting quality, intensity—drains from the gesture. Although the performers may not always be able actually to see the palm of the conductor's left hand, they must sense that the upraised palm lifts and supports their dynamic intensification.

Decrease in Dynamics: The Decrescendo

To indicate decreases in dynamics, the left hand is extended straight out from the forearm and wrist with palm down (Figure 6-2). As the hand and forearm descend, the elbow remains out in front of the body throughout the entire gesture, although some conductors may pull the elbow slightly toward the side of the body as the hand descends.

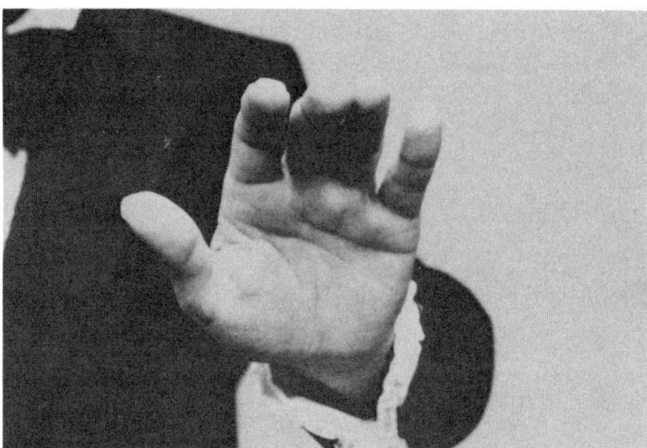

Figure 6–2. The decrescendo gesture.

• **Nota Bene**

It is a matter of educating the ensemble not to decrescendo suddenly as you turn your hand over after completing a crescendo gesture. Turning the hand over should be the preparation for the decrescendo. However, this simple movement is unfortunately often interpreted as a sudden drop in dynamics. You must educate the ensemble to give dynamically even crescendos and decrescendos.

Exercise 6-16 Begin with the left hand at approximately eye level, palm down. The left elbow should be in front of the body. The arm should be slightly bent at the elbow to avoid a look of stiffness. During four pulses, bring the hand down to approximately belt level. The hand should descend evenly and smoothly, showing no trace of the pulses being counted.

Exercise 6–17 Now combine the crescendo and decrescendo gestures. Crescendo for four pulses. After pulse 4, slowly turn the hand over and begin the decrescendo on pulse 1. Both ascent and descent must be smooth and uninterrupted. Both gestures should be straight up and down opposite the left shoulder.

Exercise 6–18 With the right hand conduct the four pattern. On pulse 1 begin a crescendo with the left hand for four pulses followed by a decrescendo for four pulses.

Exercise 6–19 Perform exercise 6–16 for durations of eight, twelve, and sixteen pulses. Do not reach the top of the gesture too quickly. Timing is absolutely essential. The hand must reach eye level exactly at the proper moment. The hand must rise vertically, smoothly, and evenly for the required number of pulses. The crescendo-decrescendo gesture should *not* swing from side to side in response to the horizontal movement in the right hand.

• To the Student

Some conductors use the turn of the hand from the crescendo position to the decrescendo position to represent the decrescendo. If they want a further diminishing of dynamics, they then either drop the hand or, with palm showing to the ensemble, pull the hand back toward the body. Whether you do this or not, it is important that your ensemble understand what you want and what gesture you will use to convey your meaning.

Additional Suggested Choral Repertoire

For Beginning Levels of Conducting

BRITTEN, BENJAMIN. *A New Year Carol.* Unison. Boosey and Hawkes, #5615.
PITONI, GIUSEPPE. *Cantate Domino.* SSA. Bourne, #ES5A.
SLEETH, NATALIE. *Christmas Is a Feeling.* Two-part. Hinshaw, #HMC-116.
STRAND, PEGGY. *Märi.* Two-part. Michael Kysar, #C102.

For Advancing Levels of Conducting

From: KJELSON, LEE, AND JAMES MCCRAY. *The Conductor's Manual of Choral Music Literature,* SB 911. Melville, New York: Belwin Mills, 1973.

PALESTRINA, GIOVANNI DA. *Hosanna in Excelsis.* SATB, pp. 13–17.
VIVALDI, ANTONIO. *Domine Fili Unigenite.* SATB, pp. 71–81.

From: *Five Centuries of Choral Music for Mixed Voices,* ED2529. New York: G. Schirmer, 1963.

BACH, J. S., arr. *Planets, Stars and Airs of Space.* SATB, pp. 134–136.
HAYDN, JOSEPH. *Sanctus.* SATB, pp. 18–24.

7 The Two Pattern/ Basic Rehearsal Techniques

Preparatory Gesture II (All Pulses)

The conductor must be able to give initial preparatory gestures on all pulses of the pattern. General rule: the pulse before the entrance serves as the preparatory gesture.

When the hand is moved into initial position to make the preparatory gesture, the hand and arm must come to a complete stop. The eyes should then sweep the ensemble or the section to be cued to be sure everyone is watching before any motion is made. Be sure you breathe as you give the preparation. This breath should be very noticeable. Do not be sneaky about your breathing at this point. Give the breath so that everyone knows it is time to breathe in preparation for the entrance.

If the work begins on pulse 4, the gesture for pulse 3 serves as the preparation (Diagram 7-1). To begin this preparation the hand should be either at or slightly to the left of the basic pulse line. Come to a complete stop. Look directly at the ensemble. Breathe as you give the preparatory gesture on pulse 3.

Diagram 7–1

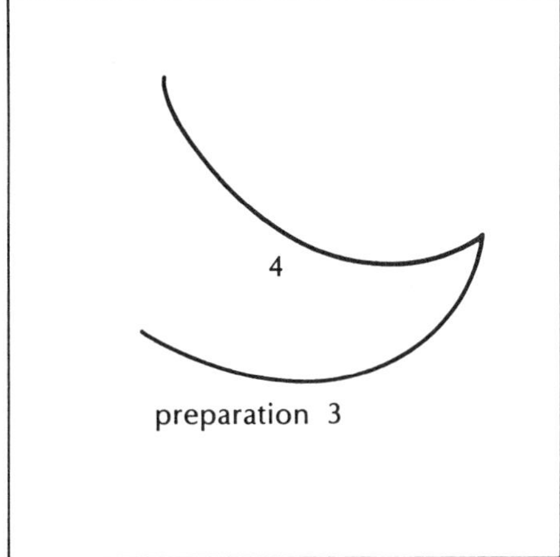

When beginning a work in triple meter on pulse 3, the gesture will be exactly as shown in Diagram 7-1. Be sure to take a strong breath on 2 as you give the preparatory motion.

Conduct Exercises 7-1 and 7-2. Sing the melodies on neutral syllables of your choosing. Be sure the initial preparation is precise, with no extraneous movement.

Exercise 7-1

Exercise 7-2

When a work begins on pulse 3, use pulse 2 as the preparatory gesture (Diagram 7-2). The hand should begin either at the basic pulse line or slightly to the right. Come to a complete stop. Look directly at the ensemble. Be sure to take an observable breath on pulse 2.

Diagram 7-2

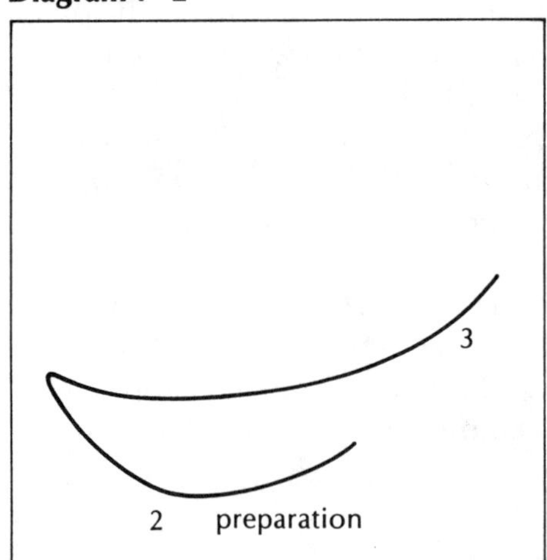

Conduct Exercise 7-3. Be sure your hand comes to a complete stop. Establish eye contact with the ensemble and then give a single gesture to prepare the performers to sing.

Exercise 7-3

If the work begins on pulse 2, the downbeat serves as the preparation. The hand should be placed on the basic pulse line and then dropped straight down (Diagram 7-3) with no other motions.

Diagram 7–3

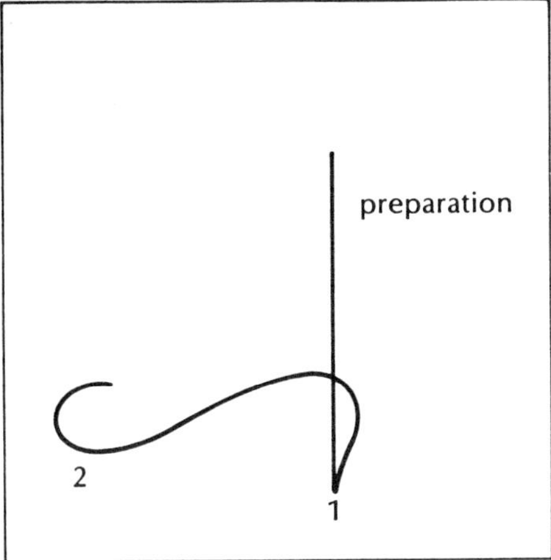

Conduct Exercise 7–4. Be sure there are no extraneous motions before the preparatory gesture is executed.

Exercise 7–4

In triple meter the preparation for entrance on pulse 2 is executed exactly the same as in Diagram 7–3 except that the resultant movement is to the outside (Diagram 7–4).

Diagram 7–4

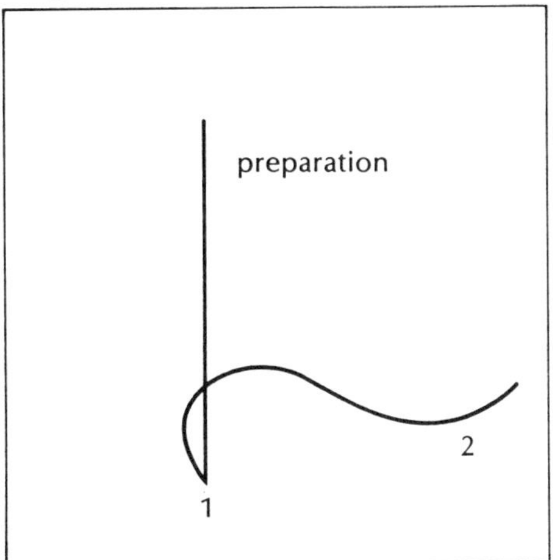

Conduct Exercise 7–5. Use a single preparatory gesture. Be sure your breath is decisive and visible.

Exercise 7–5

Occasionally you will see a conductor give a slight wrist flip at the very beginning of the preparatory gesture. In effect, this creates a double preparation, which should be avoided. If the ensemble you are conducting makes several false entrances, suspect an excessive wrist flip in the preparatory gesture as being one of the potential causes. The preparation should be a single gesture with no extraneous motions.

For additional considerations in executing preparatory gestures, see Chapter 8, "Standing on Your Head and Other Practical Matters."

Supplementary Conducting Exercises: Preparation on All Pulses

VAUGHAN WILLIAMS: The Turtle Dove

leave you for a while; If I

BARBER: Sure on this shining night

WILLAN: The Spirit of the Lord

BRAHMS: O Lovely May

Additional Suggested Choral Repertoire

For Beginning Levels of Conducting

Butler, Eugene. *How Lovely Is the House of God.* Unison. Carl Fischer, #CM 8019.
Hunnicutt, Judy. *I Cannot Keep from Singing.* SA. Augsburg, #11-0330.
Page, Sue Ellen, arr. *My Lord, What a Morning.* SSA. Hinshaw, #HMC-266.
Whitecotton, Shirley. "A Pressed Flower," from *Two Idylls.* SSA. Galaxy Music Corp., #1.2530.1.

For Advancing Levels of Conducting

From: Kjelson, Lee, and James McCray. *The Conductor's Manual of Choral Music Literature,* SB 911. Melville, New York: Belwin Mills, 1973.

Buxtehude, Dietrich. *God's Counsel Is My Wisdom.* SATB, pp. 48-57.
Brahms, Johannes. *O Lovely May.* SATB, pp. 177-181.

From: *Five Centuries of Choral Music for Mixed Voices,* ED2529. New York: G. Schirmer, 1963.

Bach, J. S., arr. *Break forth, O beauteous heavenly light.* SATB, pp. 137-138.
Billings/Gustafson. *When Jesus Wept.* SATB, pp. 97-101.
Muczynski, Robert. *Alleluia.* SATB, pp. 93-96.
Vaughan Williams, R., arr. *The Turtle Dove.* SSATB, pp. 52-55.

The Two Pattern

The two pattern, easy as it may seem, is filled with traps which frustrate conductors and performers alike. The pattern looks like a fishhook to the outside (Diagram 7-5). *It is the only pattern in which the downbeat is not straight down.* If the rebound of pulse 1 is too high, as in Diagram 7-6, the result may appear to be another downbeat.

Diagram 7-5

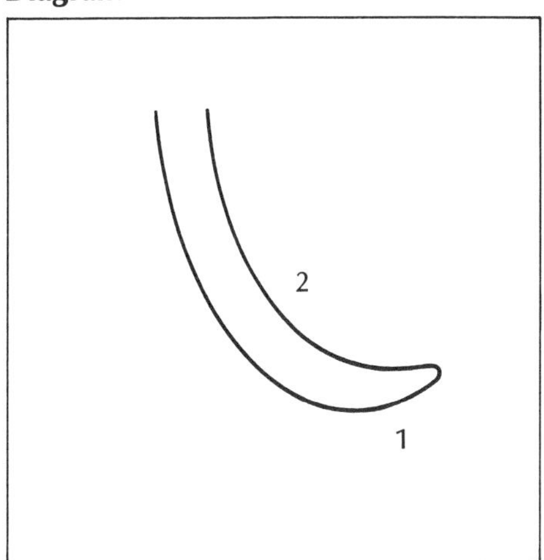

Diagram 7-6

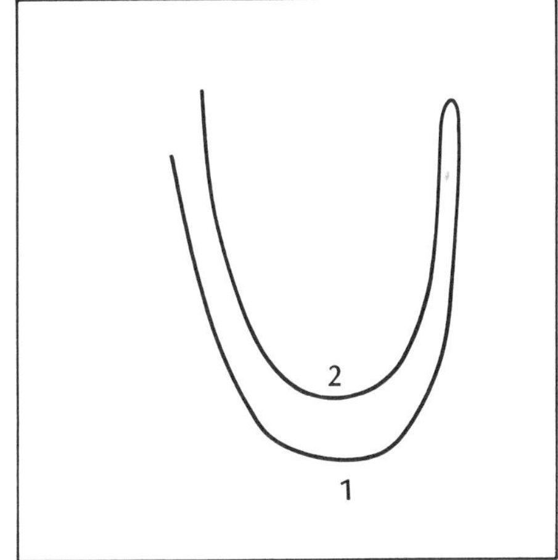

To insure that this does not happen, push the hand out to the side for pulse 1 and make the rebound short and also toward the outside, as in Diagram 7-5.

• To the Student

As soon as you learn this pattern in which the downbeat is not straight down, the danger is that you will allow it to creep into other patterns as well. Complacency may lead to a sloppy four pattern (Diagram 7-7) in which the downbeat is no longer distinct.

Diagram 7–7

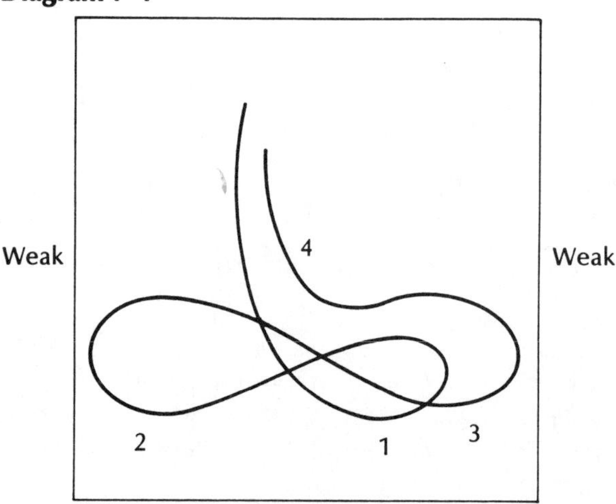

The two pattern must be considered unique, since the first pulse does not remain in the vertical conducting plane. You must not allow this sliding motion to influence other patterns. If the sliding gesture is used as a downbeat in the three pattern, hand and arm may end up far outside the conducting plane following pulse 2 (Diagram 7-8).

Diagram 7–8

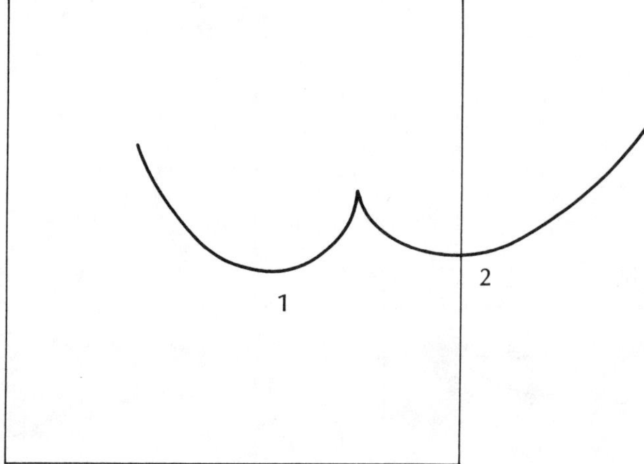

Conduct the following melodic fragments in duple meter.

Exercise 7-6

Careless Love *American Folk Song*

Love, oh, love, oh, care-less love,
Love, oh, love, oh, care - less love,

Exercise 7-7

HAYDN: The Heavens Are Telling (*The Creation*)

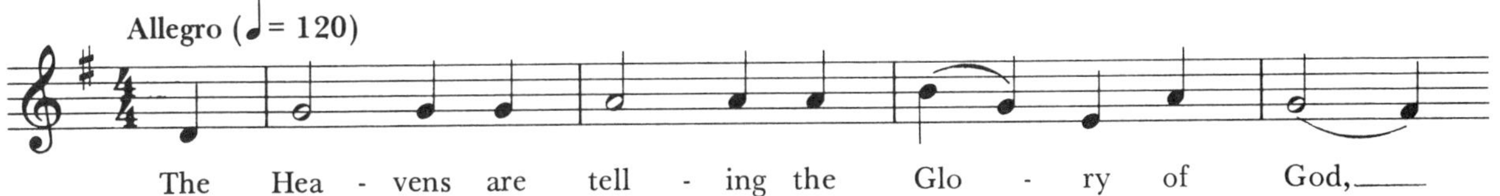
Allegro (♩= 120)
The Hea - vens are tell - ing the Glo - ry of God,

Exercise 7-8

HANDEL: Joy to the World *Hymn: Antioch*

Joy to the world! the Lord is come; Let earth re -
ceive her King;

Supplementary Conducting Exercises: The Two Pattern

MENDELSSOHN: Yet doth the Lord (*Elijah*)

Used by courtesy of G. Schirmer, Inc.

SEIBER: The Handsome Butcher (*Three Hungarian Folk-Songs*)

Additional Suggested Choral Repertoire

For Beginning Levels of Conducting

BEETHOVEN, LUDWIG VAN. *O Sanctissima.* SAB. J. Fischer and Bros., #FEC 9547.
DI LASSO/HARRIS. *O Eyes of My Beloved.* SSA. Harold Flammer, #B-5009.
HANDEL/HOPSON. *Come, Jesus, Holy Son of God.* Two-part mixed chorus. Harold Flammer, #A-5623.
HIRSCH/SIMEONE. *Anytime of the Year.* SA. Shawnee Press, #E-137.
PALESTRINA/COATES. *Ah, Look upon These Eyes.* SSA. H. W. Gray, #MOD 579.

For Advancing Levels of Conducting

From: KJELSON, LEE, AND JAMES MCCRAY. *The Conductor's Manual of Choral Music Literature,* SB 911. Melville, New York: Belwin Mills, 1973.

BILLINGS, WILLIAM. *David's Lamentation.* SATB, pp. 135–138.
FAURÉ, GABRIEL. *Libera me.* SATB, pp. 186–198.
LOTTI, ANTONIO. *Kyrie Eleison.* SATB, pp. 62–65.

From: *Five Centuries of Choral Music for Mixed Voices,* ED2529. New York: G. Schirmer, 1963.

BILLINGS/GUSTAFSON. *Chester.* SATB, pp. 112–117.
DOWLAND/WARLOCK. *What if I never speed.* SATB, pp. 108–111.
PERSICHETTI, VINCENT. *sam was a man.* Two-part, pp. 85–92.
SEIBER, MATYAS. "The Handsome Butcher" and "The Old Woman," from *Three Hungarian Folk-Songs.* SATB, pp. 64–68 and 71–74.

The Seven-Minute Rehearsal

Students usually have very limited opportunities to rehearse an ensemble while they study conducting. Many complete school without developing techniques for running an efficient, effective rehearsal. If rehearsal opportunities exist in the conducting class, the total number of students in the class determines how much time each student will be able to practice rehearsal techniques using the rest of the class as a laboratory chorus.

The following suggestions are to prepare you to rehearse your classmates for approximately seven minutes once each week. They are, however, valid procedures which will be useful later on in your conducting career. Remember: A good rehearsal is characterized by its rapidly moving pace, its high motivational level, and an expectation of musical accomplishment. Something musical happens in a good rehearsal.

Pre-Rehearsal Preparation

SELECT THE MUSIC.

If you are to select the music for your seven-minute rehearsal, consider

1. The size of the class
2. Use of two- or three-part music, depending on available voices
3. The level of difficulty versus the time limitations
4. Your accompanist

Simplicity can be a virtue. You wish to experience conducting and teaching, rather than pounding out notes. For a more detailed list of criteria for music selection, see Chapter 22.

LEARN THE MUSIC.

You must be able to

1. Sing each voice part. Play and sing each part until it is accurately learned.
2. Sing each voice part
   a. Against the accompaniment. If necessary, record the accompaniment.
   b. Against the other voice parts. Sing one part and play another, or get a fellow conducting student to sing another part against yours.
3. Sing in quartets. Switch parts so each person has an opportunity to sing all parts in a comfortable range. In order to minimize disorientation, have two people always sing their regular parts during the rotation.

Listen not only to your part but to the accuracy of the other parts, perhaps being sung in other octaves.

DEVELOP A MENTAL RECORDING OF THE WORK.

Imagine a fine, inspired ensemble performing the composition. This fantasy performance will define how you wish the finished product to sound. The difference between your fantasy performance (FP) and what you *actually* hear (AP) in the rehearsal is what you must teach (T).

$$FP - AP = T$$

Your goal in rehearsal is to bring the actual sound as close as possible to the fantasy sound. As a direct result of your teaching, the initial difference should get smaller and smaller (Diagram 7-9). In essence, you must know what you want before you can teach for it.

Diagram 7–9
Fantasy Performance

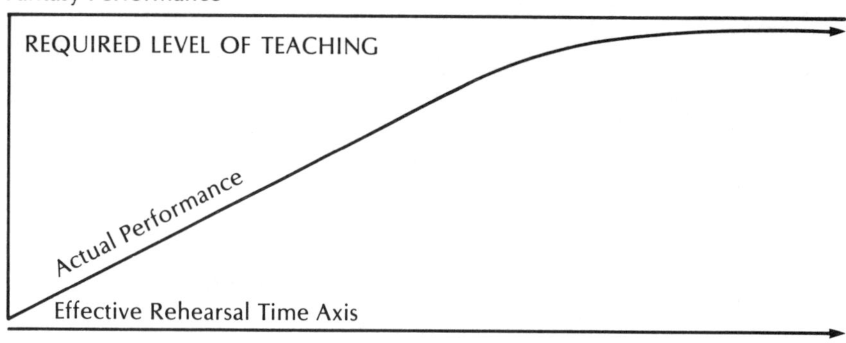

REMEMBER THE ACCOMPANIST.

When used, the accompaniment is an integral part of the composition. You must

1. Know the accompaniment to be certain it is being played correctly
2. Learn the accompaniment from the perspective of helping the accompanist play it better

CONDUCT THE SCORE TO YOURSELF.

Conduct the work, including dynamics, releases, and cues, as you

1. Speak the text in rhythm:
   a. First, each voice line completely from beginning to end
   b. Then jumping to various voice parts as cues are indicated
2. Sing the voice parts:
   a. First, each line completely from beginning to end
   b. Then jumping to various voice parts as cues are indicated

Notice the intervallic relation between entering voice parts. Where necessary, indicate how entering pitches may be found.

ISOLATE DIFFICULTIES.

Circle difficult intervals and rhythms. Chances are, if you have difficulty the ensemble will too.

The Rehearsal Plan

You should know exactly what you wish to accomplish during each rehearsal. Before the rehearsal begins, write down your goals precisely. Because you have experienced learning the music, you know where the difficult sections are. Decide which of these sections needs to be taught first and begin teaching it to the ensemble immediately after the initial run-through. The following is a sample rehearsal plan.

Giacomo Perti, "Gloria in Excelsis," S.A. (Lawson-Gould #52097)
1. Clean, energized "Gl" sound throughout
2. Read through work without stopping
3. Be sure rhythm ♫ is crisp, short throughout
4. 2/1/3 (page 2, score 1, measure 3): What voice part previously sang the first three measures of Alto (imitation of soprano)?
5. 3/2/4: check alto c-sharp, sing it high
6. 3/3/5: be sure ♩. ♪ figure in alto is accurate
7. 4/1/2: soprano c-natural
8. 4/2/1: lean in on suspension
9. Read through work again

Rehearsal Procedure

START INTO THE MUSIC IMMEDIATELY.

No words are much better than a few too many. Do not give apologies or engage in idle talk. Any delay betrays nervousness or lack of preparation on your part.

ALLOW THE ENSEMBLE TO READ THROUGH THE WORK WITHOUT STOPS.

If the ensemble should break down, you may have to go back and start somewhere again, preferably not at the beginning. Sometimes it is better just to continue to conduct the music silently, expecting the ensemble to follow along until the end of the work. This procedure tells the singers that they must keep going, that you will not stop for any reason.

LISTEN TO WHAT THE ENSEMBLE PRODUCES.

Do not sing! Listen! You have located trouble spots in the music while learning it. You have a written rehearsal plan. How well does the ensemble perform the passages you know are difficult?

REMEMBER PROBLEMS.

Remember those passages in which the ensemble has difficulty. Store them in your brain for instant retrieval later.

KEEP THE ENSEMBLE SINGING.

Make your conducting precise and explicit. Nothing fancy. The ensemble is reading. They are probably watching their music more than they are you. Just keep them moving steadily through the music.

USE POSITIVE REINFORCEMENT.

As soon as you begin to drop your hands following the final release, compliment the ensemble. ("You read that very well," or "Sopranos, your reading has improved greatly.") Be honest, however. Be certain the compliment is deserved. This compliment serves two purposes: (1) It forces you to listen for something good rather than always for what is bad or even miserable, and (2) it makes the ensemble feel good about reading.

PROCEED IMMEDIATELY TO THE FIRST SECTION IN THE MUSIC YOU WISH TO CORRECT OR IMPROVE.

Give clear, precise instructions: page number, system or score number, measure number, pulse number, and voice part, in that order. Example: Go back to page 4, second score, measure 2, pulse 1, soprano and alto parts. Instrumentalists will count backward or forward from rehearsal numbers or letters. Example: Back from letter E: one, two, three, four — the fifth measure, pulse 2, oboes. Some conductors have students number all measures in the choral score. This makes finding places in the score even easier, although the initial numbering of measures takes time and errors do occur.

COMMUNICATE THE PROBLEM CLEARLY.

After everyone in the ensemble has found the place, state exactly what you wish to correct or improve: pitches, rhythmic precision, diction, intonation, interpretation, or dynamic level. Suggest how the ensemble can improve this spot. *Cover only one point at a time.* Make your comments direct and to the point. If appropriate, *demonstrate how you wish a musical line to be performed.*

REHEARSE.

Go over the section as many times as necessary for improvement to take place. Continue to offer suggestions as to how the ensemble can sing this portion better. At this point you are a doctor of music. Do not just diagnose. PRESCRIBE!

PROCEED TO THE NEXT PROBLEM SPOT.

Check your brain file or your rehearsal plan. Again, give clear directions where you want the students to go.

WATCH THE CLOCK.

Time is of the very essence. You must decide when to stay on a section and continue to work on it and when to move to another place in the music. Gauge your time.

REPEAT THE ENTIRE WORK OR SECTION.

Just before your time is completed, conduct through the entire work or section again. Note how those portions of the music you have rehearsed have improved. Note new problems to work on during the next rehearsal. Compliment the ensemble on its improvement.

The Rehearsal in Focus

This type of rehearsal plan focuses on specific aspects in the music to work on. The plan forces attention to correct execution of pitches, rhythms, diction, and interpretation. It is far better to plan too much than to run out of material before rehearsal time is over. What is not finished today may be practiced the next time.

It is a sad state of affairs when the conductor suddenly has nothing more to say or do because the rehearsal plan has been completed ten minutes before the session is to end. The answer is not to give the choir "free time" at the conclusion of the rehearsal. They eventually will come to expect it and discipline problems may result.

The Rehearsal and Classroom Control

Many teachers have excellent classroom control because of exceptional rehearsal planning and execution. Students know when you are ill-prepared and tend to take advantage of you if they realize your preparation has not been thorough. The first step in classroom control is preparation: planning the rehearsal and implementing the plan in a professional, competent manner. Although the plan is only an imperfect guide, if you stick to it, certain necessary musical matters will get rehearsed.

The rehearsal should consist of a minimum of words and a maximum of performing. Directions and suggestions should be concise and to the point. Let your conducting gestures and nonverbal body and facial expressions convey what you want. Be certain that every time you drop your hands you begin to talk immediately. If you don't, your ensemble will. Tell them exactly where in the music they are to go, what is to be corrected, and how they should do it. Be businesslike but pleasant. An occasional splash of humor doesn't hurt. You are a leader when you rehearse the ensemble. So, *lead!*

There are many ways to get results in a rehearsal. You must discover and develop the technique that is best for you. The following rehearsal dialogue is condensed from a tape of an actual session. It is not given as a recipe for successful rehearsal procedure because, as in all teaching, there are no recipes. Rather, it is offered for your consideration of pacing, efficiency, and learning potential for the student.

Exercise 7-9 Analyze the sample rehearsal dialogue in Exercise 7-9. What factors promote rehearsal efficiency? What techniques are evident in the rehearsal? How would you improve it?

Sample Rehearsal Dialogue I

(Conductor steps to the front of the ensemble)

CONDUCTOR: Take out "Hail! Sacred Music, Hail!" of Billings. Read through it, no stops. (Ensemble reads, conductor listens carefully)

C: Good reading job. Your reading has improved greatly since our first rehearsal. Now turn to page 3, score 4, measure 2, sopranos. It's very important for this rhythm to be accurate and articulated correctly. (Conductor demonstrates)

C: Sing it, sopranos. (Sopranos sing)

C: Shorten the sixteenth notes. (Sopranos sing again)

C: No, shorter yet. Touch it and get off. (Conductor demonstrates again, sopranos sing again)

C: That's much better. Sing measures 1, 2, and 3 of that score. (Sopranos sing those three measures)

C: Same page, fifth score, measure 1. Altos, you have the same articulation problem, only more complicated. (Conductor demonstrates)

C: Everyone sing this part. Keep the sixteenth notes short. (Everyone sings)

C: Good, but don't back off the dotted eighths. Keep those notes firm. (Conductor demonstrates; everyone sings)

C: Good. Now, can you also crescendo through that line? (New item not in plan, but appropriately introduced here since rhythms and articulation should not be slighted by the introduction of the crescendo. Everyone sings)

C: Now, just sopranos and altos on your own parts, beginning with score 4, measure 5, pulse 3. Keep the sixteenths short and crescendo through the line into the next measure. (Sopranos and altos sing)

C: That's right, good job. Now look at the markings on score 6, measure 3. (Skip rehearsal plan no. 4 because time is running out.) Does anyone know what those lines over the notes are called and what they mean?

STUDENT: Tenuto.

C: Right, they are tenuto marks. What do they tell you to do? (No answer. Teacher sings line once with tenuto marks, once without)

C: Now, what was the difference?

S: The note is held full value and connected with the next note.

S: You broadened the note some.

S: You held it longer and sang it a little louder.

C: You all have portions of your statements that are correct. The tenuto mark means you should hold the note for its full value. Don't leave a gap between the notes with tenuto marks and the following sixteenth notes. Everyone try it. (Everyone sings)

C: Not bad. We'll work more on that next week. Now, from the beginning to page 4, second score. Remember the articulations of the dotted eighth-sixteenth patterns along with the crescendos. (Ensemble sings)

C: You have done very well today. OK, there's the bell. Put your music away. You're dismissed.

Exercise 7-10 Now study this sample rehearsal dialogue. What factors contribute to rehearsal inefficiency?

Sample Rehearsal Dialogue II

(Conductor steps to the front of the ensemble)

C: Hi, gang. Say, did any of you hear about Bach decomposing?

STUDENTS (groaning): That's terrible.

C: All right, will you get out "Hail! Sacred Music, Hail!" (Conductor fumbles through his stack of music to find his copy. To the side): Why do you guys keep hiding my music? (A little chuckle as students roll their eyes to the ceiling) All right, read straight through. From the beginning. (Students sing first three measures)

C: Hold it, hold it, hold it. That was terrible; read it again. (Students sing first three measures again but are interrupted)

C: Stop, stop. This is horrible. What's the matter with you guys? Can't you read? Try it again. (Exasperation shows as his voice rises in pitch. Students get through five measures this time)

C: Whoa, whoa. Haven't you guys ever seen those rhythms before? That's terrible. One more time and get it right, will you? (Students get through to measure 15, but break down once more)

C: This is torture. OK, start at measure 3.

S: Mr. Smith, what page are we on?

C: Oh, yeah, sure. Page 4. OK, let's go. (Students begin to sing)

C: Wait a minute, wait a minute. Where are you guys? Are you on the second score of that page?

STUDENTS: Oh, second score. No wonder it didn't sound right. We were on the first score.

C: Come on, wake up! What do you think this is? A picnic? We gotta get something done today. Now look, sopranos, at measure 14 your rhythm was really bad. OK, sopranos, sing it from the beginning. (Sopranos sing from beginning, but the rhythm in measure 14 collapses again)

C: Look, that rhythm is still not right. Back to the beginning and do it again. (Sopranos sing again but the result seems inevitable)

C: Sopranos? Pretty bad, but we'll have to move on now. Study your music at home and try to figure out that rhythm. I'll look at my music over the weekend too. OK, we've got five minutes before the bell rings, so put your music away.

8 Standing On Your Head and Other Practical Matters

The instrument upon which the conductor plays is the ensemble. The quality of the ensemble depends on the conductor's capacity to

1. Organize the performers into a cohesive unit
2. Teach the notes and interpretive aspects of the music
3. "Feel" and express the aesthetic essence of the music
4. Inspire and lead the performers to seek and express that aesthetic essence

If the conductor gushes forth with lovely, interpretive gestures but lacks the ability to inspire the performers, the center of the performance may be the conductor rather than the music.

THE MAIN FUNCTION OF A CONDUCTOR IS TO MAKE MUSIC.

To paraphrase one conductor, "If you have to stand on your head to get your ensemble to respond, do it." Perhaps the problem is not how to stand on your head, but rather how to do it eloquently. In any case, good conductors do that which must be done. The main concern should be: What does the ensemble need at this particular moment—in the first rehearsal? subsequent rehearsals? the dress rehearsal? the performance?

Singing with the Ensemble

It has long been considered poor practice for the choral conductor to sing with the choir. *The singing conductor does not hear as well as the listening conductor.* The ideal conductor is one who listens intently at all times to matters of balance and blend, phrasing, nuance, and articulation.

In his or her role as teacher the conductor should listen first, then stop the ensemble and verbally demonstrate pitches, rhythms, articulations, and phrasings. Sometimes, however, the conductor must sing a note or two, even an entire phrase, with a section to help the singers secure their part against the others. To perform the part independently in demonstration is not the same as singing that part against other voices. Seemingly easy intervals and rhythms may become very difficult when performed against another part. The conductor's help in singing these intervals or rhythms may put a troublesome line in perspective with the other parts.

With inexperienced choirs it is sometimes helpful for the conductor to sing for a short time while standing or sitting among the choristers. Some conductors, stressing the importance of distance between singer and conductor, may feel that this mingling with the singers is not a good policy. Others are primarily concerned with teaching in the most efficient and effective way possible. When the conductor stands among the choristers, he or she not only hears them better but also helps them with their part, becoming a model of the good choral singer, a teacher of posture, good vocal habits, and technical assurance.

There are also many church choirs which suffer from missing members both at rehearsals and on Sunday mornings. The conductor must make a choice—either sing and shore up a part or let it collapse in the name of "good" conductorship.

It is the conductor who must make the decision ultimately: "Do I need to sing?" The important word in this question is "need." The writer remembers a small-town director who always hummed very audibly with the girls' chorus. The girls did not need his humming, but he hummed anyway. To be sure, he hummed with the mixed chorus too, but at least there were other male voices to mask the sound. A basic tenet should be:

WE SHOULD DO ONLY WHAT IS HELPFUL AND NO MORE.

Physiognomical Inspiration

Think about what people look like as they listen intently to music. No matter what the mood of the music is, many listen with expressions of grim seriousness. The brow is furrowed; the head cocked to one side; the eyes are narrowed to slits as the mind ponders what the ear perceives. Such facial expressions are certainly not inspiring. Conductors must use their faces expressively, along with other body gestures, as a nonverbal means of communicating aesthetic essence while keeping their ears at maximum receptivity. A conductor's face and hands must urge the singers on. Each conductor must ask, "What do I look like when I listen intently? Will my bodily appearance help inspire the ensemble?"

Mouthing the Words

Should the conductor mouth the words? One can only ask, "Does the ensemble need this kind of help?" Beginning choirs often receive very exaggerated, grotesque mouth movements from the conductor which they might mime with approximately 50 percent accuracy. Some conductors say that without this exaggeration, the choir might deliver only 10 percent of their articulation and diction accurately. You must decide for yourself if mouthing the words is necessary.

Mouthing the words may cause two problems.

1. In polyphonic music the conductor may mouth words and rhythms that not everyone is singing. Visually this may be very disconcerting to singers when they look up for help, only to discover that the conductor is mouthing the wrong words and rhythms for them.

2. The conductor's mouth may not coincide exactly with his or her hand gestures. To get mouth and hand exactly together requires fine motor coordination. For singers to look up and see the mouth doing one thing and the hand something else is to cause confusion. Which do they follow?

Whether the conductor is engaged in singing, mouthing the words, or listening intently, his or her face must be animated and expressive. At times mouthing entrances may be of great value to the ensemble. At other times the need may not be there. The need of the ensemble must prevail. At least the singers know that the conductor who mouths the words is actively engaged in the music.

Standing on Your Head

Sometimes conductors make large, sweeping, overly emphatic gestures in rehearsal to get the ensemble to surge forward, sing out, and emote magnificently. Once the ensemble has performed a particular line several times and has the feel of it, is it possible for the conductor to use another appropriate, but less ostentatious, gesture and get the same results? The audience loves to see a conductor "stand on his head." It is a sideshow to watch the gladiators of music do their gyrations in the name of inspiration. The audience loves the conductor but does not hear the music. That is an artistic condemnation of great magnitude. The conductor who is in physical control can get the same effects with less motion by educating the ensemble. As quickly as possible the conductor must get out of the way of the music, especially the audience's perception of it.

The Initial Preparatory Gesture

The initial preparatory gesture has many functions. It must establish tempo, mood, dynamics, and articulation. The conductor must train the ensemble to observe all of these functions in a single gesture. The singers must also breathe and shape their mouths for the first sound at the same time. Although one preparatory gesture may say it all, many choral conductors conduct a full measure of preparatory pulses before the ensemble enters. If the choristers know the conductor will give three pulses before they have to take their breath—and these three pulses are really of no concern—they may turn off their minds. They may then misread the fourth pulse preparation and attack with sloppy, imprecise articulation. The result is wasted effort and loss of efficiency.

There are works, however, where a single pulse of breathing seems inappropriate. The air should enter the singer in much the same fashion as it will be expelled. In some works it seems appropriate for the singer to take in the air supply gradually over three or four pulses. Many inexperienced singers do not inhale enough air in one pulse. Experiencing the breathing action over three or four pulses allows them to fill their lungs completely as well as to enter the mood of the work more thoroughly. The conductor who uses this technique of full-measure breathing is involving the singers physically and mentally during this time. It is not just a wait-and-watch-the-conductor-beat-four process. As the breath is taken there is a gradual growth in intensity in both singer and conductor in preparation for the musical attack. These preliminary beats should be contained in front of and close to the body and be very small in size. Certainly the audience need not see them.

The conventions of conducting should not enslave us. Nor should we stray so far away that we have a nonverbal language which nobody understands. The needs of the ensemble must be met, and this demands some practical considerations. If we can in any way improve our teaching, rehearsal techniques, leadership capacity, and ability to inspire singers, we should not be so tied to the conducting conventions that we are ineffective. Our job is to make music, but we should also be sensitive enough to know when our actions get in the way of the music, the performers, or the listeners. We should only do that which we need to do and no more.

Habit is a powerful force. We get in the habit of mouthing words, singing with the ensemble, and, in effect, "standing on our heads." Are we sensitive enough to determine when the ensemble no longer needs these crutches and to stop doing what we have been doing and do only what we need to do? Can we teach the ensemble to perform without crutches and still maintain musical integrity, performance competency, and inspiration? We must be in control of our actions rather than let our habits be in control of us.

9 Gestures of Articulation/ Subdivision

Gestures of Articulation (Marcato, Staccato)

The character of the conducting gesture indicates how the singer is to articulate beginning consonants and vowels, as well as how much silence, if any, there may be between syllables and words. So far you have used the legato gesture—smooth, flowing, hand constantly in motion—indicating a liquid, connected execution of the music on the part of the performer.

The Marcato Gesture

The marcato gesture is used for more vigorous, markedly accented music. In size, the pattern may be moderate to large. The pattern is angular and the hand comes to a complete stop *at the end of each rebound.* Thus it is usually referred to as a "stopped beat" gesture. The ictus is delivered sharply and angularly, and there is no "rounding off" of the pattern as was the case in the legato gesture (Diagrams 9-1a and 9-1b). It is important to remember that the hand comes to a complete stop at the end of each rebound before moving to the ictus of the next pulse.

It is also possible to combine legato and marcato gestures in the same pattern (Diagram 9-2). The diagram shows legato pulses 1, 3, and 4, but an accented marcato gesture on 2. The preparation for the new articulation is important. After the rebound of 1, the energy in the arm and shoulder must increase greatly so that the desired marcato articulation on 2 is not misinterpreted. The ictus must be sharply delivered. After the hand comes to a complete stop following the rebound of 2, the preparation into 3 is softer, not so vigorous, more rounded, and thus not to be interpreted as another marcato pulse.

Diagram 9–1a

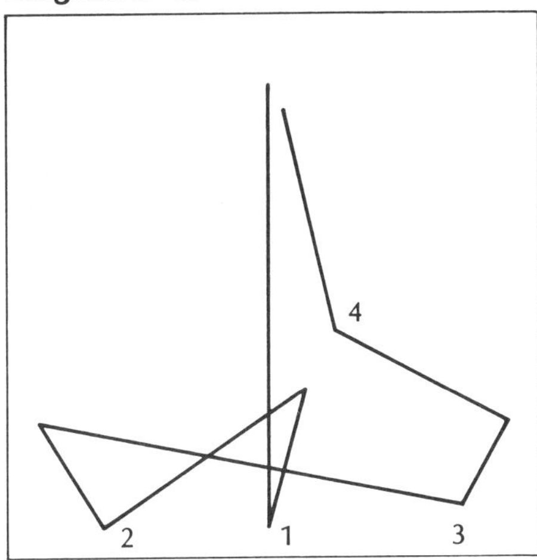

Diagram 9–1b

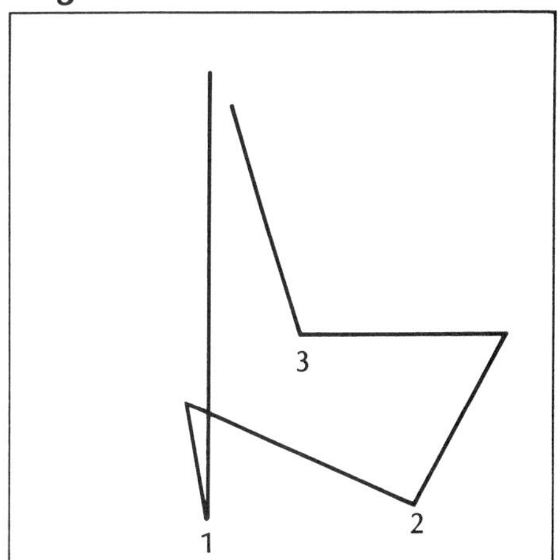

Diagram 9–2

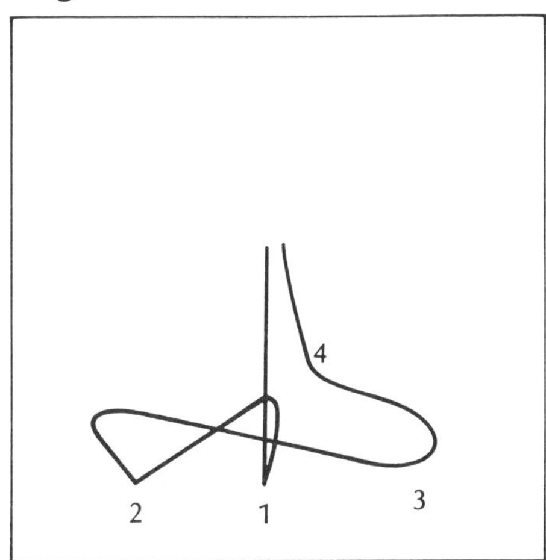

Exercise 9-1 Conduct the following melody with a marcato gesture.

The Nonexpressive Gesture

Rests indicate moments of silence. Since the conducting gesture for rests usually indicates only passage of time and some slight level of intensity, the motion is basically a nonexpressive one. The motion for the rests is smaller. The intensity tends to dissipate in the pulse pattern as it approaches the rests. To conduct the rhythm in Example 9-1 the downbeat is executed in a standard fashion.

Example 9-1:

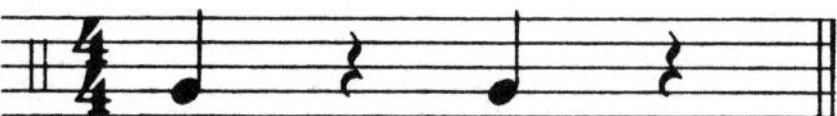

Following the rebound of pulse 1, the intensity leaves the gesture. The motion into pulse 2 is smaller, shorter. Following the rebound of 2, the arm and shoulder intensify the preparation into pulse 3, making the gesture slightly larger. This intensity remains through the rebound of pulse 3, after which the energy again dissipates until the preparation for the next performed pulse (Diagram 9-3).

Diagram 9–3

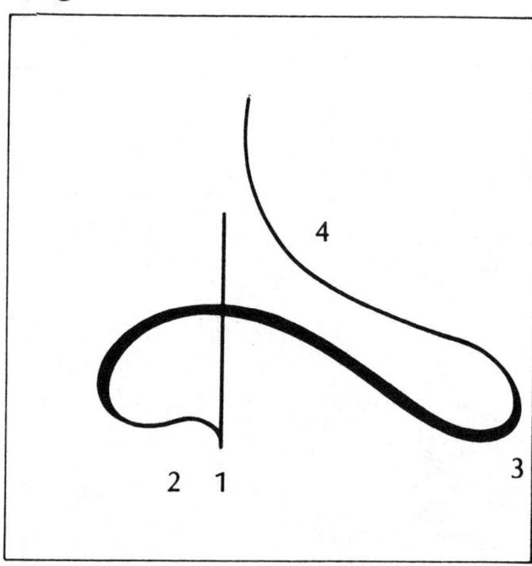

To conduct the rhythm in Example 9-2, the first 3 pulses will be "expressionless," simply marking the passing of time. These pulses will be indicated by small motions. Following the rebound of pulse 3, the hand and arm should greatly intensify and increase the size of the preparation into pulse 4 (Diagram 9-4). The result will be a sweeping sensation into pulse 4.

Example 9-2:

Diagram 9–4

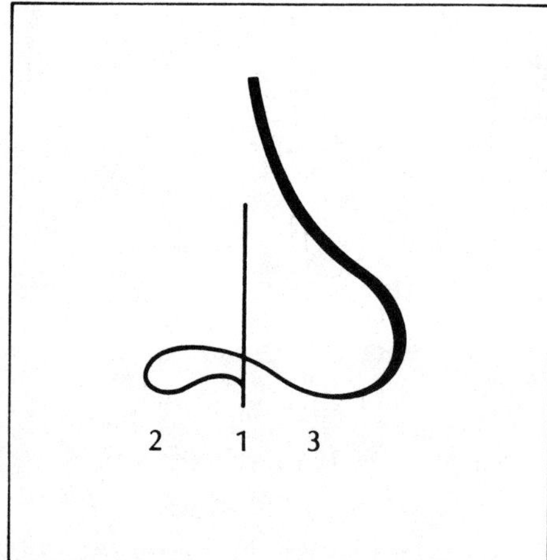

Practice conducting each of the following rhythmic exercises. Say the rhythm on "ta." The performers should not look at the music. They must be able to perform the rhythmic articulation as you prepare them through your conducting. *Note:* The symbol > is used in these exercises to denote a moderate amount of accentuation. The notes are to be noticeably attacked, yet held for full duration. The symbol —, also used for marcato, implies "a kind of "leaning" on the note, giving it special stress without noticeably attacking it."*

Exercise 9-2

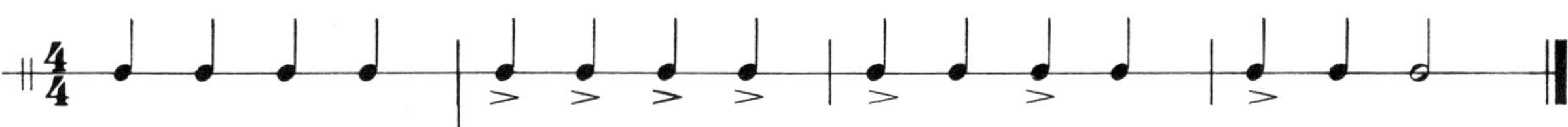

Exercise 9-3

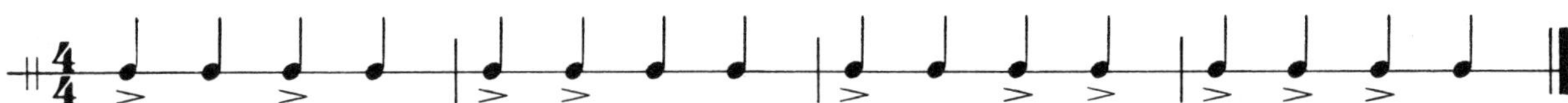

Exercise 9-4

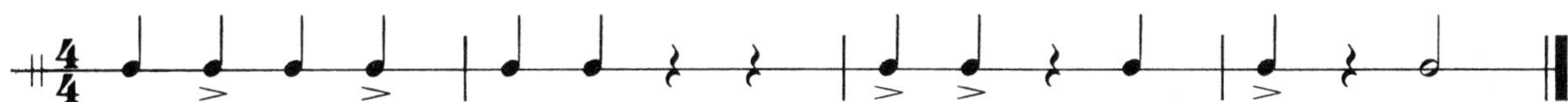

Exercise 9-5

Exercise 9-6

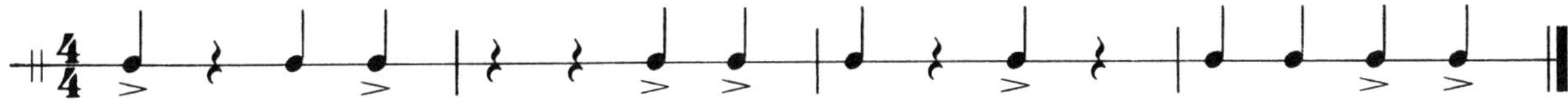

Exercise 9-7

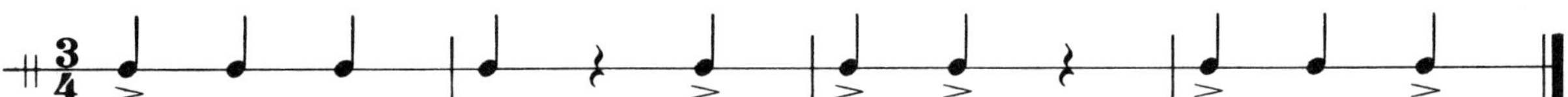

*Gardner Read, *Music Notation,* 2nd ed. (Boston: Crescendo Publishers, 1969), p. 262.

The Staccato Gesture

The staccato gesture looks very similar to the marcato except that it is smaller and less weighty. Staccato is usually reserved for softer, detached music which demands, as in the marcato gesture, that the hand come to a complete stop after the rebound (Diagram 9–5). Because of the light and bouncy character of the gesture, it is often brought up parallel to the eyes and closer to the face. The ictus of each pulse should be attacked sharply. There is very little arm movement, most of the work being done with the wrist.

Diagram 9–5

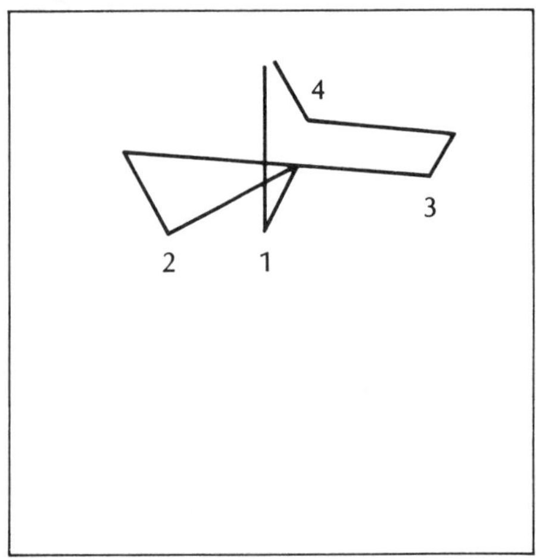

Conduct the following melody using a staccato gesture.

Exercise 9–8

Angels We Have Heard On High *French Carol Melody*

Subdivided Pulse I (Moderate and Fast Tempos)

Someday you may have the great misfortune of having the ensemble you are conducting fall apart before your very ears. Every ensemble has that potential. Your first duty is to *stop being "expressive" and go back to basics:* Work strictly to get the singers to perform precisely and rhythmically together in the same measure on the same pulse. If the performers are struggling to hold the music together, your ensemble needs the most precise pulse pattern you can deliver.

Rule 1. *Make the pulse pattern smaller.* Do not flail the air. Force the performers to focus their attention on a small, clean pulse pattern.

Rule 2. *If necessary subdivide,* showing where the "ands" are by using the wrist in the rebounds. *Each gesture for pulse and rebound is a stopped gesture,* like a small staccato gesture for both pulse and the "and." The wrist is very active in executing the rebound. The stopped beat is very helpful in showing the performers exactly where they are in the measure.

Rule 3. *Move pulses 2 and 3 clearly away from the basic pulse line.* Keep each pulse in its own proper place.

Rule 4. *Be persistent* until the group comes back together again.

Rule 5. Please, only *one downbeat per measure.*

Although one would think that a larger pattern would be easier to see, trust the experience of many conductors who have saved their ensemble by the small, angular, subdivided pulse pattern. In this instance, bigger is not better.

The fact that you stop *on the ictus* as well as the rebound differentiates this subdivided pulse gesture from the marcato gesture. In executing the gesture the hand and arm come to a complete stop at the ictus. Then a sharp wrist and forearm movement is used to indicate the subdivision "and" at the rebound (Diagrams 9-6a, 9-6b, and 9-6c).

Diagram 9–6a

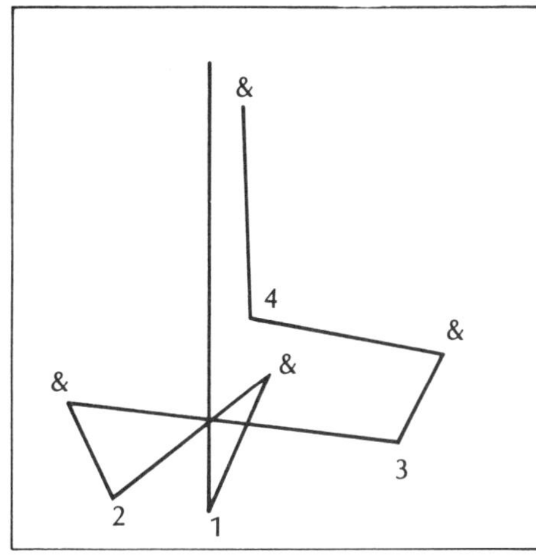

Diagram 9–6b

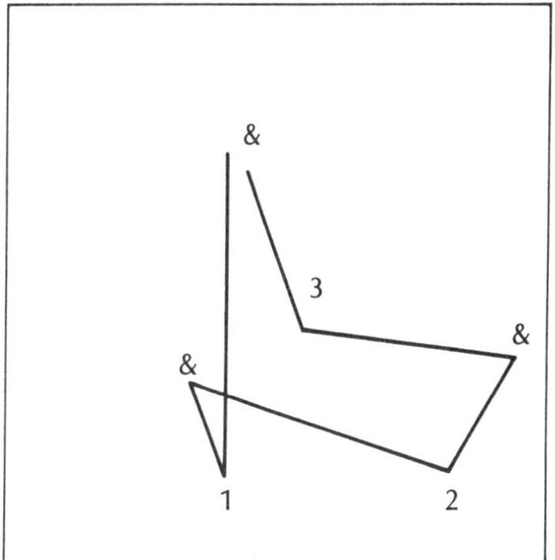

Diagram 9–6c

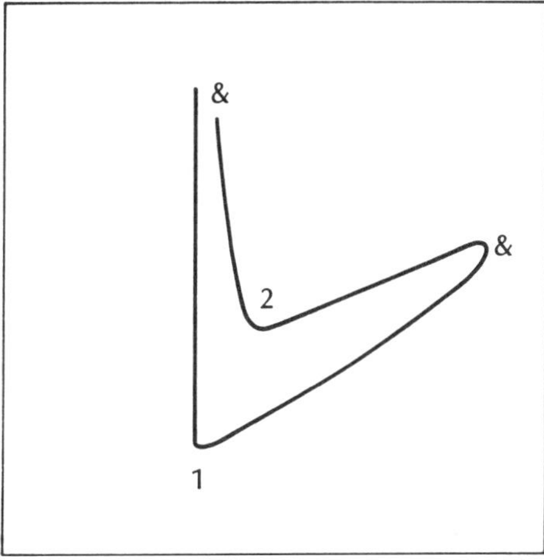

- **Nota Bene**

This subdivided beat shows the subdivision "and" of each pulse. It is clear to the point of being academic. This conducting gesture may also be used when the ensemble is entering a difficult rhythmic portion of the music and the performers need a clean, clearly delineated gesture to indicate exactly where the ictus and subdivision are. It is also extremely useful when approaching a *ritard.*

Subdivided Pulse II (Slow Tempos)

When conducting music in which the tempo is very slow, you may use another type of subdivided pulse gesture to indicate both the basic pulse and the subdivision "and." The gesture for "and" must be

1. Very close to the ictus of the pulse
2. Smaller than the pulse gesture
3. In a direction other than that of the next pulse

The subdivisions for the four and three patterns (Diagrams 9-7a and 9-7b) must be so precisely delineated that the performers will know exactly where each pulse is and where the subdivisions are.

Diagram 9–7a

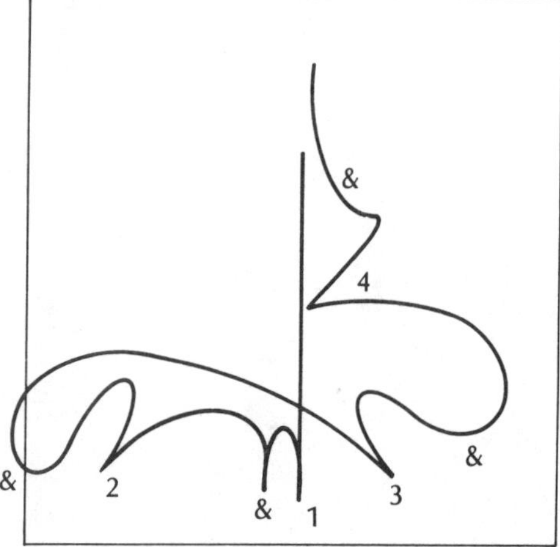

Diagram 9–7b

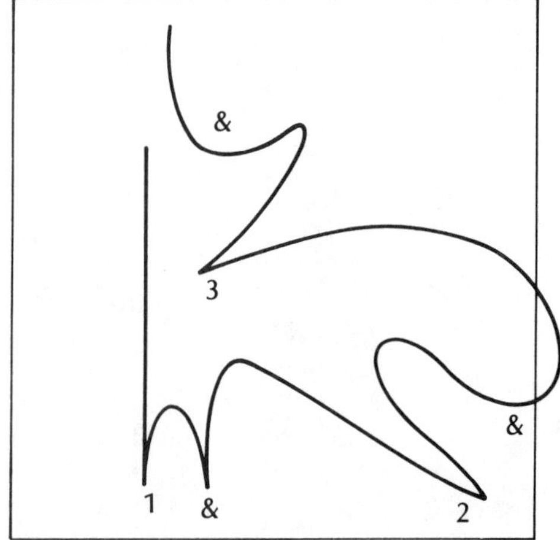

The rebound of each pulse should move back in the same direction from which the preparation for that pulse came (Diagrams 9-8a and 9-8b). Thus the rebounds of 2 and 3 tend to move back toward the basic pulse line, keeping the hand and arm from being too far extended to one side or the other.

Diagram 9–8a

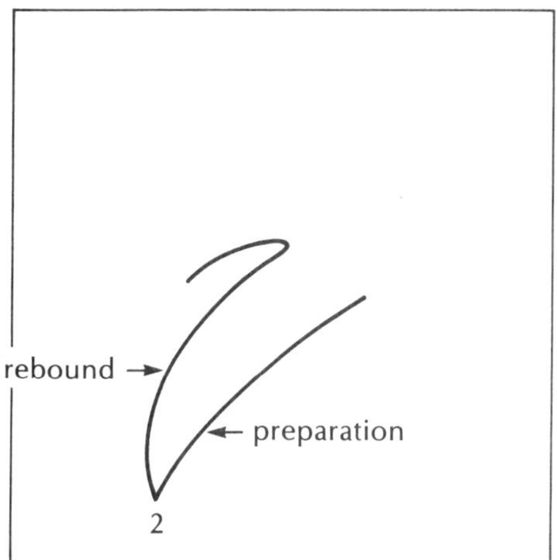

Diagram 9–8b

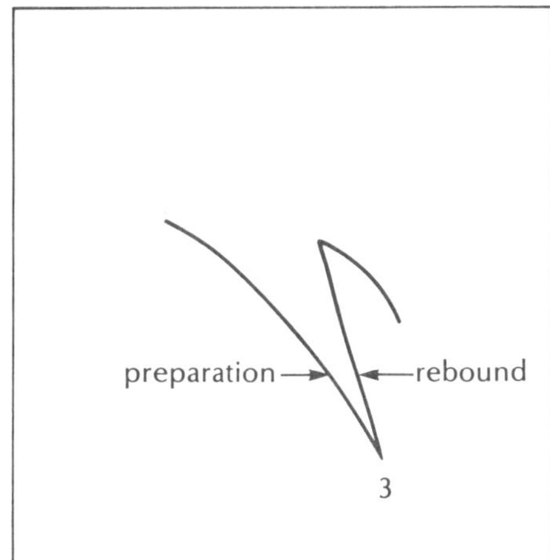

- **Nota Bene**

Some conductors will use a gesture in which the preparation of 4 actually crosses to the left of the downward pulse line. The result is a backhanded "and" of 4 (Diagram 9-9).

Diagram 9–9

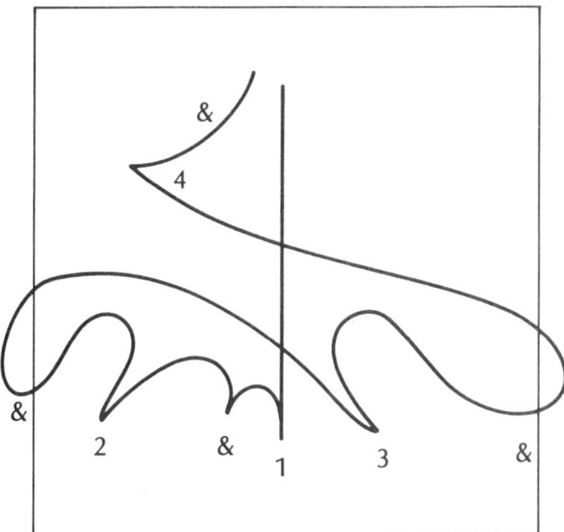

The Subdivided Two Pattern

When music demands a clearly delineated two pattern in order to show rhythmic precision or to hold the ensemble together, the gesture is executed as an angular two pattern with rhythmic rebound (Diagram 9-10). Note that the downbeat can actually be, and should be, straight down for this gesture. The gesture, as with the subdivided four and three patterns, is a stopped gesture, with stops occurring directly on the pulse and the "and" of the pulse.

Diagram 9–10

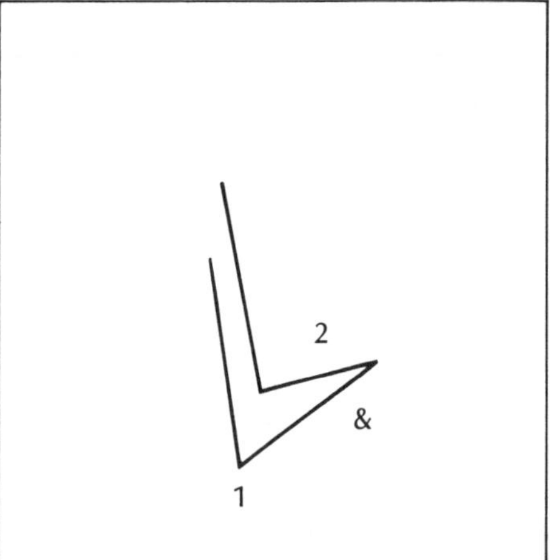

When the music is in a slow two meter, necessitating subdivision, some conductors will simply conduct a four pattern, as if the music were in $\frac{4}{8}$ rather than $\frac{2}{4}$. It is imperative that you inform your ensemble which gesture will be used to conduct a particular meter if it varies from the traditional.

Other conductors will use the subdivided two pattern. The downbeat may either be straight down (Diagram 9–11a) or slightly to the side (Diagram 9–11b). Pulse 2 may also cross the basic pulse line, resulting in a backhanded "and" of 2 (Diagram 9–11c). Note that the rebound of pulse 1 in diagram 9–11b is very angular, back in the direction of the preparation for pulse 1. This gesture keeps the hand and arm from being extended too far to the outside for the subdivision "and."

In the subdivided patterns there is, of course, more motion per measure than there is for those measures that are not subdivided. But all suggestions about the latter made thus far apply. Be sure you do not roll the wrist or forearm or pull the second pulse toward the body. Hands and fingers should be left in the same position relative to the wrist and arm unless the music demands they be moved otherwise for shading and phrasing purposes.

Diagram 9–11a

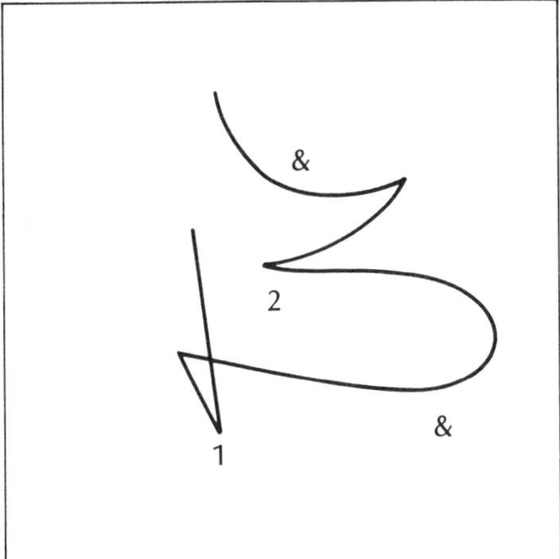

Diagram 9–11b

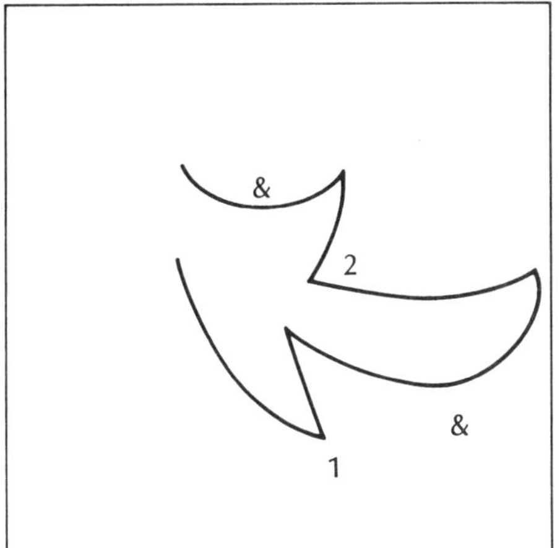

Diagram 9–11c

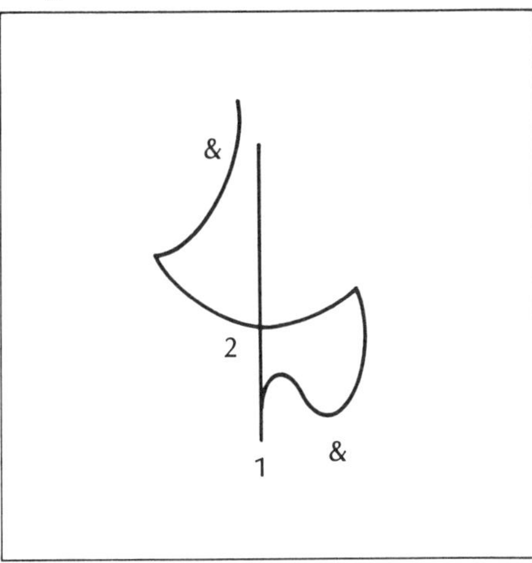

Conduct the following melodies using the appropriate subdivided pattern.

Exercise 9-9

Exercise 9-10

Exercise 9-11

Supplementary Conducting Exercises: Subdivided Pulses

HAYDN: Sanctus (*Harmoniemesse*)

HANDEL: Behold the Lamb of God (*Messiah*)

way, tak - eth a - way the
way the sins
cresc.
tak - eth a - way the
tak - eth a - way the

SOPRANO
f
Sure-ly, sure - ly He hath
ALTO
f
Sure-ly, sure - ly He hath
TENOR
f
Sure-ly, sure - ly He hath
BASS
f
Sure-ly, sure - ly He hath
borne our griefs, and car - ried our sor - rows,
borne our griefs, and car - ried our sor - rows,
borne our griefs, and car - ried our sor - rows,
borne our griefs, and car - ried our sor - rows,

MOZART: Requiem aeternum (*Requiem*)

Published by Edwin F. Kalmus, n.d.

10 Ending The Work

Fermatas I (Final Fermatas)

Fermatas cause considerable problems for conductors because they occur in many different musical contexts. A fermata usually signifies a hold, the length of which is to be determined by the conductor. However, in Baroque chorales the fermata indicated the end of a phrase and not necessarily a hold. In da capo works from the Baroque period the fermata indicated the end of the work.

The major concern here is with the held fermata. The length of the hold is at the discretion of the conductor, who must consider the effect it may have on the dramatic impact of text and music. There are no definitive rules on how long a fermata should be held, although musical propriety and good taste should be considered when making a decision.

Because no tone should "sit still," you must show in your fermata gesture that the tone continues musically to develop. You must either increase or decrease intensity and/or dynamics. The conducting hand must continue to move throughout the gesture. If you wish the final note to crescendo, increase the intensity in your body, hand, and arm. To decrescendo, the intensity must be diminished as your hand moves through the fermata gesture.

You must be sure that the fermata has its intended effect, i.e., a hold beyond the normal duration of the tone. Your timing is not only important for aesthetic reasons: you also do not want your hand and arm to be overly extended to the outside.

Final Fermata: Four Pattern

If the fermata occurs on pulse 1 of the final measure (Examples 10–1a and 10–1b), the pulses are melded into a single diagonal gesture.

Example 10-1a: **Example 10-1b:**

If the fermata occurs on a final whole note, as in Example 10–1a, count the full measure in your head, add an appropriate duration, then give the release (Diagram 10–1a). If the fermata is on a final quarter note, as in Example 10–1b, add an appropriate duration after the downbeat, then give the release (Diagram 10–1b). In general, if the fermata occurs on the first pulse of the last measure, all gestures will look the same, no matter whether the final note value is a whole note or an eighth note.

Diagram 10–1a

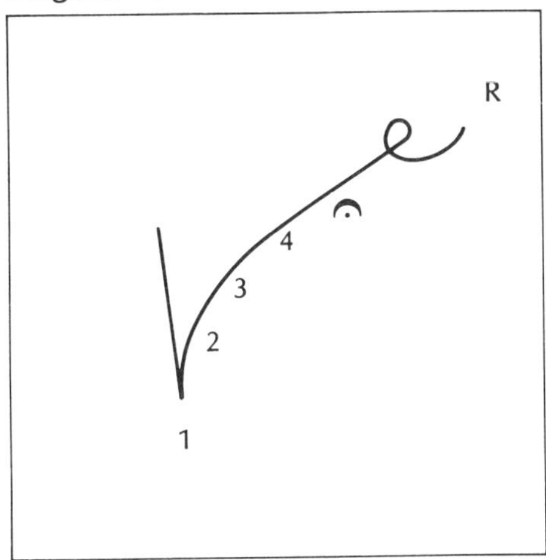

Diagram 10–1b

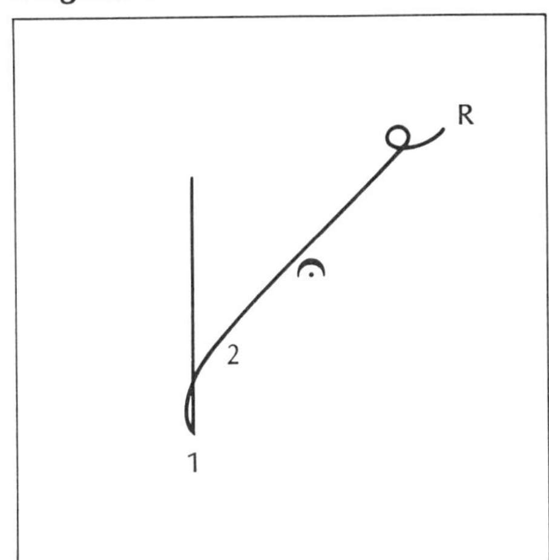

Another school of thought suggests conducting the entire note value over which the fermata is placed, then adding an appropriate duration for the fermata. If the fermata is over a final whole note the conductor would actually conduct the entire measure, and, after pulse 4, add an appropriate duration for the fermata. The use of this technique is a personal decision. The left hand may be used to hold the ensemble by using a crescendo gesture to show an increase in intensity for the duration of the fermata.

When the fermata occurs on pulse 2 of the final measure (Examples 10–2a and 10–2b), the diagonal gesture begins immediately after the ictus of pulse 2 (Diagrams

Example 10-2a: **Example 10-2b:**

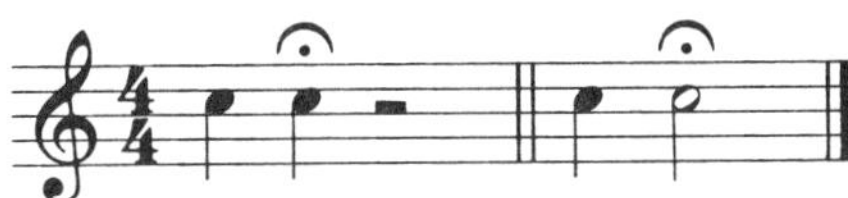

Diagram 10–2a

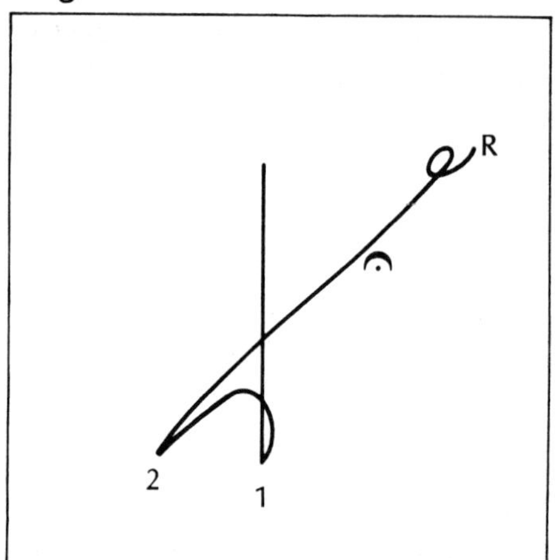

Diagram 10–2b

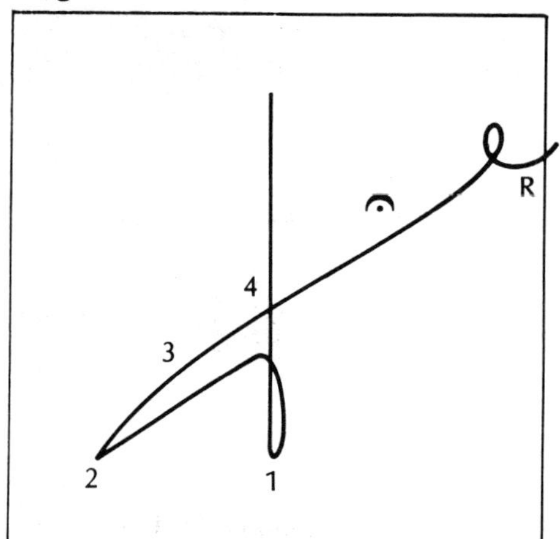

10–2a and 10–2b). Note that the rebound of 2 is absorbed in the diagonal gesture. The diagonal is back over the basic pulse line. Timing the gesture is again critical so that you are not overly extended to the outside when you make the release.

When the fermata occurs on pulse 3 of the last measure (Example 10–3), the most important aspect to consider is again where the hand will be when the final release is made (Diagram 10–3). To keep the release gesture within limited range, the gesture into pulse 3 must be shorter than usual, barely past the basic pulse line. The diagonal movement will thus be more sharply angled to keep the entire gesture within limits.

Example 10-3:

Diagram 10–3

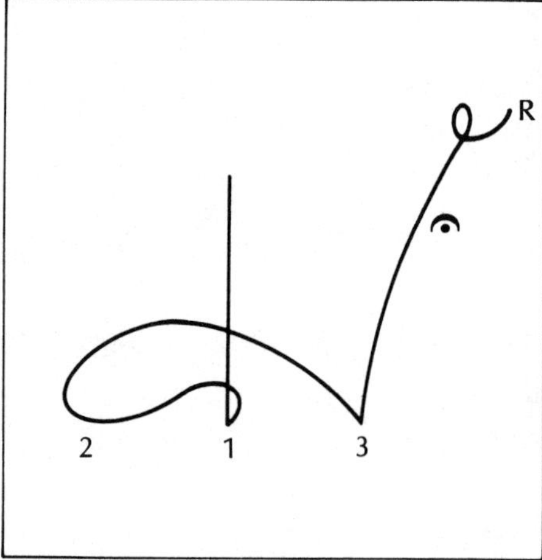

When the fermata occurs on the final pulse of the measure in four meter (Example 10-4), the diagonal gesture is begun after the ictus of pulse 4 (Diagram 10-4).

Example 10-4:

Diagram 10–4

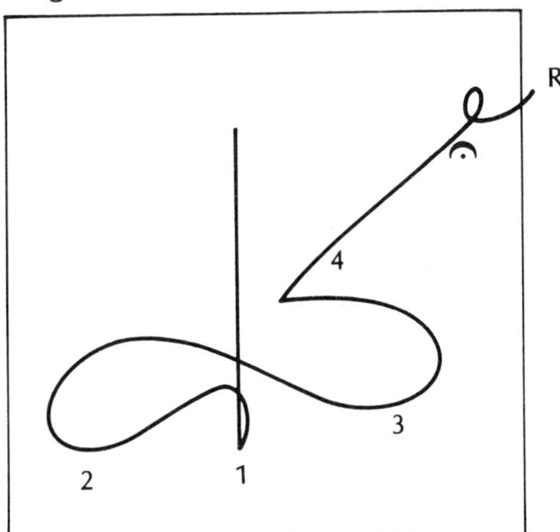

In other instances when you need more distance, the ictus of 4 may be executed to the left of the downbeat line (Diagram 10-5).

Diagram 10–5

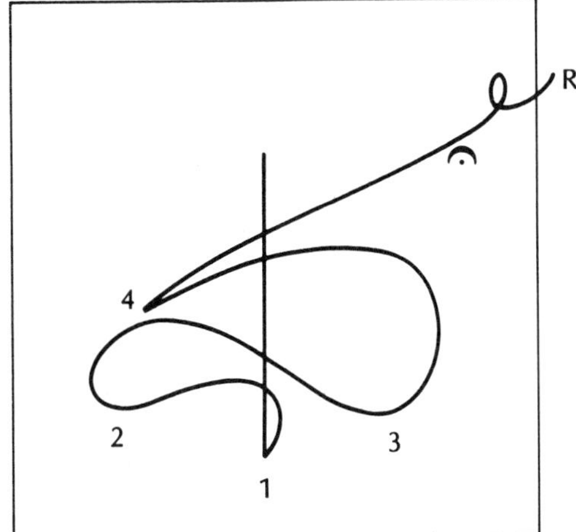

• Nota Bene

No matter where the ictus for the final pulse is, it is important that the conducting hand be in an appropriate position for the release. As you study the music and practice the conducting gestures for each fermata, you will have to decide:

1. When the basic pattern must be modified
2. How long the fermata is to be held
3. How far the hand must travel before the release

It is important to remember that the hand should continue to move throughout the entire gesture. You must *plan* where your hand will be at the time of the release.

Final Fermata: Three Pattern

In the three pattern the fermata gesture and release are similar to those in the four meter (Diagrams 10–6a, 10–6b, and 10–6c). When the fermata occurs on pulse 2, the ictus for 2 should be executed very close to the downward pulse line. Otherwise the hand may be in an awkward position for the release.

Diagram 10–6a. Fermata on 1

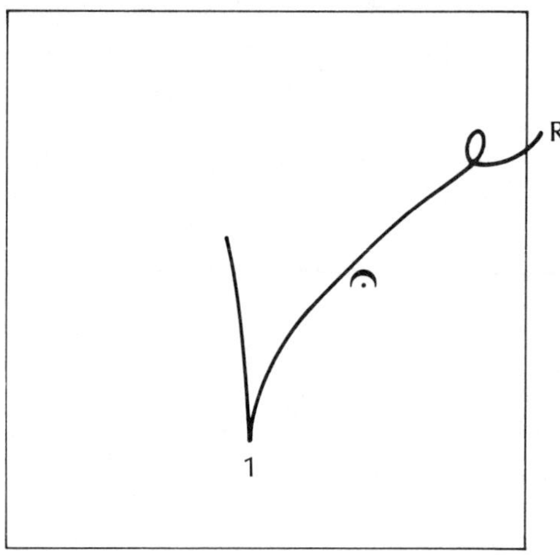

Diagram 10–6b. Fermata on 2

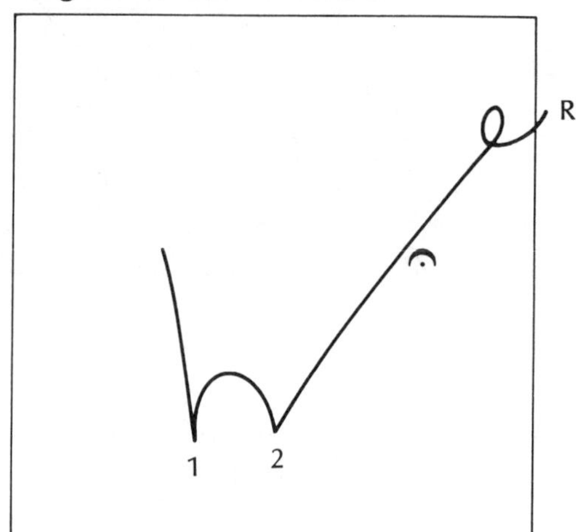

Diagram 10–6c. Fermata on 3

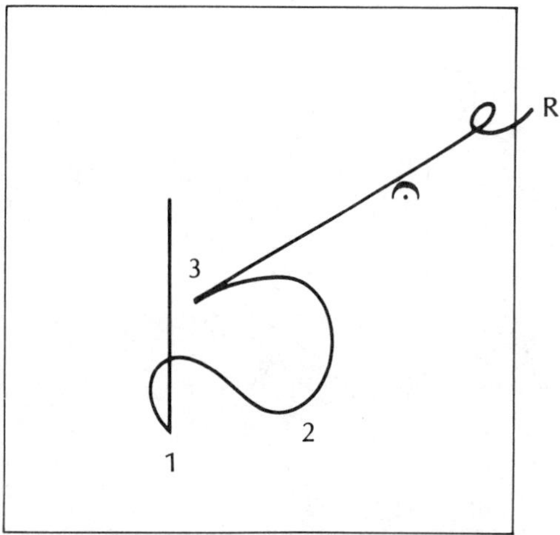

Final Fermata: Two Pattern

The gesture for the fermata on pulse 1 is similar to the other gestures on the same pulse (Diagram 10-7). Note that instead of using the "fishhook" motion for pulse 1, this pulse can be executed straight down.

Diagram 10–7

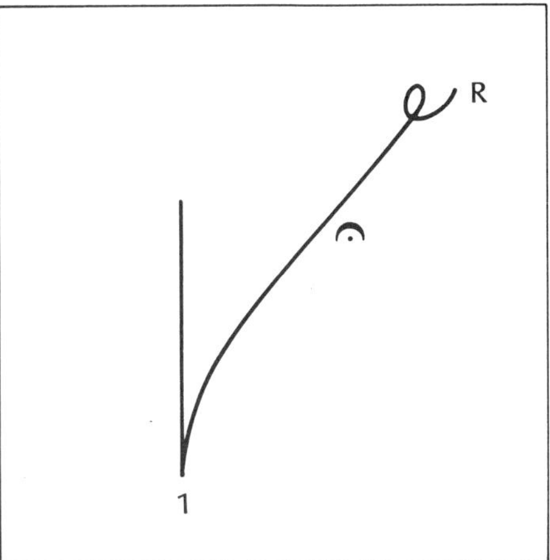

When the fermata occurs on pulse 2, the ictus of 2 should be executed at the basic pulse line (Diagram 10–8a) or even slightly to the left of the line (Diagram 10–8b) to give additional space for the diagonal movement of the fermata gesture.

Diagram 10–8a

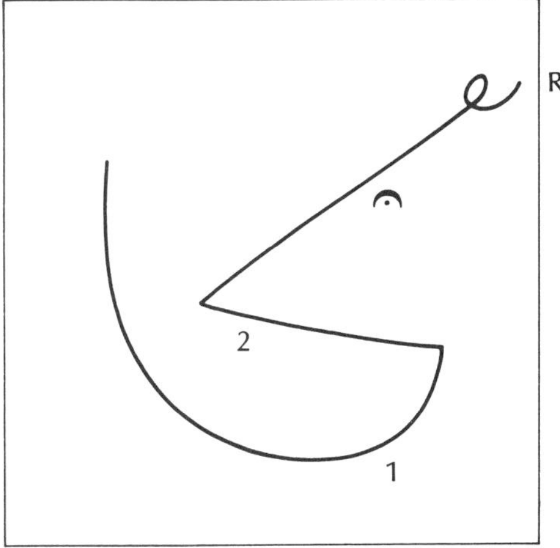

Diagram 10–8b

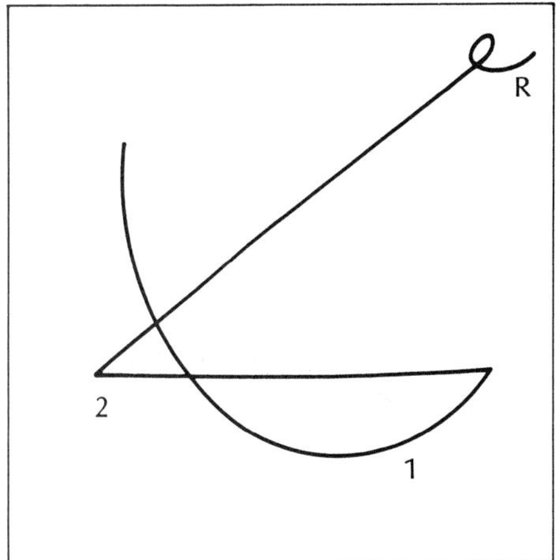

• Nota Bene I

The fermata gesture resulting in a release at the end of the work tends to move in a diagonal direction up and slightly away from the body toward the ensemble. The arm reaches slightly outward toward the ensemble as if straightening at the elbow. It should be noted, however, that the arm should not straighten entirely. This would give the release a very stiff look.

• Nota Bene II

The release in all of these examples is done primarily with the wrist, although its character depends on the music. For a rousing *fff* release, the release circle may be considerably larger and the rebound from the release ictus much more abrupt. The larger the loop, the more the forearm must move and the faster the hand must travel to get to the release point. This has the effect of increasing intensity. Note that the rebound is very short and abrupt, and your hand must come to a complete stop before dropping to your side.

The Morendo Gesture

Not all music ends with rousing, intensity-increasing character. Sometimes it is appropriate to end with a decrescendo or morendo ("dying away"). Instead of an intensity-increasing diagonal gesture moving up and away from the body, the diagonal gesture is downward and slightly toward the body. In the morendo gesture your elbow comes down toward your side. The release should be soft and gentle. In the case of a morendo ending, it should be subtle, almost imperceptible, yet exact and precise. A simple rotating curl of the fingers to make the release loop should be enough. At other times a gentle patting gesture with the fingers may be used. The wrist should hardly move.

If a fermata occurs on pulse 1 of any of the patterns, the gesture will look like Diagram 10-9. Because the pulse pattern is smaller and the gesture for the fermata downward, the ictus for the downbeat may be closer to face level so that the diagonal gesture will have an appropriate distance to travel. By moving the entire gesture up closer to face level, the diagonal may move downward to approximately belt level as long as nothing is in the way to block the ensemble from seeing the release gesture.

Diagram 10–9

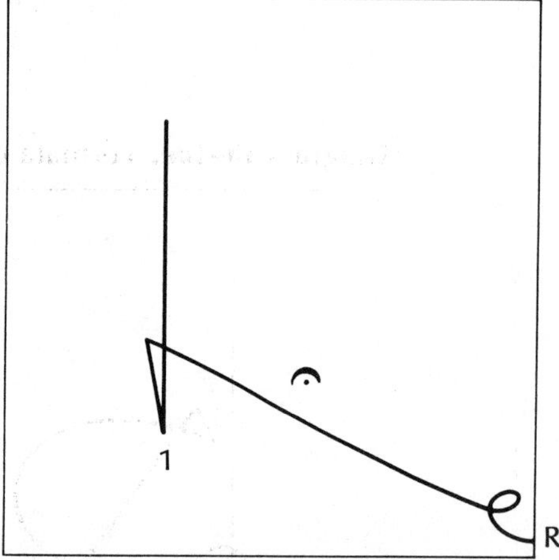

The fermata gestures resulting in a decrescendo or a morendo are shown in Diagrams 10-10a through 10-10f.

Four Pattern

Diagram 10–10a. Fermata on 2.

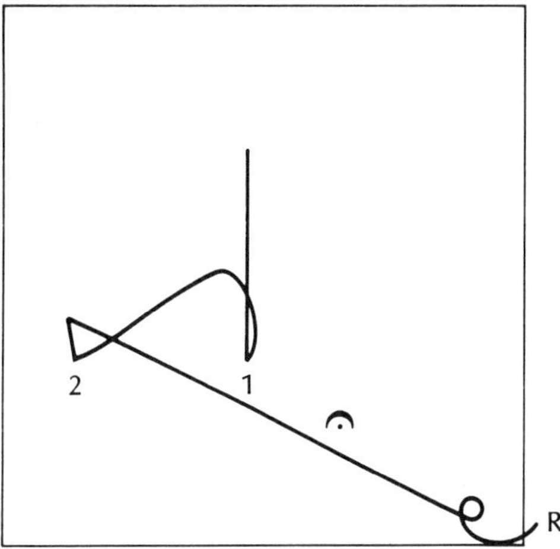

Diagram 10–10b. Fermata on 3.

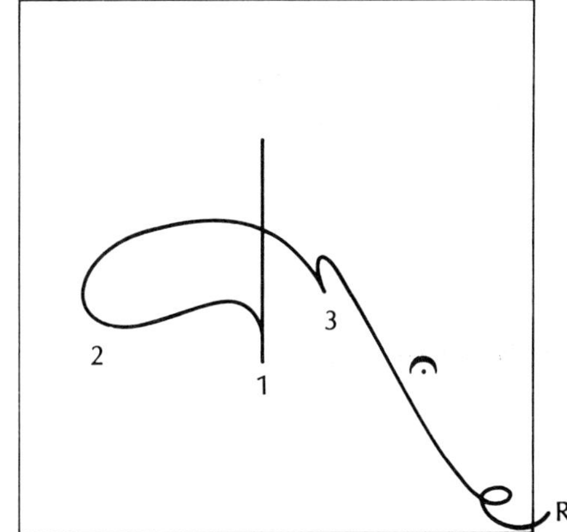

Diagram 10–10c. Fermata on 4.

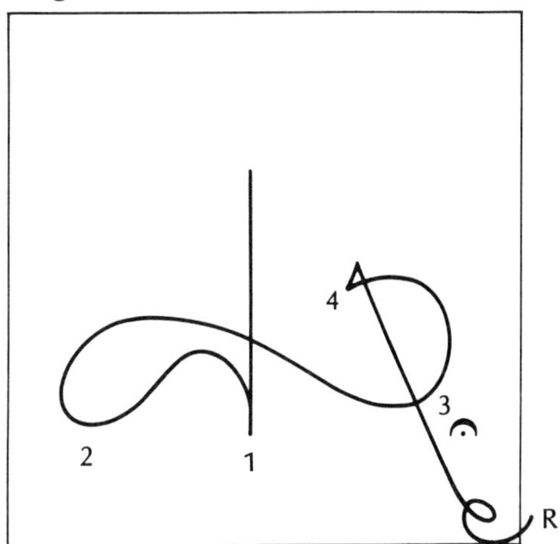

Three Pattern

Diagram 10–10d. Fermata on 2.

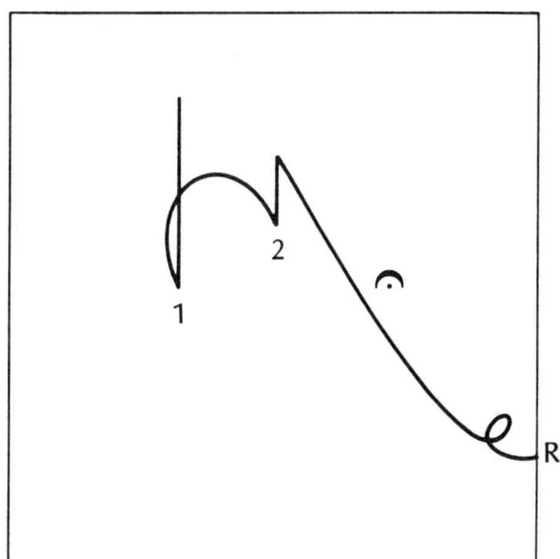

Diagram 10–10e. Fermata on 3.

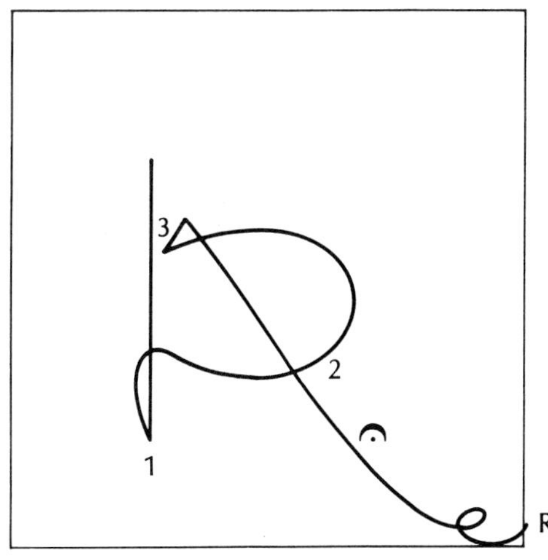

Two Pattern

Diagram 10–10f. Fermata on 2.

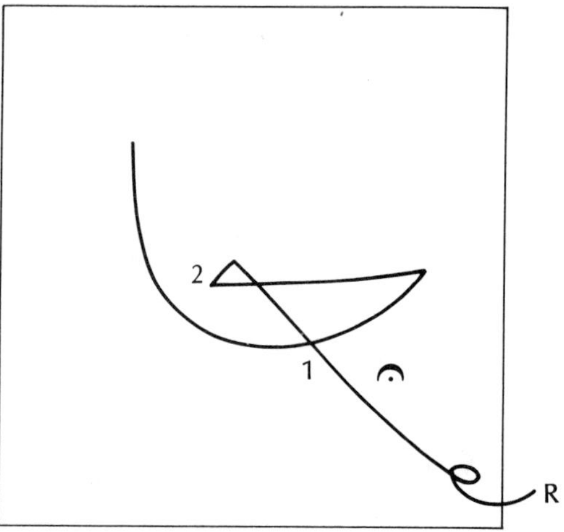

- **Nota Bene**

Note that the downward diagonal is preceded each time by a small rebound after the ictus. Because the downward diagonal is contrary in direction to any rebound normally given, the rebound must be given to show precisely the ictus of the pulse.

Supplementary Conducting Exercises: The Final Fermata

IPPOLITOF-IVANOF: Bless the Lord, O my soul

FAST: Let Me Grow Lovely, Growing Old

BARBER: Sure on this shining night

BRAHMS: Wondrous cool, thou woodland quiet

SEIBER: The Old Woman (*Three Hungarian Folk-Songs*)

Additional Suggested Choral Repertoire

For Beginning Levels of Conducting

STRAND, PEGGY. *Märi.* Two-part. Michael Kysar, #C102.
YOUNG, BRECK. *Red Rosey Bush.* SSA. Carl Fischer, #CM 5282.

For Advancing Levels of Conducting

From: KJELSON, LEE, AND JAMES MCCRAY. *The Conductor's Manual of Choral Music Literature,* SB 911. Melville, New York: Belwin Mills, 1973.

CROCE, GIOVANNI. *O Vos Omnes.* SATB, pp. 21-23.
FAURÉ, GABRIEL. *Libera me.* SATB, pp. 186-198.
LOTTI, ANTONIO. *Kyrie Eleison.* SATB, pp. 62-65.
PALESTRINA, GIOVANNI DA. *Hosanna in Excelsis.* SATB, pp. 13-17.

From: *Five Centuries of Choral Music for Mixed Voices,* ED2529. New York: G. Schirmer, 1963.

BACH J. S. *Come, soothing death.* SATB, pp. 6-8.
BILLINGS/GUSTAFSON. *When Jesus Wept.* SATB, pp. 97-101.
MENDELSSOHN, FELIX. *He, watching over Israel.* SATB, pp. 25-31.
VAUGHAN WILLIAMS, R., arr. *The Turtle Dove.* SSATB, pp. 52-55.

11 Mixed Meters/Other Release Gestures

Mixed Meters

The student of conducting must have the conducting patterns so well in hand that shifting from one meter to another can be handled without a conscious thought process. Meters often change in contemporary music. The same meter does not always remain constant throughout the musical work. The following exercises should be conducted in two different ways. First, conduct each meter in the exercise twice, i.e., $\frac{4}{4}$, $\frac{4}{4}$, $\frac{3}{4}$, $\frac{3}{4}$, etc., allowing the equivalency of two measures for each meter. Use the three tempos suggested. Then conduct each meter only once, as given, allowing the equivalency of only one measure for each meter. Use the three tempos suggested. Memorize the exercises. Begin slowly at first, being sure each sequence of meters can be completed accurately and confidently.

Exercise 11-1 ♩= 60, ♩= 90, ♩= 120

$\frac{4}{4}$ $\frac{3}{4}$ $\frac{4}{4}$ $\frac{2}{4}$ $\frac{3}{4}$ $\frac{2}{4}$ $\frac{4}{4}$

Exercise 11-2

$\frac{3}{4}$ $\frac{4}{4}$ $\frac{2}{4}$ $\frac{4}{4}$ $\frac{3}{4}$ $\frac{2}{4}$ $\frac{3}{4}$

Exercise 11-3

$\frac{4}{4}$ $\frac{3}{4}$ $\frac{4}{2}$ $\frac{4}{4}$ $\frac{2}{4}$ $\frac{3}{2}$ $\frac{4}{4}$

In Exercise 11-3 the quarter note remains constant throughout the exercise. In the $\frac{4}{2}$ and $\frac{3}{2}$ measures use a subdivided beat, literally eight and six pulses per measure, respectively.

Supplementary Conducting Exercises: Mixed Meters

BARBER: Sure on this shining night

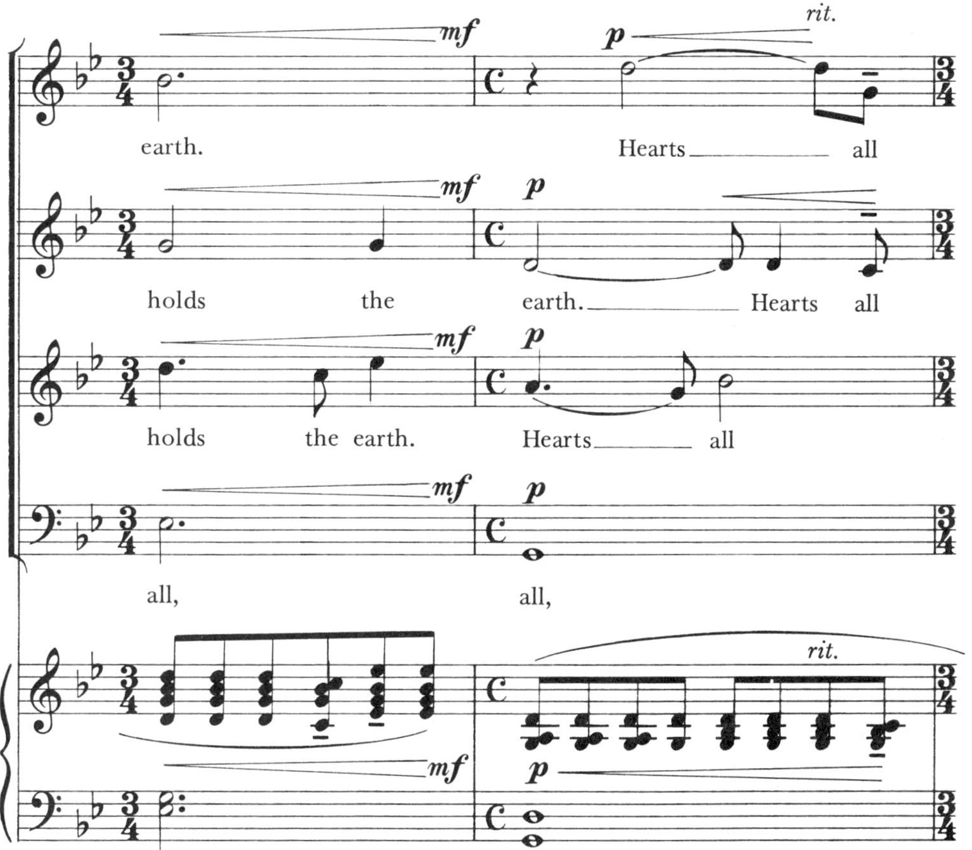
mf
p
rit.
earth.
Hearts all
holds the
earth. Hearts all
holds the earth.
Hearts all
all,
all,

Very light and crisp
SOPRANO
O
hark!
ALTO
O
hark!
TENOR
pp
Hark! hark, the lark. Hark the lark. Hark, hark the lark.
BASS
pp
Hark! hark, the lark. Hark the lark. Hark, hark the lark.
[PIANO]
pp (use as needed)
O
Hark!
O
O
Hark!
O
Hark the lark. Hark, hark the lark.
Hark the lark. Hark, hark the lark.

HOLST: Lullay my Liking

Additional Suggested Choral Repertoire

For Beginning Levels of Conducting

BARTÓK, BÉLA. *Three Hungarian Folk Songs.* SSA. Boosey and Hawkes, #5488.
THOMPSON, RANDALL. *Velvet Shoes.* SA. E. C. Schirmer, #2526.
VAUGHAN WILLIAMS, R. *Lullaby.* SSA. Oxford University Press, #44.603.

For Advancing Levels of Conducting

From: KJELSON, LEE, AND JAMES MCCRAY. *The Conductor's Manual of Choral Music Literature,* SB 911. Melville, New York: Belwin Mills, 1973.

HEISINGER, BRENT. *O Praise the Lord.* SATB, pp. 223–235.

From: *Five Centuries of Choral Music for Mixed Voices,* ED2529. New York: G. Schirmer, 1963.

BARBER, SAMUEL. *Sure on this shining night.* SATB, pp. 1-5.
HOLST, GUSTAV. *Lullay my Liking.* SATB, pp. 149–150.
MUCZYNSKI, ROBERT. *Alleluia.* SATB, pp. 93-96.
VAUGHAN WILLIAMS, R. *Let us now praise famous men.* SATB, pp. 102–107.

The Release Gesture IV (Other Types)

Conductors use a variety of release gestures. The beginning conductor should remember that the gesture must be effective, appropriate to the music, and unique for clarity's sake.

Along with the circular release gesture recommended throughout this book, a very popular and commonly used release among choral conductors is the thumb-forefinger release. At the moment of release the thumb and forefinger come together. There is no preparation loop. As preparation, most conductors open the palm toward the ensemble just before the moment of release. Eye contact is absolutely essential, since the gesture is considerably more subtle than that preceded by the preparatory loop. If this release is used at the end of a work, the thumb and forefinger may stay together until after the rebound, when the arm is dropped to the side. If this release is used within the composition, the thumb and forefinger should separate immediately. Because this type of release lacks a pronounced preparatory gesture, it should be moved to face level so that eye contact can help indicate a release is coming.

Danger I. If the conductor pulls pulse 2 of the four pattern toward the body, a thumb-forefinger release on pulse 2 will not be seen by half the ensemble. View of the release gesture will be blocked by the conductor's forearm and hand. The release gesture must remain out in front of the body.

Danger II. If the conductor executes this release on pulse 3 of the four pattern and at the same time rolls the wrist and forearm counterclockwise, the palm of the hand will end up completely facing the outside. Rolling the forearm will force the elbow up. The view from the audience will not be very desirable, since the arm will flap considerably.

Another type of release is the heel-bump release. As preparation, the hand is tilted back so that the full palm is facing the ensemble. The hand is vertical to the ground, with fingers straight up in the air. The moment of release is indicated by bringing the hand downward with palm open to the ensemble and bumping the release ictus with the heel of the hand. The fingers do not move. The ensemble's attention must be directed to the heel area of the hand. There should be a small rebound following the release. This is an effective gesture if you are asking for a decrescendo. In some instances your palm may be open to the ensemble for an entire measure: for example, as you indicate a decrescendo on the final two measures of a piece (Example 11-1).

Example 11-1:

Eye contact is very important to indicate that a release is about to be made.

In the finger-tap release, the wrist draws the hand back as a preparatory gesture. As the hand moves forward again, the fingers simply tap the ictus of the release pulse. The fingers move slightly to indicate the exact moment of release. This release can be used for subtle as well as forceful, sharp releases. The gesture is often used following a fermata or for a final release. It is not often used for an internal release.

For exciting, loud climactic endings the conductor may use what might be called a fist-grab release. Normally this is given intensely and dynamically. As preparation the hand moves toward the ensemble, fingers beginning to close. At the moment of release, the fingers snap shut in a fist, virtually grabbing the sound away from the ensemble. There may be a considerable rebound from the force of hitting the release ictus. This rebound may carry the conductor's hand over his head. After a slight pause at the top of the rebound the conductor may drop the hand to his side, or open the hand, palm up, and acknowledge the ensemble for the "magnificent" ending. At this point, the director usually steps to one side so that the audience has a full view of the ensemble.

The fade-away release occurs on a morendo ending. The hand is very slowly dropped, palm down, indicating a decrescendo. As the performers become inaudible they do not reenter. The ensemble stops of its own accord when the collective air runs out. The hands or fingers do not signal an actual release, just a constant decrescendo. When the sound has ended, the conductor's hand may stop momentarily before dropping to the side, or it may, if already close to the side, continue to drop slowly until it gets there.

• To the Student

Most of these releases, except the fist-grab release, may be executed with both hands. Mirror releases, especially final releases, appear to give the ensemble more solidity, more assurance, and more precision. Practice these releases with one hand and then both hands until they feel comfortable.

12 The Six Pattern/ Fermata Studies

The Six Pattern

When the tempo of music written in six meter is relatively quick, the music is usually conducted in a standard two pattern (Diagram 12-1). When the tempo of the music is slow, however, necessitating that each eighth note receive a pulse, the pattern is usually divided into two groups of three pulses each (Diagram 12-2).

Pulses 2 and 3 are placed to the inside, pulses 4 and 5 to the outside. Pulses 2 and 4 should be placed close to the basic pulse line so that the hand and arm are not overextended for pulses 3 and 5.

Diagram 12–1

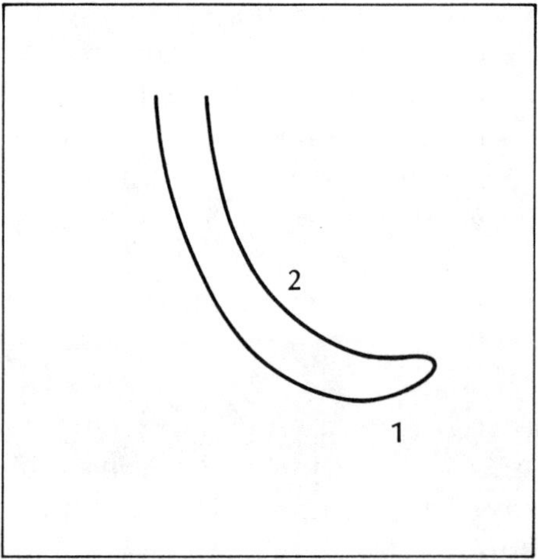

Diagram 12–2

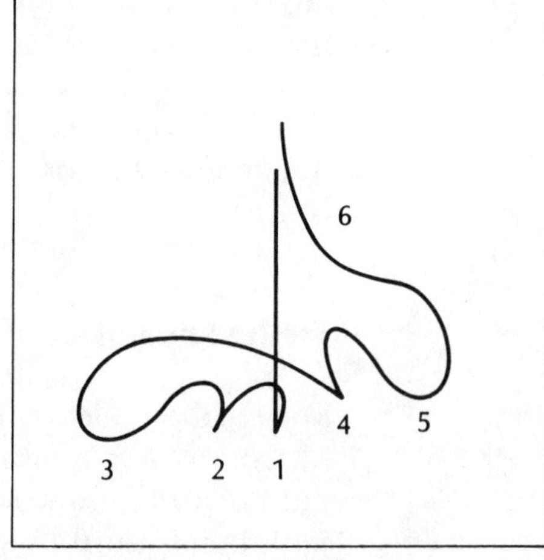

• To the Student

As you observe yourself in the mirror, be sure that pulse 2 and 3 of the six pattern are placed along the horizontal line. You should reach for pulse 3, rather than pull pulse 3 toward your body. Keep your hand and arm out in front of your body.

Conduct the following melodies, using both the two pattern and the six pattern.

Exercise 12-1

Exercise 12-2

Exercise 12-3

Supplementary Conducting Exercises: $\frac{6}{8}$ Meter

Drink to Me Only with Thine Eyes *Old English Folk Song*

Drink to me on - ly with_ thine eyes,_ And I___ will pledge with mine.
Or leave a kiss but in___ the cup___ And I'll___ not look for wine.

MOZART: Laudate Domine (*Vesperae solennes de confessore*)

tr
f
tr
fi - li - o et spi - ri - tu - i san - cto,
f
fi - li - o et spi - ri - tu - i san - cto,
f
fi - li - o et spi - ri - tu - i san - cto,
f
fi - li - o et spi - ri - tu - i san - cto,
f

Additional Suggested Choral Repertoire

For Beginning Levels of Conducting

HANDEL/HOPSON. *Come, Jesus, Holy Son of God.* Two-part mixed voices. Harold Flammer, #A-5623.

NELSON, RON. "I Will Not Leave You Comfortless," from *Four Anthems for Young Choirs.* Two-part. Boosey and Hawkes, #5576.

WHITECOTTON, SHIRLEY. "The Skylarks," from *Two Idylls.* SSA, Galaxy Music, #1.2530.1.

Fermatas II (Internal Followed By Rest)

In the following examples the fermatas are followed by a rest. A release must be executed by the conductor on the rest. The fermata is indicated by a diagonal movement of the hand.

Fermata on 1: Four Pattern

When the fermata occurs on pulse 1, as in Example 12-1, the diagonal hand movement follows the rebound of pulse 1 (Diagram 12-3). A sharper rise to the diagonal fermata line keeps the hand close to the downward pulse line. At the top of the diagonal the hand may stop momentarily before moving to the left of the downward pulse line for the release on pulse 2. The release on 2 is at approximately eye level. Following the release the hand should continue into the pattern for pulse 3.

Example 12-1:

Diagram 12–3

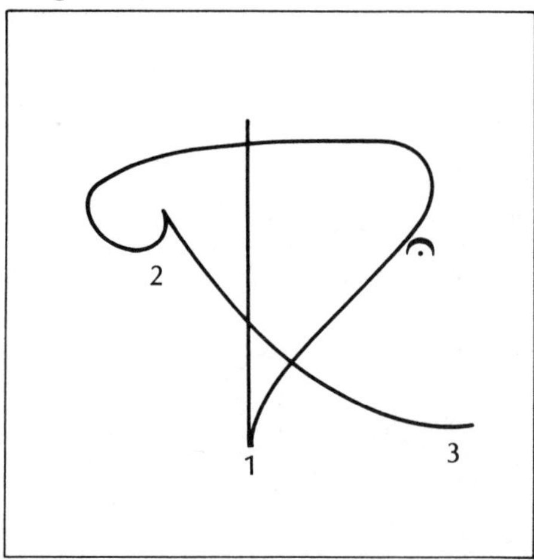

Fermata on 1: Three Pattern

When the fermata occurs on pulse 1 in triple meter (Example 12-2), the preparatory release loop is given at the top of the diagonal, putting the hand in exact position for the release on pulse 2 (Diagram 12-4).

Example 12-2:

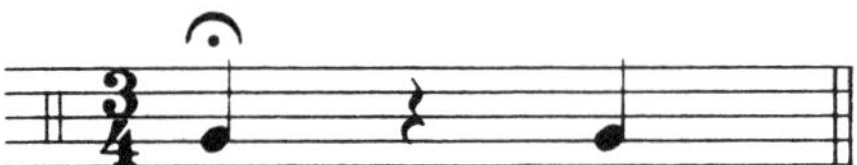

Diagram 12–4

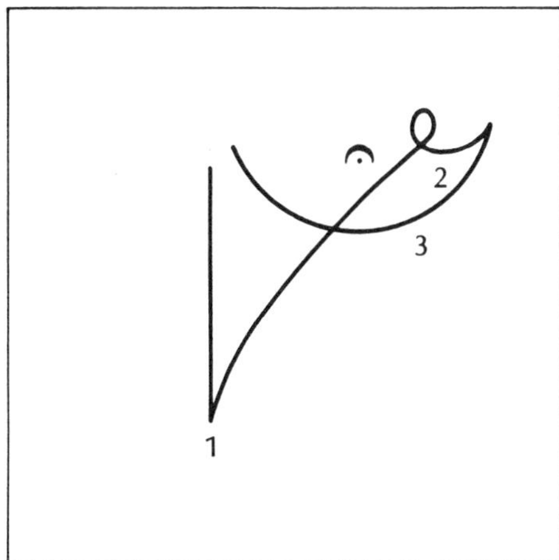

Because the release on 2 should be given at approximately eye level, pulse 3 should descend below the release ictus of pulse 2. Since the loop will carry the hand even farther out to the side, it is imperative that the diagonal rise sharply so the hand is not extended too far to the side after the loop has been executed.

Fermata on 2: Four Pattern

When the fermata is on pulse 2, as in Example 12-3, the diagonal fermata gesture moves across the vertical pulse line. The gesture looks exactly like a release on 3, although the diagonal gesture must move more slowly to indicate the fermata. At the top of the diagonal the wrist executes the loop, putting the hand in the correct position for the release on 3 (Diagram 12-5).

Example 12-3:

Diagram 12–5

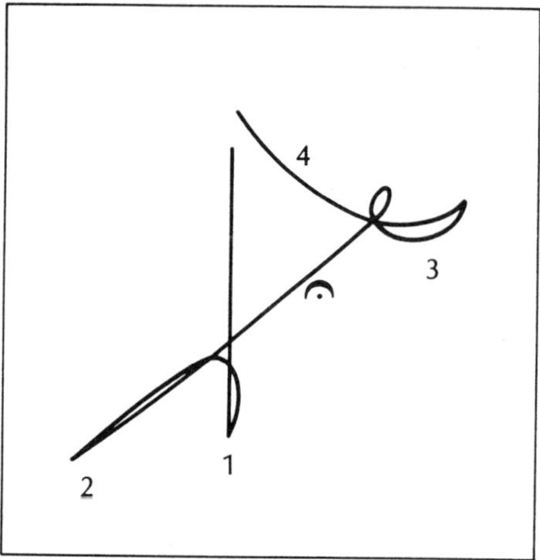

Fermata on 2: Three Pattern

When the fermata occurs on pulse 2 in triple meter, pulse 2 is executed very close to the vertical basic pulse line. The diagonal fermata gesture rises sharply. The release is executed with a hand-arm-wrist movement "over the top" of the pattern toward the basic pulse line. The release loop actually moves beyond the basic pulse line so that the release on 3 allows the rebound to be straight up. The hand is now in position for the downbeat (Diagram 12-6).

Diagram 12–6

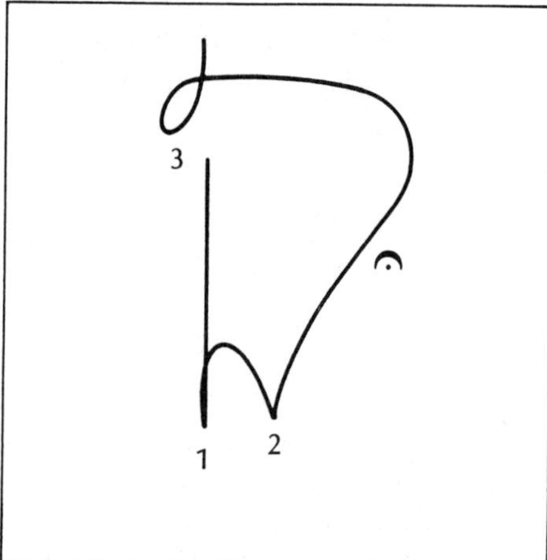

Fermata on 3: Four Pattern

When the fermata occurs on pulse 3, as in Example 12–4, pulse 3 must be very close to the basic pulse line and the diagonal gesture must rise sharply (Diagram 12-7).

Example 12-4:

Diagram 12–7

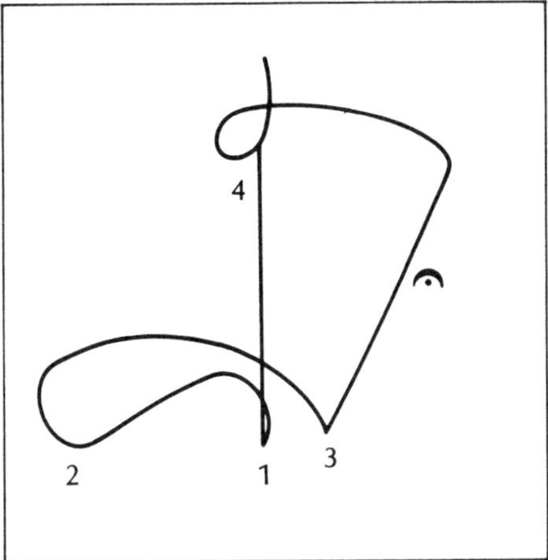

The release is again "over the top" of the pattern, with the preparatory loop crossing the basic pulse line. The hand rises on the rebound of the release, in position for the downbeat of the next measure.

There are some instances in which pulse 3 may occur to the left of the basic pulse line (Diagram 12–8), allowing more distance for the diagonal fermata gesture to travel.

Diagram 12–8

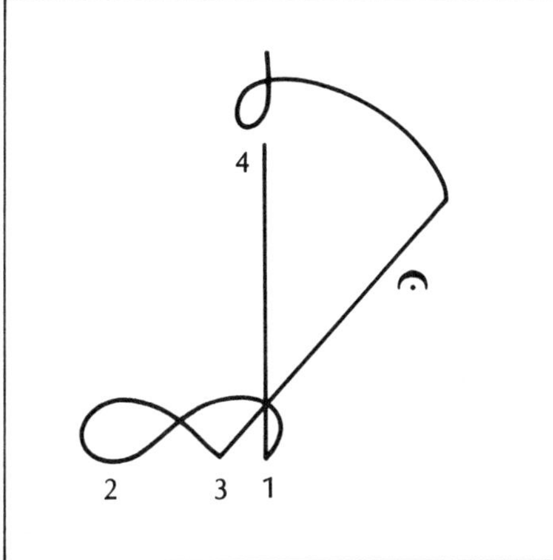

Fermata on the Final Pulse of the Measure

When the fermata occurs on the final pulse of the measure, as in Example 12-5, the gesture must be carefully controlled. The preparatory gesture for the final pulse must remain low in the pattern. The ictus should occur approximately *on the basic pulse line.* The diagonal is the same as in the other patterns. The release is executed "over the top," as in the other releases studied. It is important to remember, however, that the release occurs on the first pulse of the next measure and that *the rebound of the release is actually the rebound of pulse 1.* Although the hand is in position for a downbeat, it does not give the downbeat, but instead continues on into pulse 2. The hand will move to the left for pulse 2 in a four pattern (Diagram 12-9a), and to the right for pulse 2 in a three pattern (Diagram 12-9b).

Example 12-5:

Diagram 12–9a

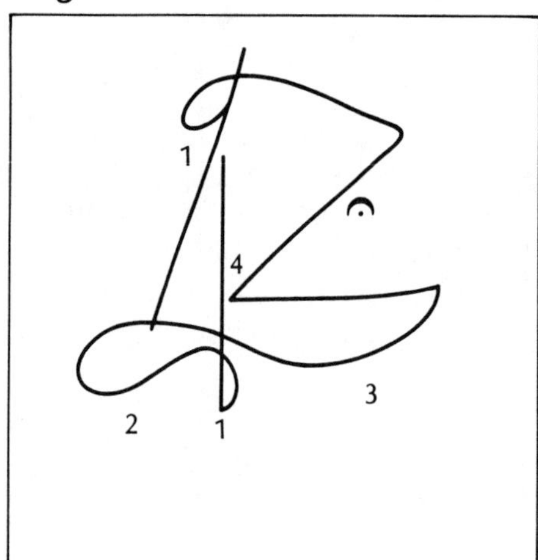

Diagram 12–9b

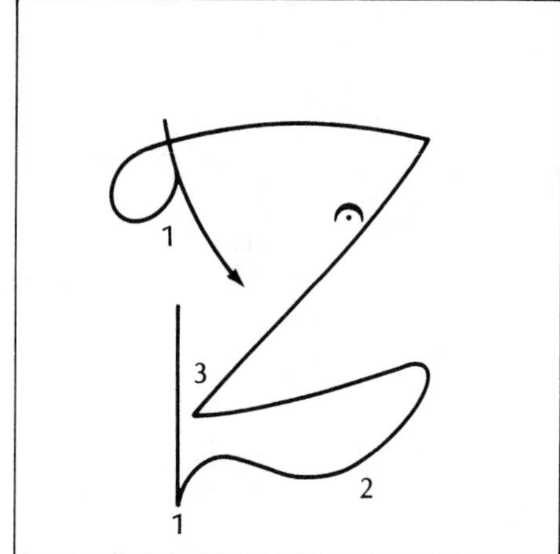

• To the Student

Fermata gestures must be practiced many times until they become automatic. Use the mirror. Watch the wrist on the release. Do not allow the diagonal line to move too far to the outside. The speed with which you move the diagonal line will determine how long you hold the fermata. In all cases the fermata gesture must continue to move before the release preparation is executed. *Keep the fermata gesture moving!!!*

Conduct the following exercises. Be sure to maintain eye contact with the ensemble throughout the fermata gesture and the release.

Exercise 12-4

Exercise 12-5

13 The One Pattern/ Additional Fermata Studies

The One Pattern

Some music goes so quickly the conductor can only give one pulse per measure. The gesture for the one pattern looks like a long, slender, vertical oblong (Diagram 13–1). The ictus of pulse 1 should be cleanly and precisely executed, although the gesture may be slightly rounded at the ictus point.

Diagram 13–1

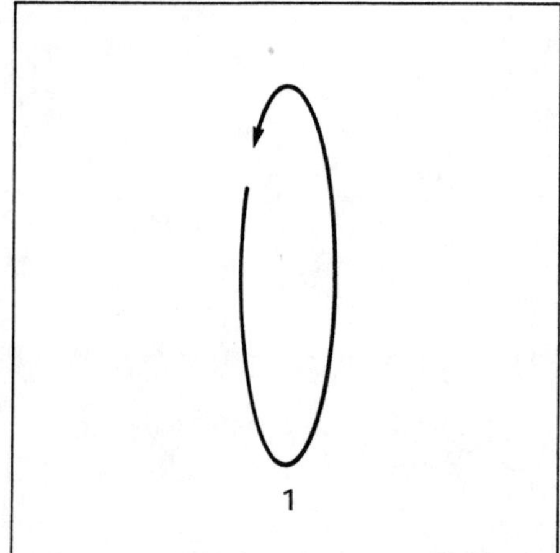

Conduct the following melodies using the one pattern.

Exercise 13-1

Exercise 13-2

Supplementary Conducting Exercises: The One Pattern

ROHWER: Tanzlied

Musik in der Schule, Band II, Moeseler Verlag Wolfenbuettel; trans. Brian Busch.
Text and melody: Jens Rohwer
From: Jens Rohwer, "Das Wunschlied," Möseler Verlag, Wolfenbüttel und Zürich/Voggenreiter Verlag, Bonn-Bad Godesberg

MORLEY: Sing we and chant it

Fa la la la la la la la, Fa la la la.
Fa la la la la la, Fa la la la la.
Fa la la la la la, Fa la la la.
Fa la la la la, Fa la la la.
Fa la la la la la la, Fa la la la la la.

Additional Suggested Choral Repertoire

For Advancing Levels of Conducting

From: Kjelson, Lee, and James McCray. *The Conductor's Manual of Choral Music Literature,* SB 911. Melville, New York: Belwin Mills, 1973.

Ravenscroft, Thomas. *Tomorrow the Fox Will Come to Town.* SATB, pp. 34–36.

From: *Five Centuries of Choral Music for Mixed Voices,* ED2529. New York: G. Schirmer, 1963.

Morley, Thomas. *Sing We and Chant It.* SATB, pp. 44–48.

Preparatory Gesture III (Subdivision Preparation)

A customary problem when conducting works which begin on a subdivision of a pulse is to get the ensemble to enter *on time* and with the proper articulation. The preparatory gesture for works which begin on a subdivision is exactly the same as if the work began on the next pulse. Thus the ensemble has less than a full pulse to interpret the conductor's gesture. Your gesture must be firm, precise, and command considerable authority.

To conduct a work beginning on a subdivision of a pulse (Examples 13-1a and 13-1b), the general rule is to give as preparation the pulse gesture which precedes the entrance. Example 13-1a begins on the "and" of pulse 1. To conduct this example, bring your hand to a complete stop on the basic pulse line. Sweep the ensemble with your eyes to be certain everyone is watching. Then drop your hand forcefully straight down, giving pulse 1 as the preparation for entrance. Take a quick, forceful breath as you give this pulse. Your downbeat and subsequent rebound will be more angular than usual. You may also attack the downbeat with a bit more energy. Remember that the ensemble must take a quick breath with you on the downbeat and be prepared to sing on the "and" of pulse 1. A solid downbeat will help the ensemble take a more forceful breath. A slightly angular rebound with a small wrist flip will help define the exact point at which the ensemble should begin.

Example 13-1a: **Example 13-1b:**

If the work begins on a subdivision smaller than "and" (Example 13-1b), the initial preparation pulse must be even more forceful, more angular, the intake of air even more abrupt. To conduct Example 13-1b, give the initial downbeat with vigor. Be sure there is plenty of eye contact before you begin. Your intake of air as you execute the downbeat must be very visible, even audible.

The same procedure is followed for all attacks on subdivisions of the other pulses. The pulse just before the subdivision is given as preparation. If a work begins on a subdivision of pulse 2, then 2 is given as the preparation. If a work begins on a subdivision of pulse 3 or 4, then pulse 3 or 4, correspondingly, is given as the preparation.

• To the Student

Works which begin on subdivisions of the pulse often cause problems for the conductor. Be sure your hand comes to a complete stop before giving the preparation. Sweep the ensemble with your eyes to be certain you have everyone's attention. Eye contact is critical. Give the pulse forcefully. Take a strong, solid, even audible breath as you give the pulse. Before you prepare to conduct Exercises 13-3 to 13-10, review pp. 89-92.

It is your responsibility to teach the performers to take the quick "catch" breath and enter in the appropriate tempo if they have not experienced this type of attack before. It may be necessary to practice just the attack several times during each rehearsal until it is secure. You must be sure that *your* preparation of the gesture is disciplined and secure before attempting it with an ensemble. For most works, the preparatory gesture suggested above is appropriate and adequate. There may be other works, however, in which additional pulses are appropriate to allow the performers more time to inhale an adequate air supply (see Chapter 8, "Standing on Your Head and Other Practical Matters").

Conduct Exercises 13-3 to 13-10. Do each exercise slowly, moderately fast, then fast. Also use legato, marcato, and staccato articulations.

Exercise 13-3

Exercise 13-4

Exercise 13-5

Exercise 13-6

Exercise 13-7

Exercise 13-8

Exercise 13-9

Exercise 13-10

Supplementary Conducting Exercises: Subdivision Preparation

BARTHOLOMEW (arr.): Shenandoah

BRAHMS/KJELSON: O Lovely May

IPPOLITOF-IVANOF: Bless the Lord, O my Soul

Additional Suggested Choral Repertoire

For Beginning Levels of Conducting

FAST, WILLARD. *Be Not Afraid Because the Sun Goes Down.* SATB. G. Schirmer, #11936.
REVICKI, ROBERTO. "Paper," from *Random Thoughts.* SSA. Boosey and Hawkes, #5366.

For Advancing Levels of Conducting

From: KJELSON, LEE, AND JAMES MCCRAY. *The Conductor's Manual of Choral Music Literature,* SB 911. Melville, New York: Belwin Mills, 1973.

BRAHMS, JOHANNES. *O Lovely May.* SATB, pp. 177-181 (beginning of second section, p. 178, measure 12).
HAYDN, JOSEPH. *Awake the Harp.* SATB, pp. 106-115.

From: *Five Centuries of Choral Music for Mixed Voices,* ED2529. New York: G. Schirmer, 1963.

BARTHOLOMEW, MARSHALL, arr. *Shenandoah.* SATB, pp. 79-84.
IPPOLITOF-IVANOF, M. *Bless the Lord, O my soul.* SATB, pp. 13-17.
SCANDELLO, ANTONIO. *The Little White Hen.* SATB, pp. 56-61.

Fermatas III (Internal With Breath)

Often a breath is either marked or implied following a fermata (Example 13-2). One may state a general rule for executing fermatas of this type: *When a fermata occurs on a pulse and is followed by an implied or marked breath, execute the release for breath on the same pulse as the fermata.*

Example 13-2:

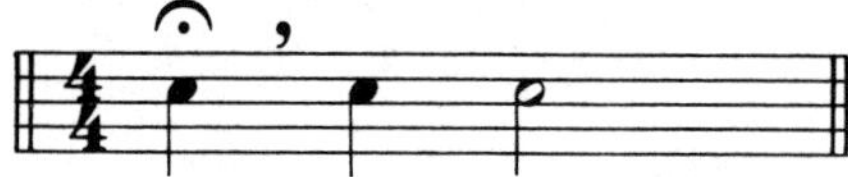

To conduct Example 13-2, execute the downbeat followed by the diagonal fermata gesture. The diagonal gesture should be steep in angle, not pulling too far from the vertical pulse line. The release for breath is "over the top," occurring where a release on pulse 1 would normally occur (Diagram 13-2). The release is at approximately eye level.

Thus the hand executes a fermata on pulse 1, then executes a release on *another pulse 1* before completing the pattern. The result is an extra pulse in the measure since there is the equivalence of two downbeats. This extra pulse cannot be given on pulse 2, since the ensemble must sing on 2. The ensemble must therefore breathe on pulse 1 in order to sing on 2. The conductor must breathe forcefully following the release.

Some conductors may prefer the inside release (Diagram 13-3).

Diagram 13–2

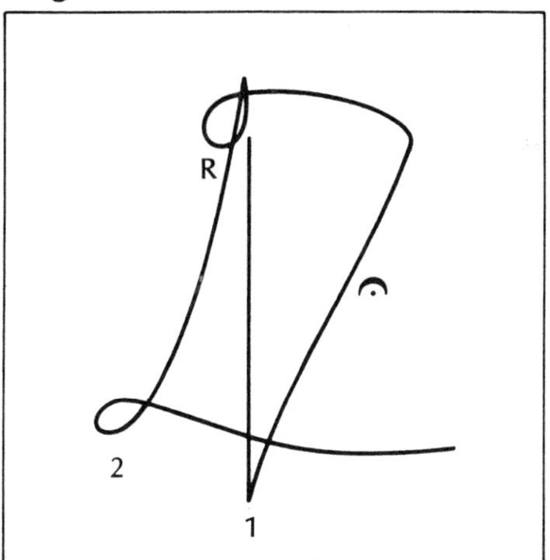

Diagram 13–3

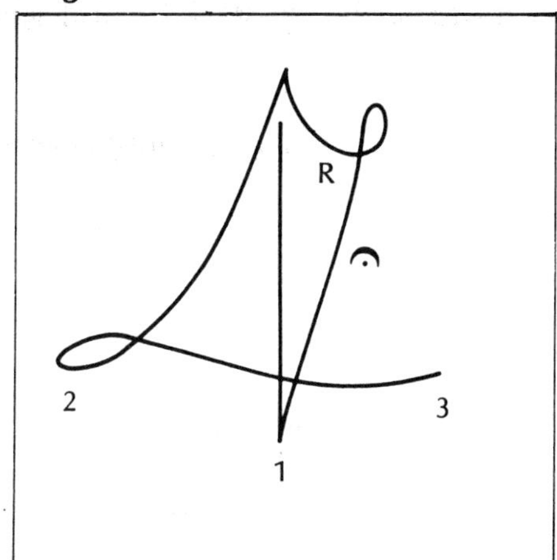

Fermata on 1: Three Pattern

When the fermata occurs on pulse 1 in triple meter, the release is also executed on a second downbeat, followed by a motion to the outside into pulse 2 (Diagram 13–4). The release and rebound are the preparation to sing on pulse 2.

Danger: If you execute the release (R) at the top of the fermata diagonal (Diagram 13–5), the gesture into pulse 2 may extend your arm too far to the outside.

Diagram 13–4

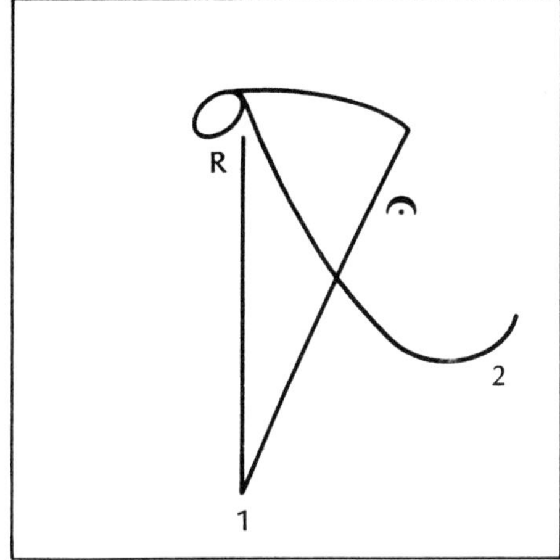

Diagram 13–5

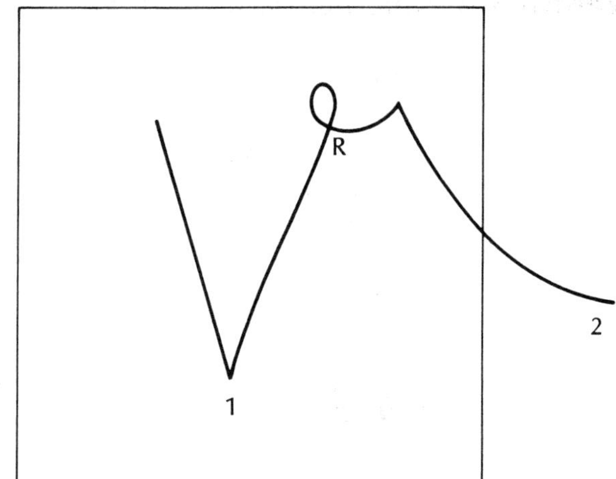

Fermata on 2: Four Pattern

When the fermata occurs on pulse 2 followed by a breath mark (Example 13–3), the release is executed on pulse 2, necessitating a second pulse 2 in the measure. The

Example 13-3:

release following the diagonal fermata gesture is executed "over the top" of the pattern to the left of the basic pulse line. The release, approximately at eye level, is higher than the initial gesture into 2 (Diagram 13-6). The hand then moves to the outside for pulse 3.

Again, some conductors may prefer the inside release (Diagram 13-7).

Diagram 13-6

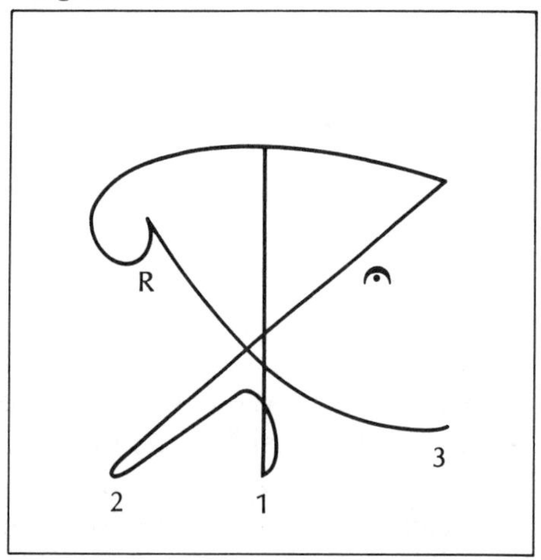

Diagram 13-7

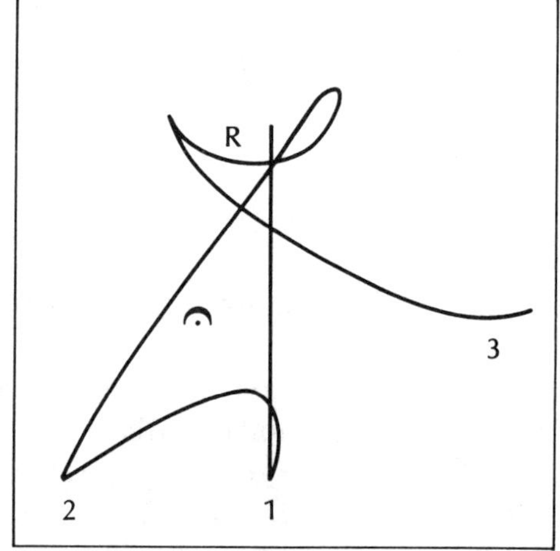

Fermata on 2: Three Pattern

When the fermata occurs on pulse 2 in triple meter, the initial pulse 2 must be executed very close to the basic pulse line. The diagonal fermata gesture should rise sharply so that the release gesture does not place the hand and arm too far to the outside (Diagram 13-8). The release, executed at the top of the diagonal at approximately eye level, is higher than the initial second pulse.

Diagram 13-8

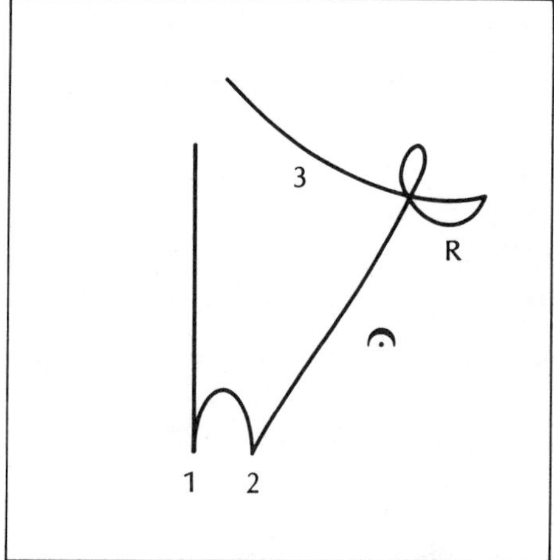

Fermata on 2: Two Pattern

In a two pattern the release loop moves slightly to the left of the basic pulse line (Diagram 13-9). At the completion of the loop, the hand and arm are in position to rise straight up in preparation for the downbeat.

Diagram 13–9

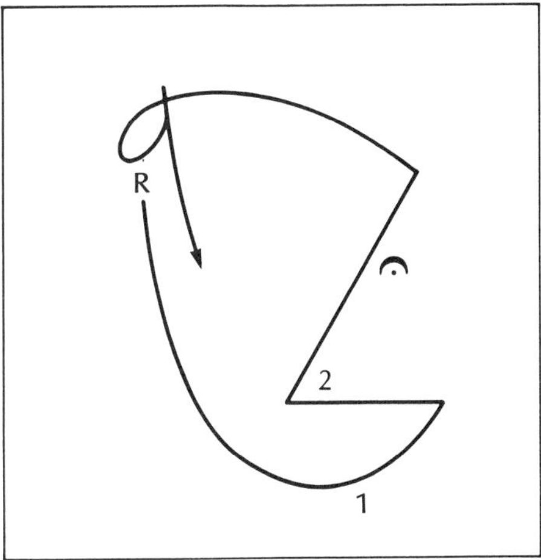

Fermata on 3: Four Pattern

When the fermata occurs on pulse 3 (Example 13-4), the release is executed on a second pulse 3. The initial 3 must be executed close to the vertical pulse line. The fermata diagonal moves up sharply. The release is executed higher than the initial pulse 3. This will place the hand and arm in the proper position to execute pulse 4 (Diagram 13-10). The release on the second pulse 3 of the pattern is thus the preparation for the ensemble attack on 4.

Example 13-4:

Diagram 13–10

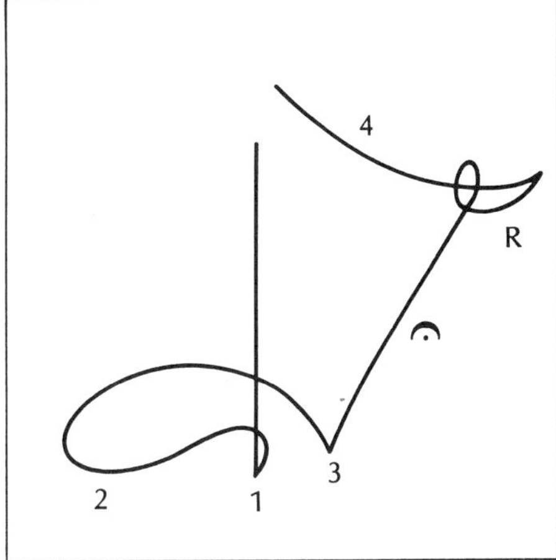

Fermata on 4: Four Pattern

When the fermata is on pulse 4, as in Example 13–5, the release must be executed along the basic pulse line so that the hand is in position to give the next downbeat (Diagram 13–11).

Example 13-5:

Diagram 13–11

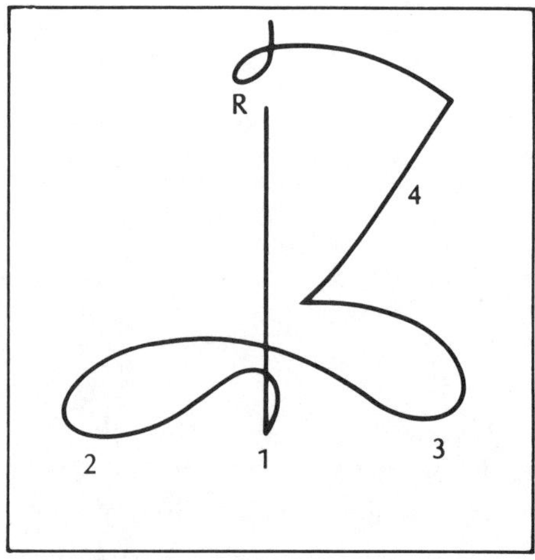

• To the Student

In all of these examples the most important technical aspect has been the position of the release. In effect you have added an extra pulse to these measures, each time duplicating in some way the pulse on which the fermata occurred.

The fermata gesture is one of great importance. It is also one which often generates great confusion among the performers. You must exercise great care in the execution of the gesture. Some conductors, rather than using the diagonal fermata gesture, will raise the hand straight up for the fermata. Experiment with both types of gestures on your own. Be sure you use the mirror to check the position of the fermata gesture and the release.

Exercise 13–11 Conduct the following melody. The ensemble is to breathe after each fermata.

Fermatas IV (Internal Without Breath)

If there is *no breath* indicated following the fermata, the precise continuation of the music needs careful preparation. Following the diagonal or straight-up gesture for the fermata, the preparation for the next pulse consists of a wrist flip of the hand along the diagonal or vertical line. This wrist flip is given on the "and" subdivision of the fermata pulse. If the fermata is on pulse 4, the timing might be schematized as shown in Diagram 13-12.

Diagram 13–12

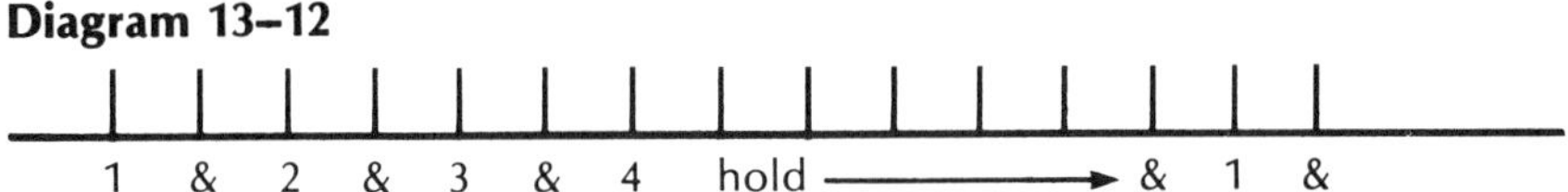

Realizing that the length of the fermata is at the discretion of the conductor, you must think the "and" subdivision in the tempo of the music following the fermata. Diagram 13-13 shows the direction of hand motion when the fermata is on pulse 4, as well as the position of the wrist flip to indicate the preparation for the next pulse.

Diagram 13–13

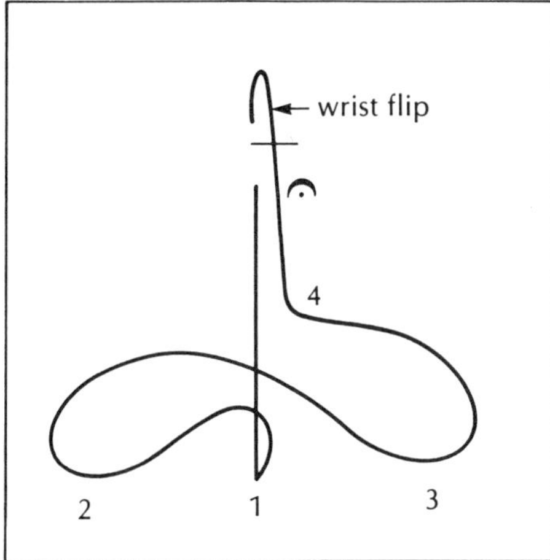

Note that the fermata gesture moves nearly straight up when the fermata is on pulse 4, so that the hand is in position following the wrist flip to execute the downbeat.

Exercise 13-12 Conduct the following melody. The ensemble is to breathe only at the breath marks provided.

If the fermata occurs on pulse 1, the wrist flip is given in the same direction as the fermata gesture, either diagonally or straight up (Diagram 13-14). After the upward wrist flip on the "and" of pulse 1, the hand and arm move into pulse 2 in continuation of the pattern.

Diagram 13–14

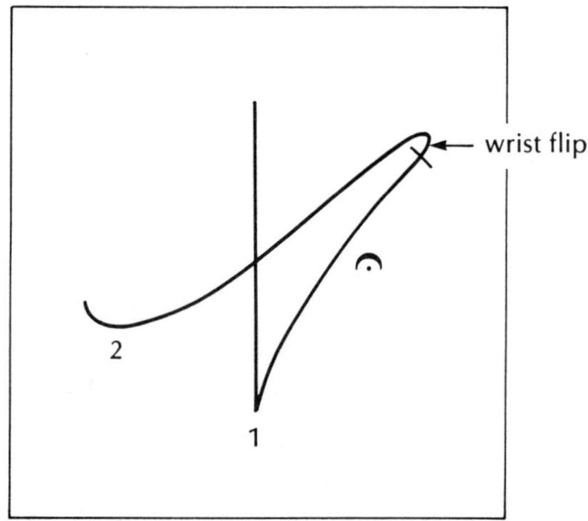

Be certain that there is no extraneous motion which would cause the performers to stop the tone and take a breath. The left hand, with palm facing upward as if executing a crescendo, may be used to "hold" the ensemble so that no breath occurs after the fermata gesture or the wrist flip.

Exercise 13-13 Conduct the following melody. The ensemble is to breathe only at the breath marks provided.

When the fermata is on pulse 2, the hand moves diagonally toward the downward pulse line (Diagram 13-15). The wrist flip is given on the "and" of pulse 2. The hand then moves into pulse 3, in continuation of the pattern.

Diagram 13–15

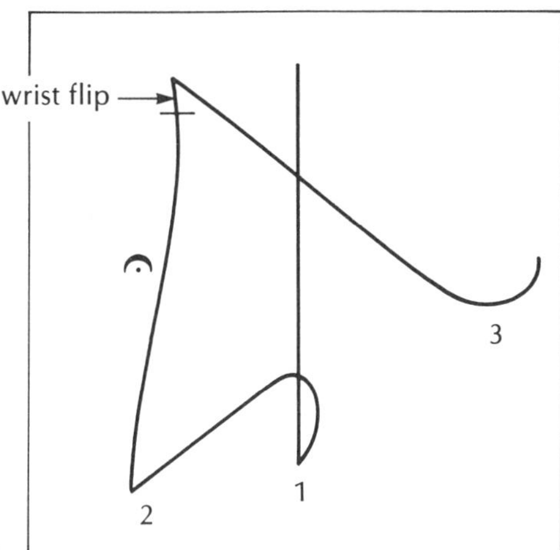

Exercise 13–14 Conduct the following melody. The ensemble is to breathe only at the breath marks provided.

If the fermata occurs on pulse 3, pulse 3 must remain close to the basic pulse line (Diagram 13–16). The diagonal fermata gesture must move far enough to the outside to allow an appropriate gesture into pulse 4 with a rebound which places the hand in exact position for the next downbeat.

Diagram 13–16

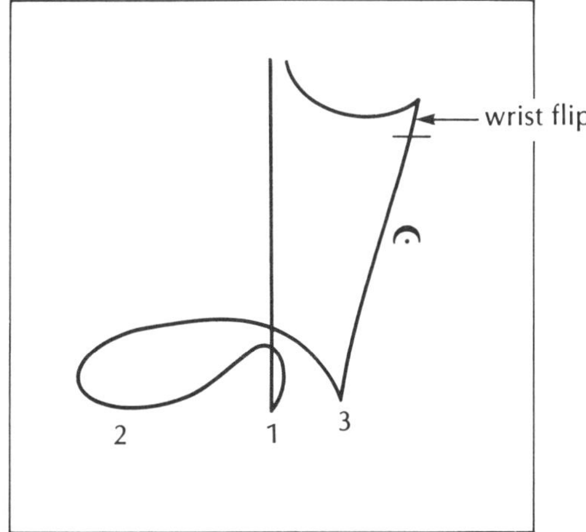

Exercise 13–15 Now conduct the following melody. The ensemble is to breathe only at the breath marks provided.

Exercise 13-16 This exercise combines fermatas on all pulses. The ensemble is to breathe only at breath marks. In the event that the ensemble cannot hold the phrase as long as you would like, devise ways of solving the problem.

PART II

Advanced Conducting Gestures

14 Asymmetrical Meters

Patterns in Moderate and Slow Tempos

Asymmetrical meters usually consist of accentual groupings of two and three pulses. The conductor must analyze the groupings within a measure and select a pattern accordingly.

The Five Pattern

Quintuple meter is usually grouped either as 3 + 2 pulses or 2 + 3 pulses. The change from one group to the other is indicated by crossing the basic pulse line as in Diagrams 14–1a and 14–1b.

Diagram 14–1a

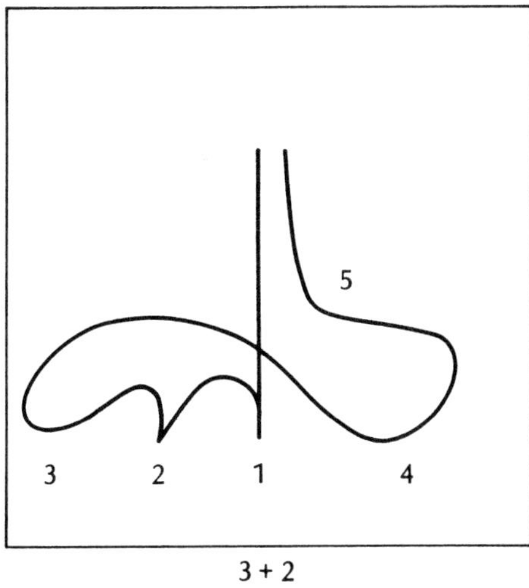

3 + 2

Diagram 14–1b

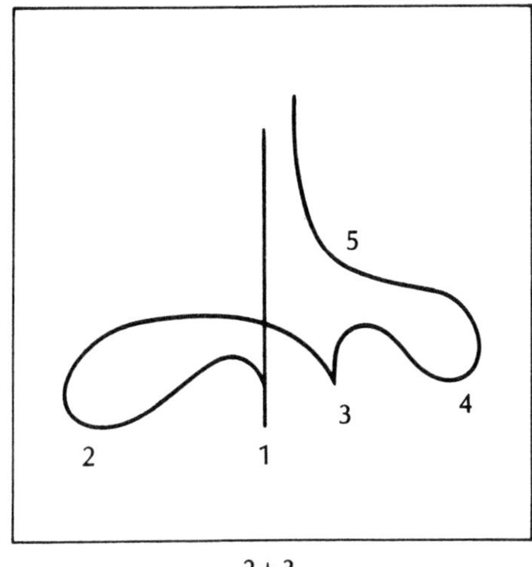

2 + 3

The Seven Pattern

The seven meter has three common divisions: 2 + 2 + 3 (Diagram 14–2a), 3 + 2 + 2 (Diagram 14–2b), and 2 + 3 + 2 (Diagram 14–2c).

Diagram 14–2a

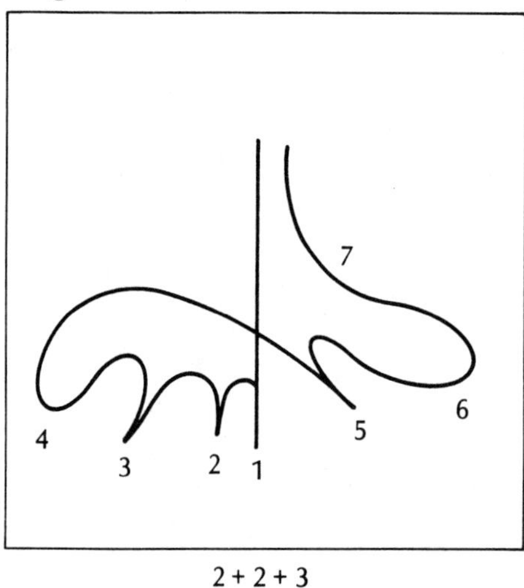

2 + 2 + 3

Diagram 14–2b

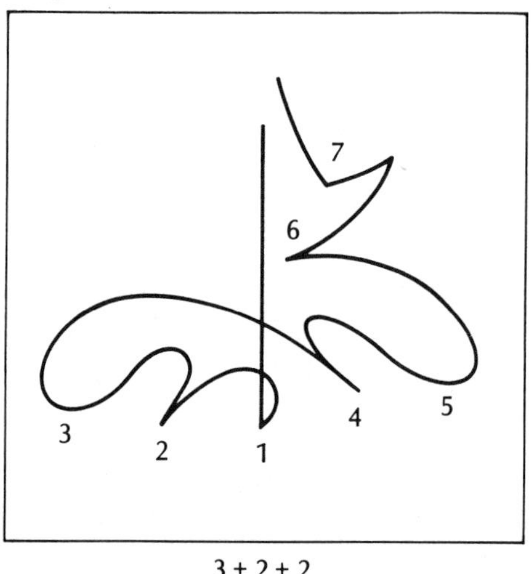

3 + 2 + 2

Diagram 14–2c

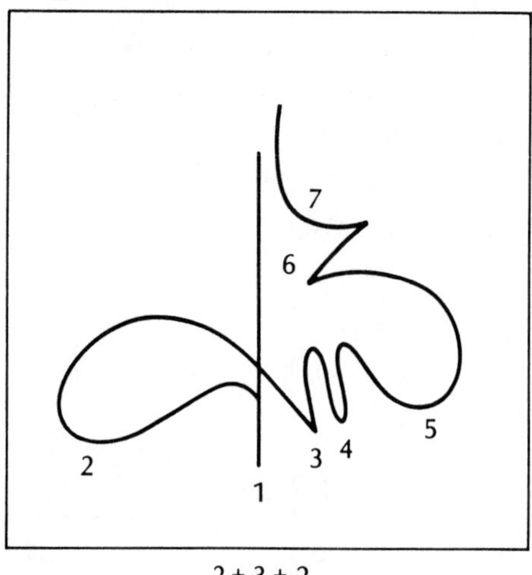

2 + 3 + 2

There are many acceptable variations on these patterns, including executing the penultimate pulse *to the left* of the basic pulse line. This results in a backhanded final pulse. The primary concern of the ensemble, however, is to be able to determine where the conductor changes from one grouping of pulses to the next.

The Nine Pattern

When the nine pulses are evenly divided, the basic subdivided three pattern is used as the framework (Diagram 14–3).

Diagram 14–3

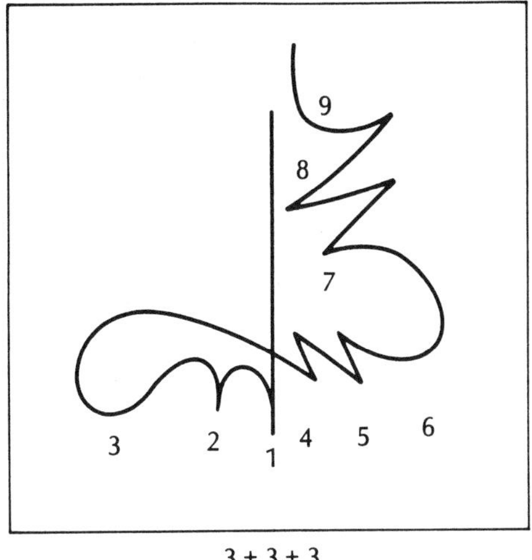

3 + 3 + 3

Diagram 14–4

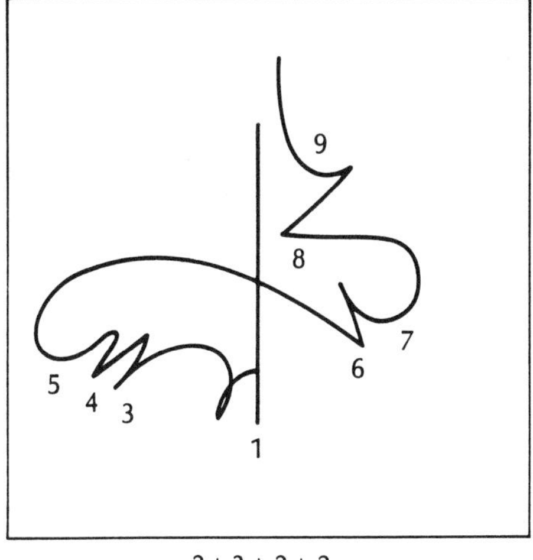

2 + 3 + 2 + 2

When the nine pulses are divided in combinations of twos and threes, as in 2 + 3 + 2 + 2, the basic four pattern is used as the framework (Diagram 14–4).

The Eleven Pattern

It is important for the conductor to delineate clearly the change of direction for each group of pulses. If the grouping of the eleven meter is 2 + 3 + 2 + 2 + 2, the pattern would look like Diagram 14–5.

Diagram 14–5

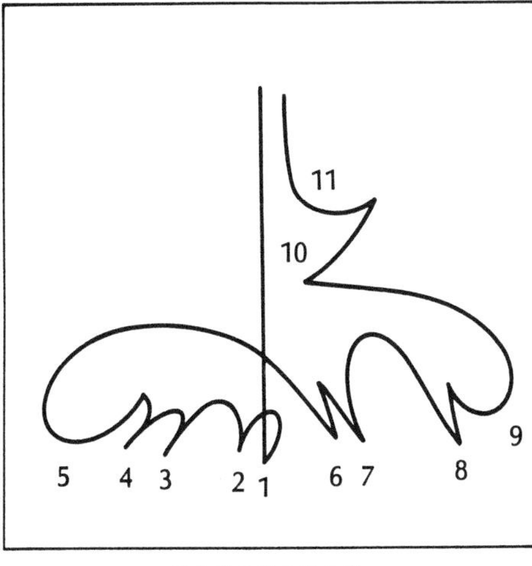

2 + 3 + 2 + 2 + 2

The Twelve Pattern

The standard subdivided four pattern is used when the twelve meter is evenly divided into groups of three (Diagram 14–6). The conductor will have to determine the most appropriate pattern when the twelve meter is divided otherwise.

Diagram 14–6

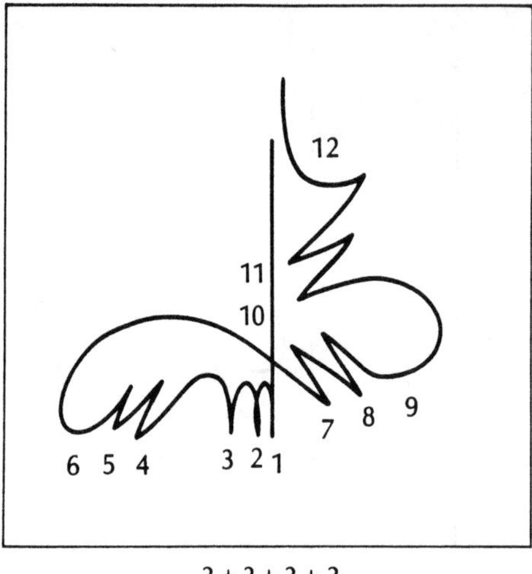

3 + 3 + 3 + 3

- **To the Student**

Each change of pulse groupings must be clearly shown. A larger gesture into each grouping should be given to indicate the change. All potential combinations have not been given here. You will have to decide the pattern from analysis of the groupings in the music you conduct.

Patterns in Fast Tempos

Asymmetrical meters have become widely used in contemporary music. When the tempo is so fast that it is impossible to conduct each pulse, pulses must be combined. Usually pulses are combined into groups of twos and threes according to accentuation. When the groups have been determined, they are then placed within standard conducting patterns.

Asymmetrical Meters in 5

A meter in 5 is usually grouped as 3 + 2 or 2 + 3 (Example 14-1). The number of groupings indicates the pattern to be used. The two pattern is usually used to conduct meters in 5 (Diagrams 14-7a and 14-7b).

Example 14-1:

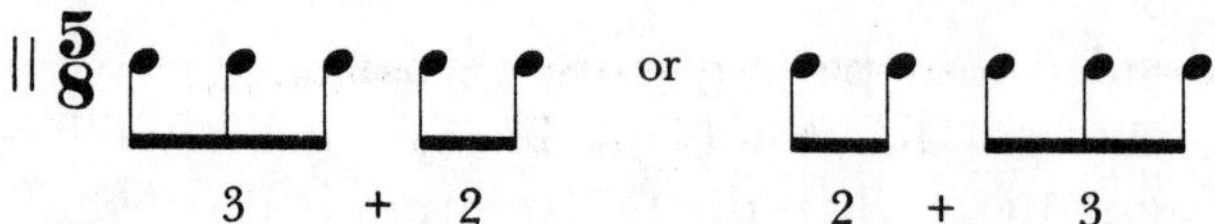

Diagram 14–7a

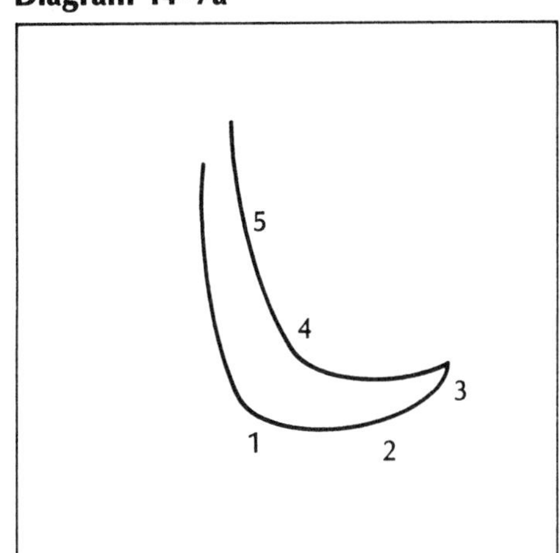

Diagram 14–7b

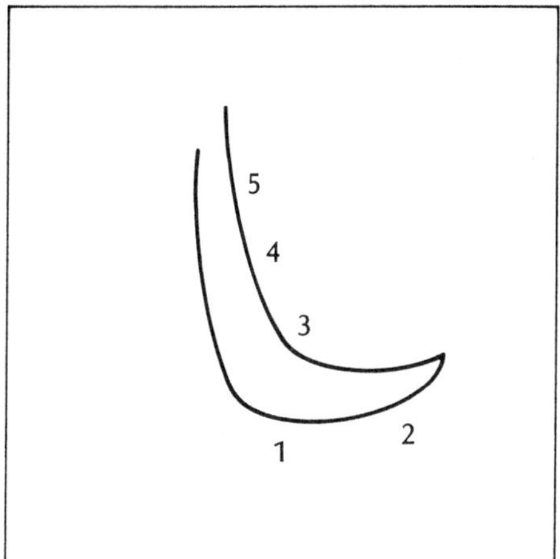

The size of the pattern may be large or small, depending on the dynamic level indicated in the music. If the ensemble finds singing music in asymmetrical meters difficult, keep your pattern more precise and compact. The portion of the pattern with the grouping of three tends to move slightly more slowly than the portion combining the two grouping. The three grouping has a sensation of lift, or waiting slightly, so that all pulses are accounted for within the gesture. Sometimes a stop gesture is used for the grouping of three. The hand moves immediately to the end of the rebound, stops, then waits for the number of pulses to be completed. The eighth notes in Example 14-1 are to be performed as absolutely equal in length. Timing is essential. Being late into the next pulse grouping is a danger. You must set your internal clock ticking to mark even subdivisions of the pulse so that the music moves steadily through time.

Conduct the following musical exercises. Determine the accentuation of the pulses and the pattern to be used according to the grouping of notes.

Exercise 14-1

Asymmetrical Meters in 7

The seven meter may be grouped in three different ways: 3 + 2 + 2; 2 + 3 + 2; or 2 + 2 + 3. The number of groupings indicates the use of a three pattern in the execution of meters in 7 (Diagrams 14–8a through 14–8c).

Diagram 14–8a

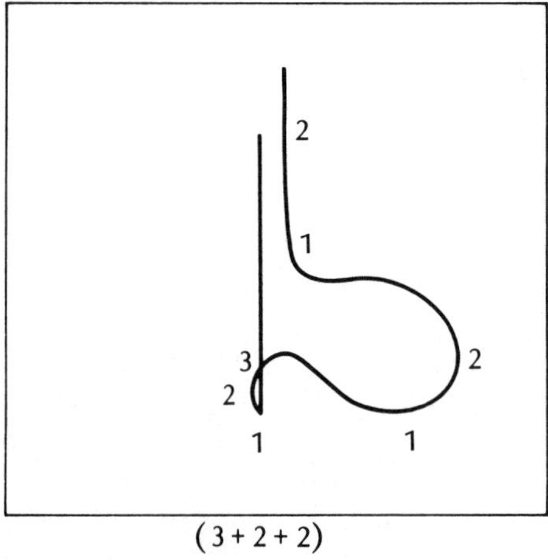

(3 + 2 + 2)

Diagram 14–8b

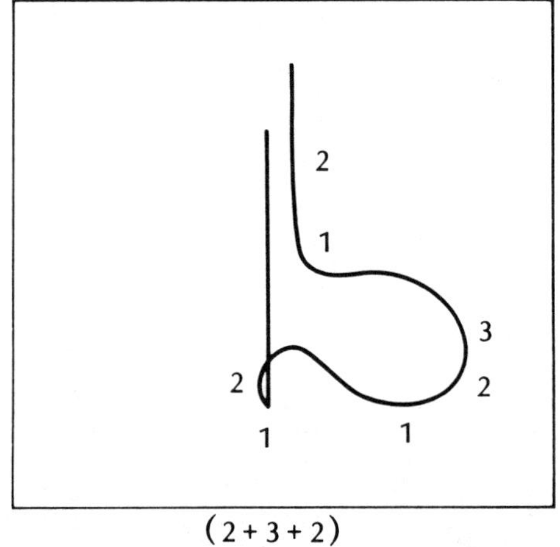

(2 + 3 + 2)

Diagram 14–8c

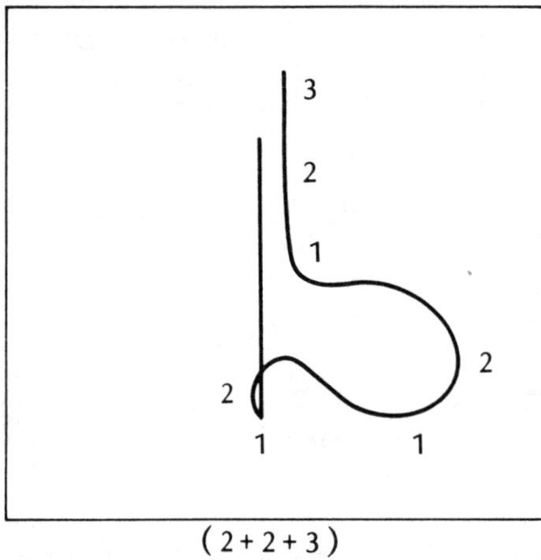

(2 + 2 + 3)

You must be certain all pulses are equal in duration. Note that the hand either moves more slowly or stops completely within a grouping of three pulses. Timing is essential. The ictus of each pulse group must be precisely in tempo.

Conduct Exercises 14-3 to 14-5.

Exercise 14-3

Exercise 14-4

Exercise 14-5

Asymmetrical Meters in 8

When conducting asymmetrical meters in 8, the number of groupings again indicates the use of the three pattern. Combinations of pulses for meters in 8 may be: 3 + 3 + 2; 3 + 2 + 3; and 2 + 3 + 3 (Diagrams 14–9a through 14–9c).

Diagram 14–9a

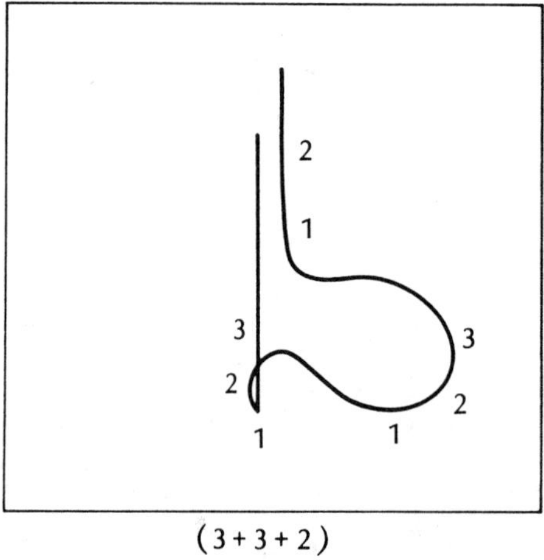

(3 + 3 + 2)

Diagram 14–9b

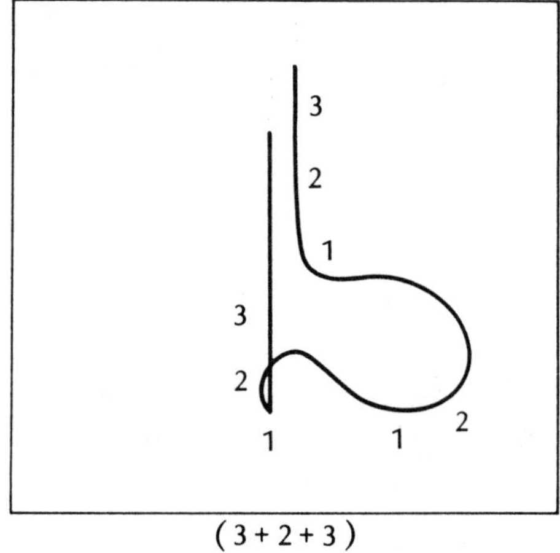

(3 + 2 + 3)

Diagram 14–9c

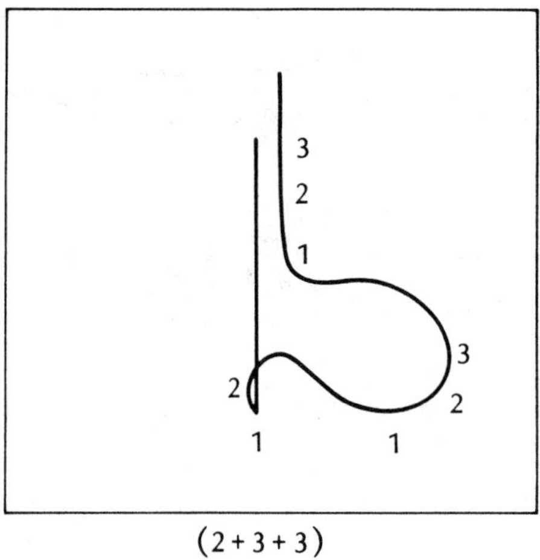

(2 + 3 + 3)

• Nota Bene

It is not the preparation into the three grouping that slows down, lifts, or drags, but rather the rebound following the ictus of the three grouping.

Conduct Exercises 14-6 to 14-8.

Exercise 14-6

Exercise 14-7

Exercise 14-8

Asymmetrical Meters in 9

As well as the traditional division of meters in 9 into three metrical groups of three pulses each, the following combinations are also possible: 2 + 2 + 2 + 3; 2 + 3 + 2 + 2; 2 + 2 + 3 + 2; and 3 + 2 + 2 + 2. The number of groupings suggests the use of a four pattern (Diagrams 14–10a through 14–10d).

Diagram 14–10a

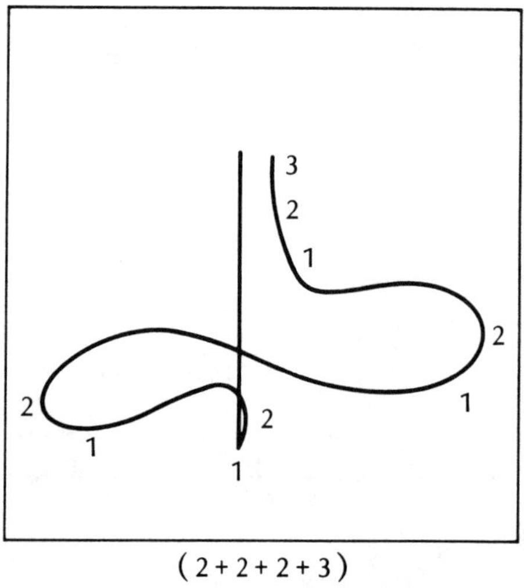

(2 + 2 + 2 + 3)

Diagram 14–10b

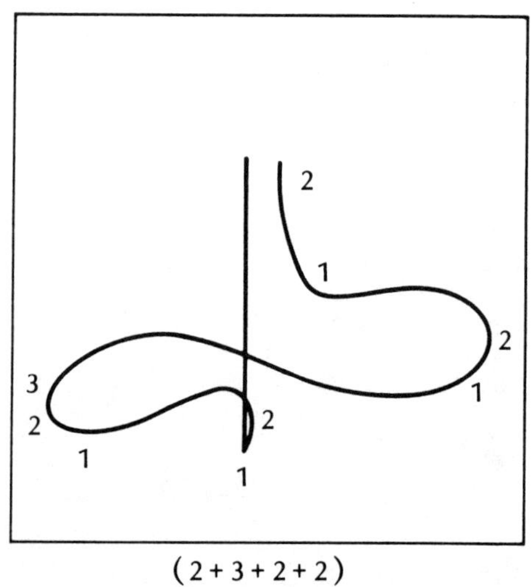

(2 + 3 + 2 + 2)

Diagram 14–10c

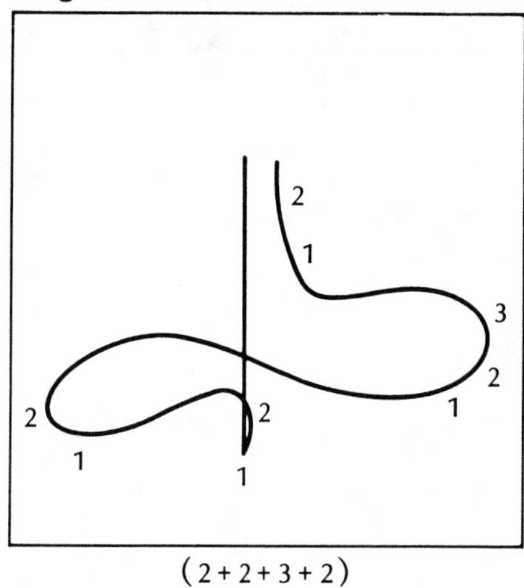

(2 + 2 + 3 + 2)

Diagram 14–10d

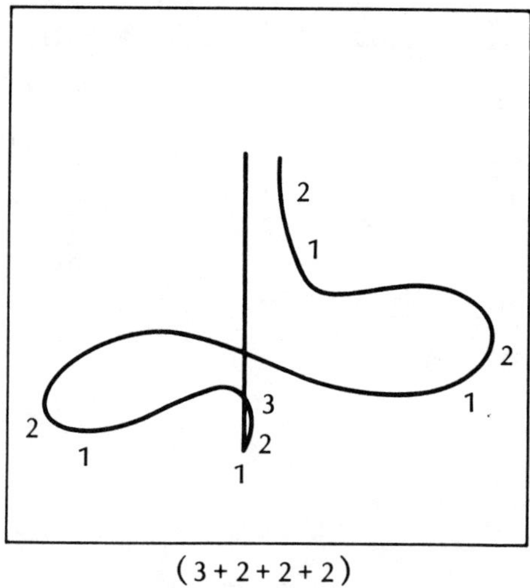

(3 + 2 + 2 + 2)

Note again that the hand slows or stops completely when conducting the groupings of three within the pattern. Because of the precision demanded when performing asymmetrical meters, the patterns tend to become much more angular with many more stop gestures used than in symmetrical meters.

Conduct Exercises 14-9 to 14-12.

Exercise 14-9

Exercise 14-10

Exercise 14-11

Exercise 14-12

Other Asymmetrical Combinations

All other combinations may be determined in the same manner. A meter in 12 might be 3 + 2 + 2 + 3 + 2. The standard five pattern would be used. Additional clues would be needed to determine if a 3 + 2 or a 2 + 3 combination should be used (Diagrams 14-11a and 14-11b).

Diagram 14–11a

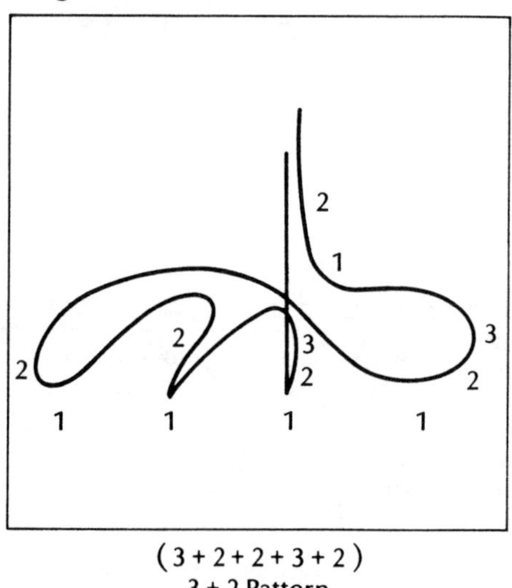

(3 + 2 + 2 + 3 + 2)
3 + 2 Pattern

Diagram 14–11b

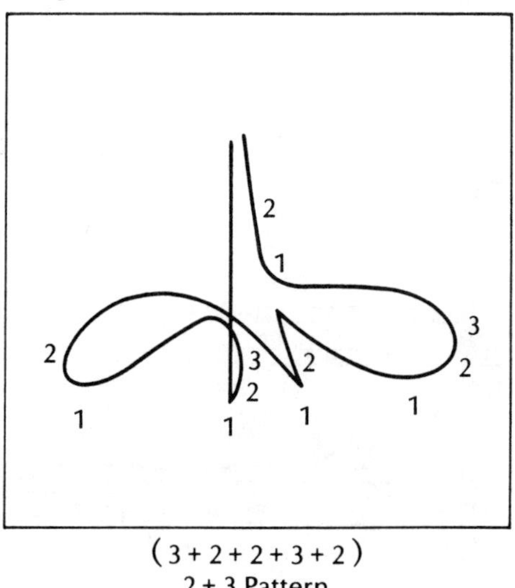

(3 + 2 + 2 + 3 + 2)
2 + 3 Pattern

Many works are written in shifting asymmetrical meters. Your mind must be keen and your hands sure when conducting these shifting patterns. The ensemble depends on your precision and accuracy when performing such works. A single mix-up of meters in the middle of a work can cause that work to collapse. Your preparation of the score must be very thorough.

Conduct the following exercises. The ensemble should speak the underlying quarter-note or eighth-note pulse on a neutral syllable. The ensemble should not look at the meter patterns but rather "read" them from your hand gestures. The quarter-note or eighth-note pulse remains constant throughout each exercise (Example 14-2). These exercises should be rehearsed until the gestures are so exact and precise the ensemble can read the pulsation patterns from your hand gesture.

Example 14-2:

Conductor: ♪= 200

(use 8th note underlying pulse) $\frac{2}{4}$ $\frac{3+2}{8}$ $\frac{3+3+2}{8}$

Ensemble speaks: *da* da *da* da *da* da da *da* da *da* da da *da* da da *da* da

Exercise 14-13 ♩ = 200

2/4 3/4 2/4 4/4 3+2/4 2+3/4 3+3/4 2+2+2/4

Exercise 14-14 ♩ = 200

2/4 3/4 3+2/4 2+3/4 4/4 2/4 3+2+2/4 2+3+2/4 2+2+3/4 4/4

Exercise 14-15 ♪ = 200

2/4 3/8 3/4 3+2/8 4/4 2+3/8 4/8 2/8 3/4 2+3+2/8 3/4

Exercise 14-16 ♪ = 200

3+2+2/8 4/4 2+2+3/8 3/4 3+2/8 4/4 2+3/8 3/4 3/8 2/4

Exercise 14-17 ♪ = 200

2/4 3+3/8 3/4 2+2+2/8 4/4 4/4 3/4 2/4 3+3/4 2+2+2/4

Exercise 14-18 ♩ = 200

3/4 3+2/4 2/4 3+2+3/4 1/4 2+3+2/4 4/4 2+3+3/4 4/4

Exercise 14-19 ♪ = 200

4/4 3+2/8 3+2/4 2/4 2+3+3/8 1/4 2+3/8 3/4 3/8 3+2+2/8 2/4 3+2+3/8

Exercise 14-20 ♪ = 208

3+2/8 3+3+3/8 2+2+2+2+2/8 3+2/8 2+3+2/8 2+2+3/8

Exercise 14-21 ♪ = 208

3/8 2/2 6/8 4/8 2/8 4/4 3/4 2/8 3/8 3+2/8 2/4

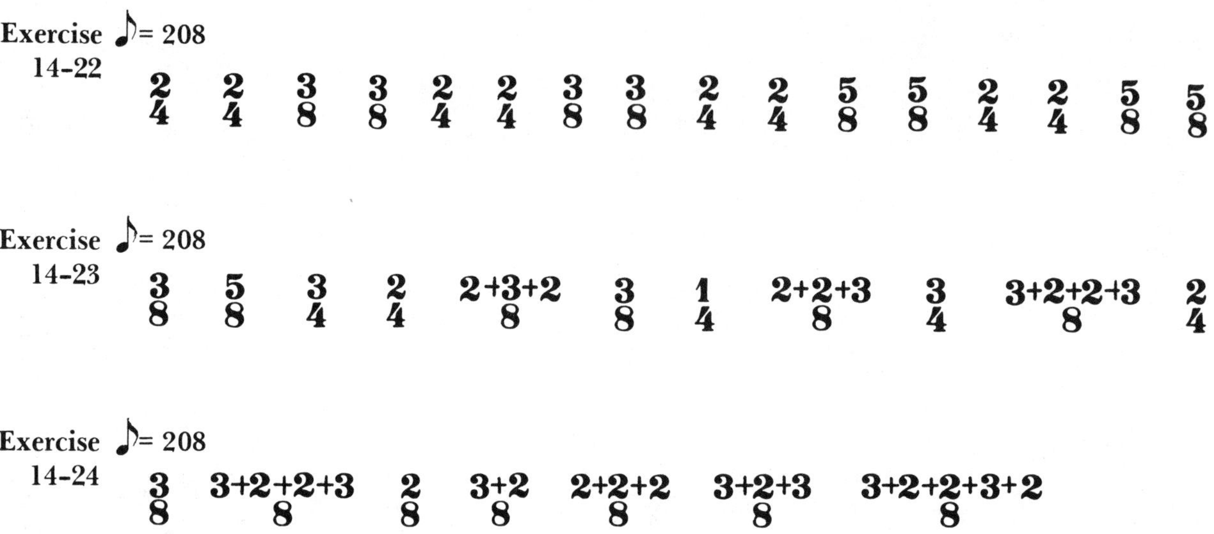

Supplementary Conducting Exercises

DIEMER: The Prophecy

PIERCE: Dance of the One-Legged Sailor

mf
Come ye mates and let me tell ye a -
man who loved to laugh and sing
mf
Come ye mates and let me tell ye a -
man who loved to laugh and sing
mf

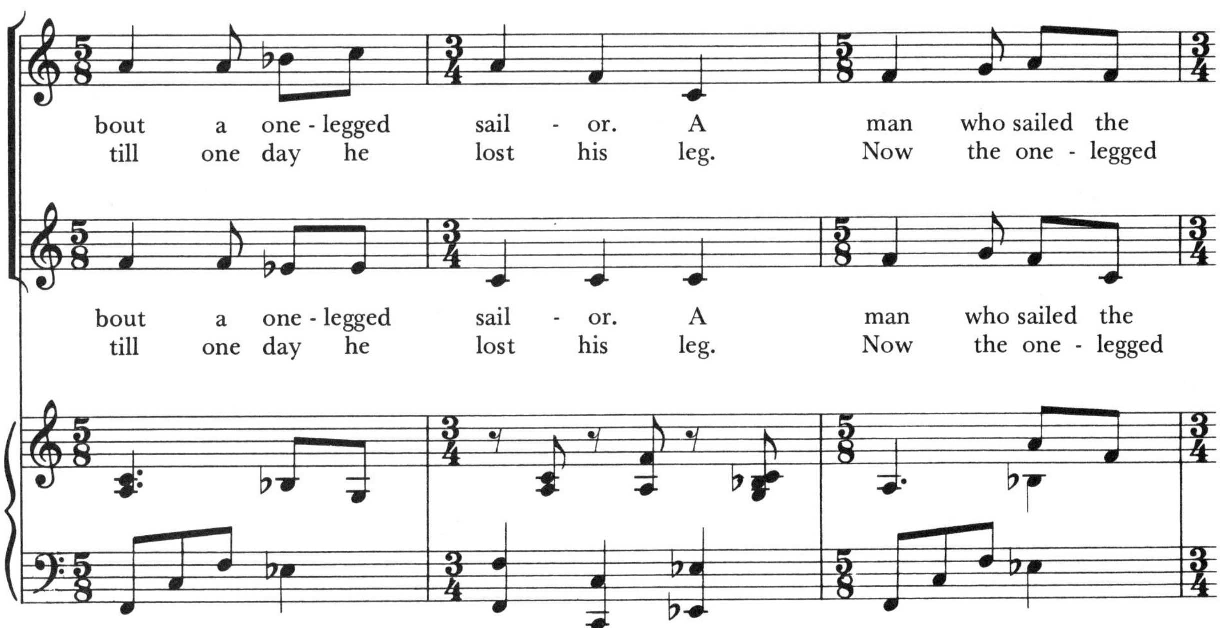
bout a one - legged sail - or. A man who sailed the
till one day he lost his leg. Now the one - legged
bout a one - legged sail - or. A man who sailed the
till one day he lost his leg. Now the one - legged

BYRD: Though Amaryllis Dance

dance in green, like Fair - y Queen,
force him not, sith God it wot,
dance in green, like Fair - y Queen, like Fair - y
force him not, sith God it wot, sith God it
dance in green, like Fair - y Queen, and sing full
force him not, sith God it wot, the more I
in green, like Fair - y Queen,
him not, sith God it wot,
green, in green, like Fair - y Queen,
not, him not, sith God it wot,

15 Cueing With Body Turns

When conducting a large ensemble there will be times when you must shift or turn your body to make various gestures toward certain sections of the ensemble. In order to turn your body to the left, pivot slightly on the ball of your right foot and move your left foot back and slightly out. Move the left foot far enough so that you face squarely the section you intend to conduct (Diagram 15-1).

Diagram 15–1

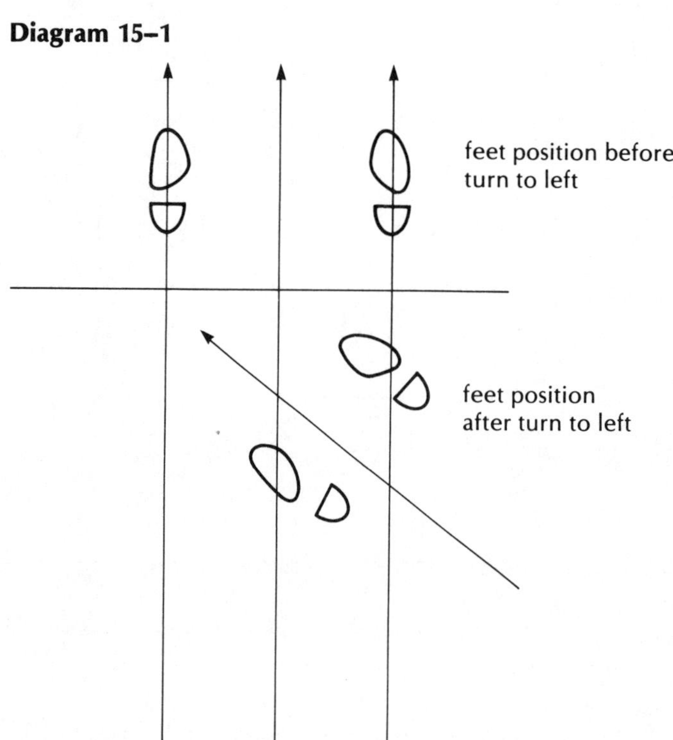

To turn to the right, pivot on the left foot and move the right foot back and out so that you face squarely the section you wish to conduct (Diagram 15-2).

Diagram 15–2

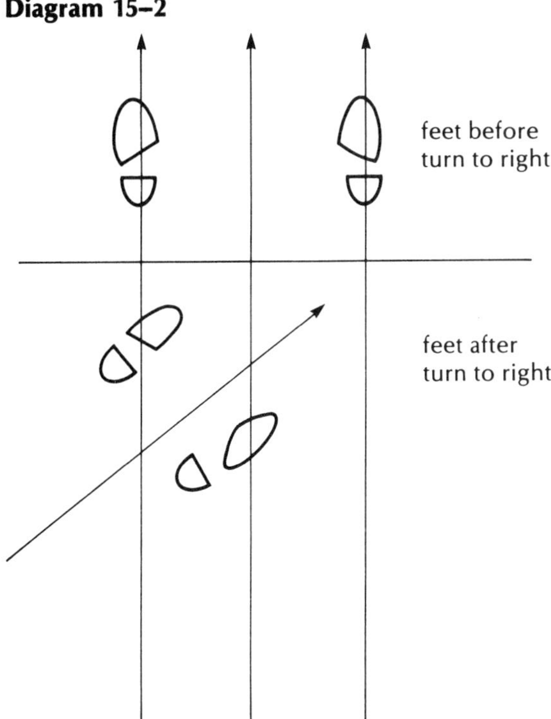

- **Nota Bene**

At times it is possible to twist the trunk of the body slightly to make a particular gesture to the left or right. Too much twist, however, turns the conductor into a corkscrew, thereby damaging his or her stature and posture. Be aware of what you look like to an ensemble and an audience as you make various gestures to the left and right of the ensemble.

General Suggestions

Turning the body and shifting the feet causes a shift in the conducting plane. The plane shifts to the left or right as you turn but maintains its position in front of the body. The plane thus moves *with* the body. As you practice the following cueing gestures, the following suggestions will help you maintain a clear, concise pattern:

1. The feet begin to move on the pulse preceding the cue.
2. The eyes are already focused on the section to be cued at least a full pulse before the cue is executed.
3. The ictus of the cue gesture moves approximately to eye level so that face, eyes, and hand participate together in the cue.
4. The hand should not cover the eyes when making a cue, nor should the eyes look at the hand while giving the cue. Look directly at the section being cued.

5. The cue must be in the character of the music to be performed.
6. The relationship of hand, wrist, and arm do *not,* as a rule, change. *The body simply carries the hand, arm, and wrist as it turns.* The cue is delivered as if you were stationary facing the section.
7. A slight finger movement may be used to indicate the exact moment of ictus.

It is important that the downbeat is executed as a downbeat (straight down), and that the anacrusis (upbeat) is executed in an upward motion. Because of the turn of the body, the following diagrams will sometimes show more lateral motion than up-and-down motion. Up and down should only be perceived in the relationship of hand and arm to body, not in terms of the space used to complete the gesture. It is important that you keep this fact in mind:

THE DOWNBEAT IS STILL DOWN; THE UPBEAT IS STILL UP.

Diagram 15–3 shows a cue to the left on pulse 1 of measure 2. On pulse 4 of measure 1, shift your feet, turning to the left. Even on pulse 3 of this first measure your head and eyes should already begin moving toward the section to be cued. The hand executes the cue on pulse 1 of measure 2 approximately at eye level. Note that the hand then drops down into the normal conducting plane to execute pulse 2. The body begins to return to the initial position on pulse 2, reversing the shift of feet so that pulse 3 is delivered as you face the entire ensemble.

Diagram 15–3

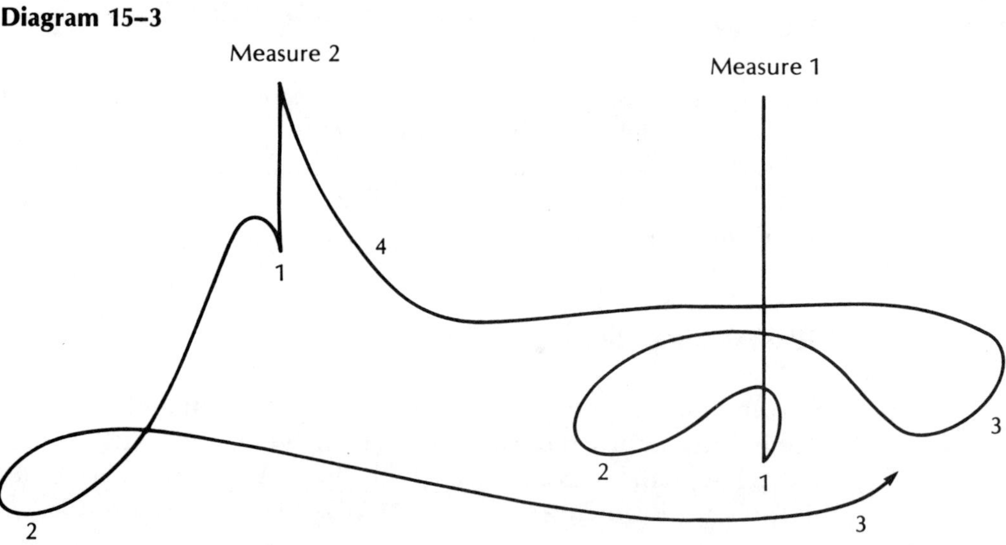

- **Nota Bene**

The hand and arm stay in position relative to the body no matter what the body is doing. *The body carries the hand and arm into each new position.*

Turn to the Left, Cue on 2

If you are cueing to the left on pulse 2, your eyes and head should move to the left during the downbeat. Look directly at the section to be cued. During the rebound of pulse 1 the body turns (Diagram 15-4) and the cue on pulse 2 is executed along the shifted plane. The hand is opposite the face for the cue gesture. As soon as the cue has been executed, body and head immediately begin to return to the neutral, central position so that pulse 3 is delivered in the original plane of conducting. Note that in the diagram, the rebound of pulse 1 appears to move on a diagonal. *As the body turns,* however, *the rebound actually maintains a vertical relation to the body. Downbeat and rebound are still straight down and straight up in relation to the body.*

During the preparation for pulse 2 the left foot actually becomes planted in its new position before the ictus of the cue is executed. This completion of body movement before the ictus gives the cue gesture solidity and stability.

Diagram 15-4

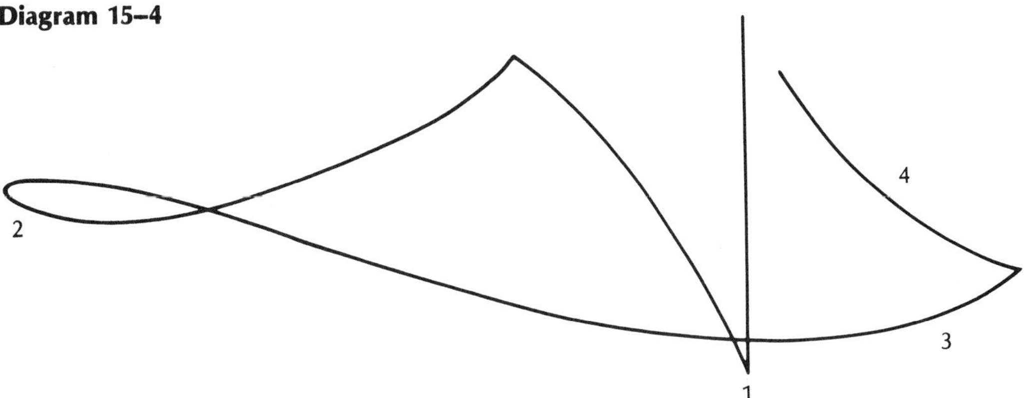

Turn to the Left, Cue on 3

The cue gesture on pulse 3 is somewhat unusual because it is followed by a very long rebound gesture to move the hand into position to execute pulse 4 (Diagram 15-5). As the body turns on pulse 2, the hand moves higher to face level. The pulse

Diagram 15-5

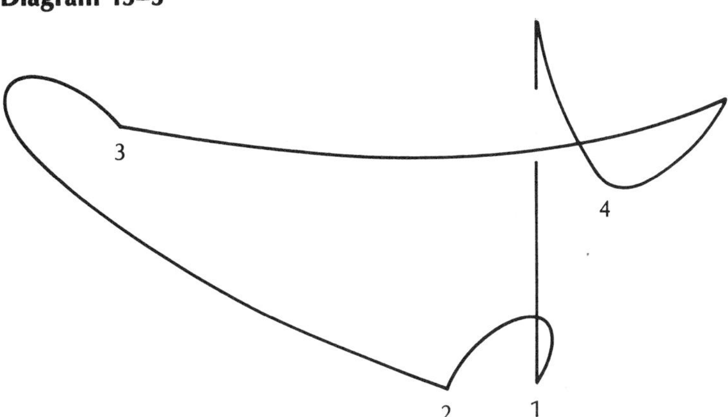

on 3 appears to be a small bump in the pattern, usually made with a slight wrist action to indicate the exact occurrence of the ictus. The following rebound is parallel to the ground and *in the same direction* as the preparation for 3, as Diagram 15-5 shows. This long rebound moves the hand into position to execute a slight downward gesture for the ictus of pulse 4.

• To the Student

The cue on 3 with body turn to the left is a very awkward gesture which must be practiced many times for smooth coordination of hand and body. It is difficult to maintain hand, arm, and body alignment as the body returns to a neutral position because the rebound is in the same direction as the preparation of the pulse.

Turn to the Left, Cue on 4

The cue on pulse 4 falls very naturally within the turn of the body. Maintenance of hand and arm position in relation to the body is relatively easy, although the following downbeat can sometimes be weak and ineffective due to the turning of the body back to the neutral position (Diagram 15-6).

Diagram 15-6

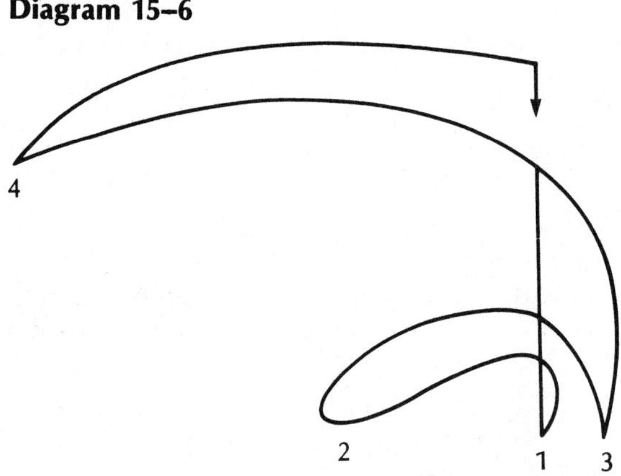

Care must be taken to place the downbeat along the vertical downbeat line in the neutral position. The ictus of this downbeat should not be approached diagonally. After the ictus on pulse 4 the body returns to the neutral conducting position and the downbeat is executed in the neutral position. The primary danger in cueing on 4 with a body turn is that the rebound of 4 will be too high. The rebound should be short and only slightly away from the direction of the ictus. The hand should not rise above the forehead during the gesture.

Do the following exercises slowly at first. Study each gesture as you make it. Observe yourself in the mirror. Check your posture, your hand, arm, and body position, and also your feet position as you do each exercise.

Exercise 15-1 Practice turning to the left and cueing on each pulse of the pattern until the gesture feels comfortable.

Exercise 15-2 Practice turning to the left and cueing on pulses 1 and 3, then 2 and 4. Always turn back to a neutral position on the pulses between the cues.

Turn to the Right: Cue on 1

The suggestions given above also pertain to cues given with a body turn to the right. The following diagrams give an indication of the general direction of the movement.

Diagram 15-7

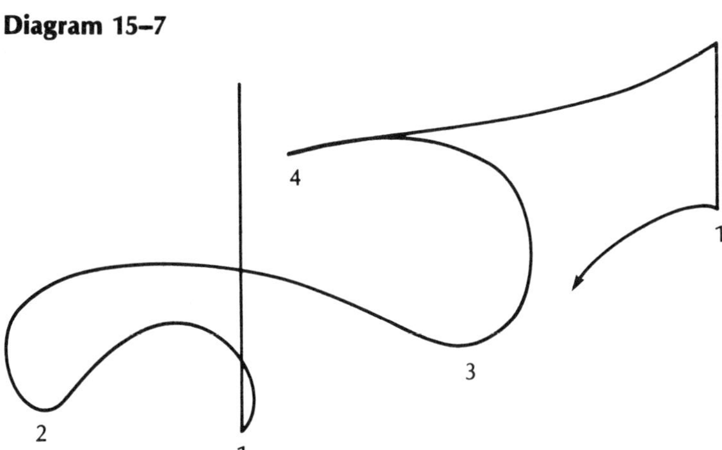

Diagram 15-7 shows a turn to the right being executed on the rebound of pulse 4. The cue on the downbeat is executed in the shifted plane approximately at eye level. After the cue is delivered, the hand and arm return to the neutral conducting position. It is somewhat easier to turn on pulse 3, since the hand and arm are already moving in that direction (Diagram 15-8). However, at times you may not have pulse 3 to turn on and then the turn must be made on pulse 4. You must be sure that pulse 3 stays down in the conducting plane. Bringing the hand up to face level too early may induce an entrance from the ensemble one pulse too soon.

Diagram 15-8

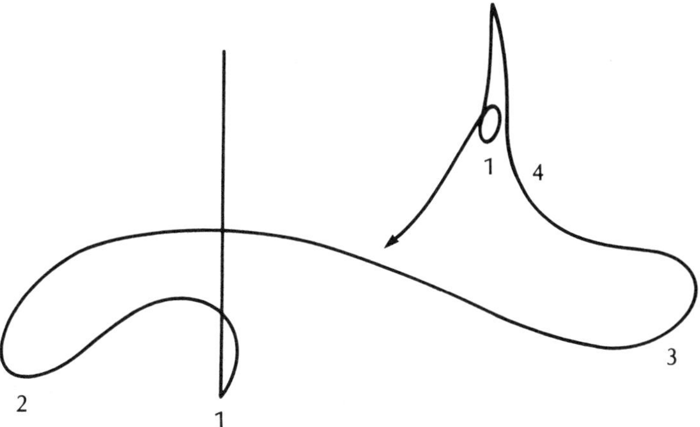

Turn to the Right, Cue on 2

The cue on pulse 2 with body turn to the right ranks in difficulty with the cue on 3 with a body turn to the left. Note that the ictus for the cue on pulse 2 is merely a bump in the line, usually executed with the wrist. The rebound, *in the same direction as the preparation,* carries the hand to the left of the basic pulse line in the neutral plane so that pulse 3 can be made, as is customary, to the right of this line (Diagram 15–9).

Diagram 15–9

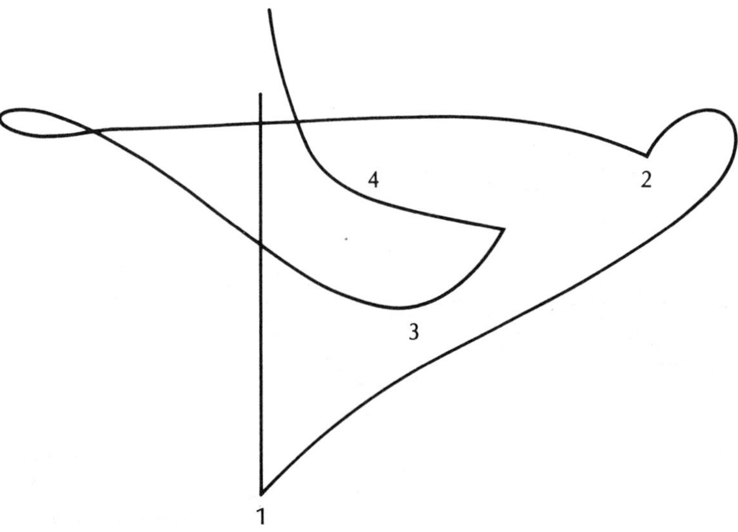

Turn to the Right, Cue on 3

Because the gesture for the cue on pulse 3 is in the general direction of the body turn, it is easier to make than the previous cue on 2. The preparation for 3 is brought to eye level. The ictus for 3 is executed with a slight drop of the wrist and hand to indicate the exact moment of the cue (Diagram 15–10).

Diagram 15–10

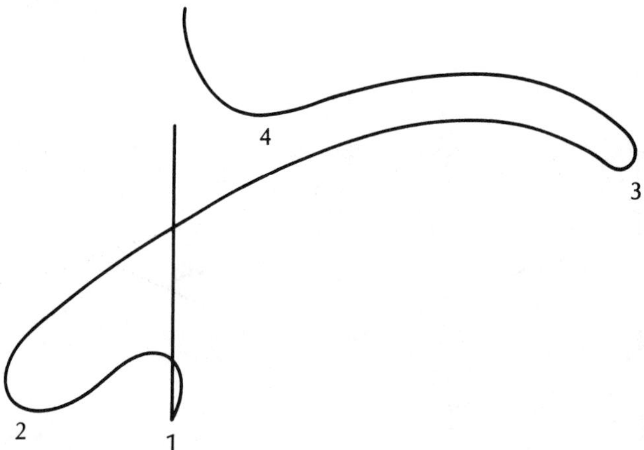

Turn to the Right, Cue on 4

The cue on pulse 4 occurs as a wrist action to indicate the ictus. The hand continues in the same basic direction for the rebound in order to be in the correct location to give the downbeat in the neutral position (Diagram 15–11).

Diagram 15–11

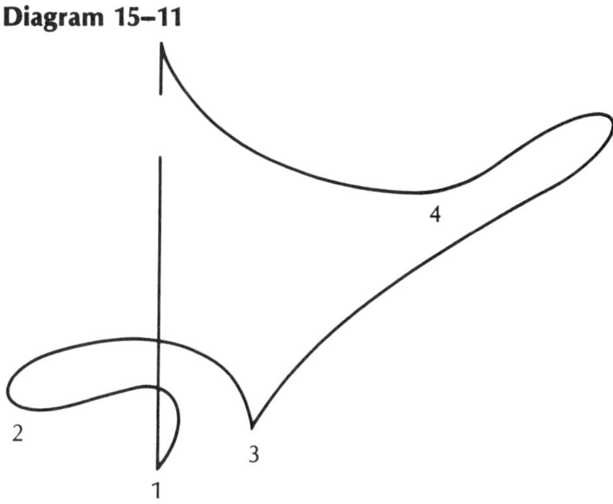

The following exercises should be done slowly at first. Study each gesture as you make it. Observe yourself in the mirror. Check your posture, your hand, arm, and body position, and also your feet position as you do each exercise.

Exercise 15–3 Practice turning to the right and cueing on each of the pulses in the measure until the gesture becomes comfortable.

Exercise 15–4 Practice turning to the right and cueing on pulses 1 and 3, then 2 and 4. Be sure to return to a neutral position after each cue.

Exercise 15–5 Practice turning to the left to give a cue on pulse 1, then to the right to give a cue on pulse 3 (Diagram 15–12).

Diagram 15–12

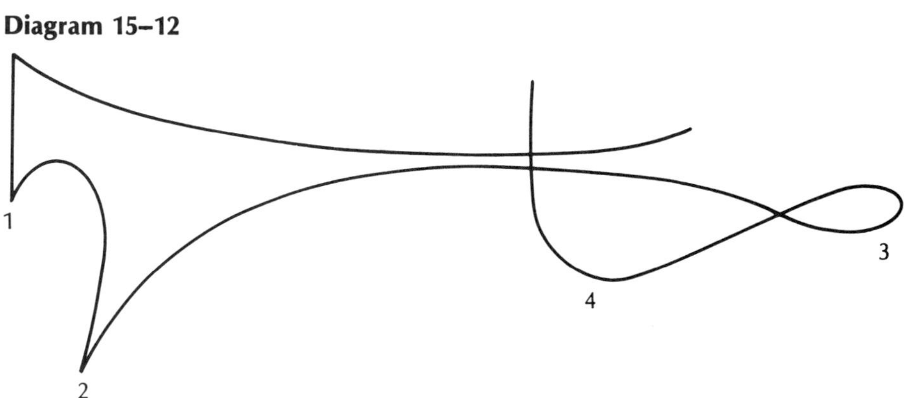

Exercise 15-6 Practice turning to the left to give a cue on pulse 2, then to the right to give a cue on 4.

Exercise 15-7 Reverse the direction of the turn in Exercises 15-5 and 15-6.

Exercise 15-8 Apply the same gestures to cues in the three pattern.

For Exercises 15-9 to 15-17, divide the ensemble into three groups and arrange them as in Diagram 15-13. Conduct these *polychoral* works, turning to the appropriate group as indicated. When only two ensembles are called for, divide Ensemble C so that half moves to Ensemble R, half to Ensemble L. Check your hand and arm position in relation to your body as you make each turn toward the ensemble. Be sure your cues are exact, precise, and in the character of the music.

Diagram 15-13

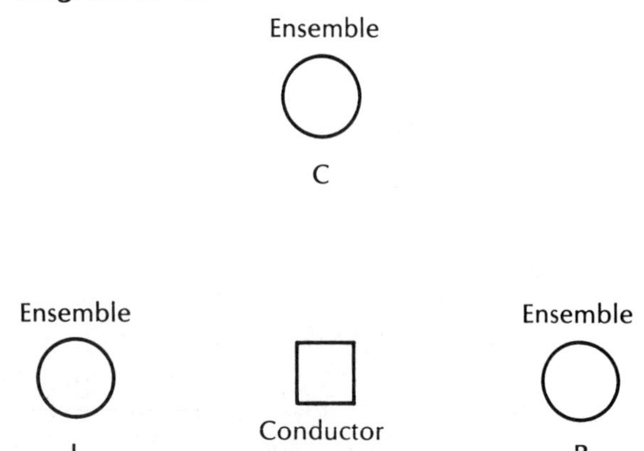

Sing the exercises on a neutral syllable. Concern yourself only with the cueing of each entrance and the final release. Memorize each exercise so that you can look up for each cue. Turn the body to indicate cues to the left (L), center (C), and right (R).

Exercise 15-9

Exercise 15-10

Exercise 15-11

Exercise 15-12

Exercise 15-13

Exercise 15-14

Exercise 15-15

Exercise 15-16

Exercise 15-17

16 Conducting Gradual Changes in Tempo

Clarity is essential as changes in tempo begin to occur. The accuracy of the ictus is probably more important than maintaining the pattern. Indicate to the ensemble that a change of tempo is about to occur by enlarging your pattern, changing your physical position, or bringing your left hand into play.

The *Ritardando*

When a *ritardando* is called for, mentally subdivide the measure into smaller note values before the change begins. As that subdivision begins to slow down, you may eventually have to subdivide the various pulses physically until you establish a new tempo, return to the original tempo, or end the work.

In Example 16-1 the *ritardando* closes the work. As early as the first measure, begin to think eighth-note subdivision. The first 8th-note pair in measure 2 should be conducted using an angular stopped gesture. The second pair of eighth notes should be subdivided, giving each eighth note an ictus (Diagram 16-1).

Example 16-1:

Diagram 16–1

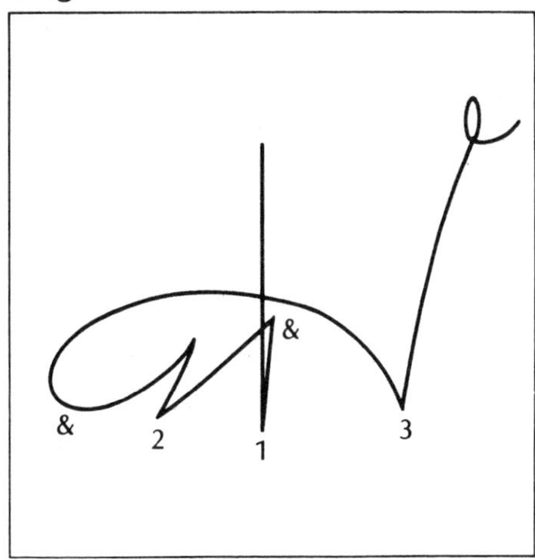

Exercise 16-1 Conduct the following.

BACH: Our freedom, Son of God, arose (*The Passion According to St. John*)

In Baroque choral literature you will find examples of *ritardando* which demand a double subdivision (Example 16-2). The conducting pattern for this example is shown in Diagram 16-2.

Example 16-2:

Diagram 16–2

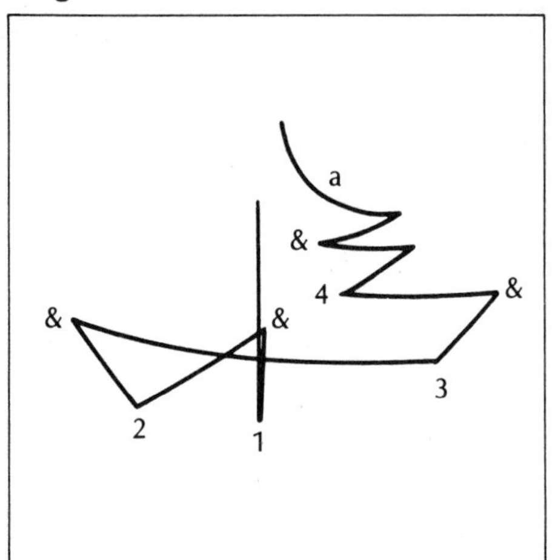

Diagram 16–3

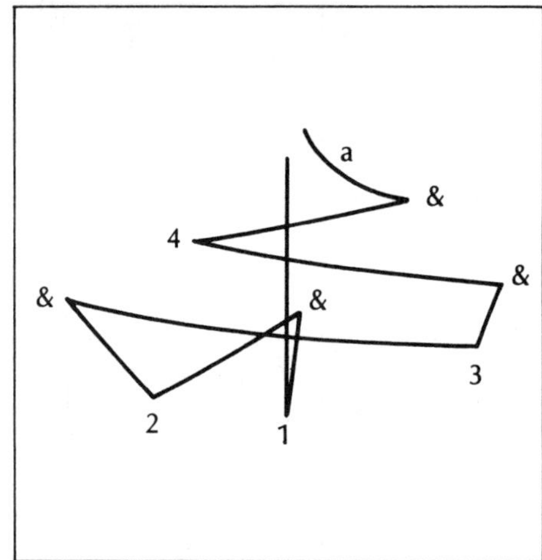

On the last pulse, each note is given an ictus for absolute clarity. An alternate pattern is shown in Diagram 16–3.

In the following exercise the next to the last measure should be conducted very angularly. If a *ritard.* is used in the penultimate measure, it should not begin until pulse 3. Pulses 3 and 4 may still be conducted angularly within the pattern. The final measure should be subdivided so that each syllable of "cru-ci-fy" receives an ictus (Diagram 16–4). Note that because this diagram is not three-dimensional, Diagram 16–4 shows three vertical strokes in different places. These three strokes should be on the downward pulse line.

Diagram 16–4

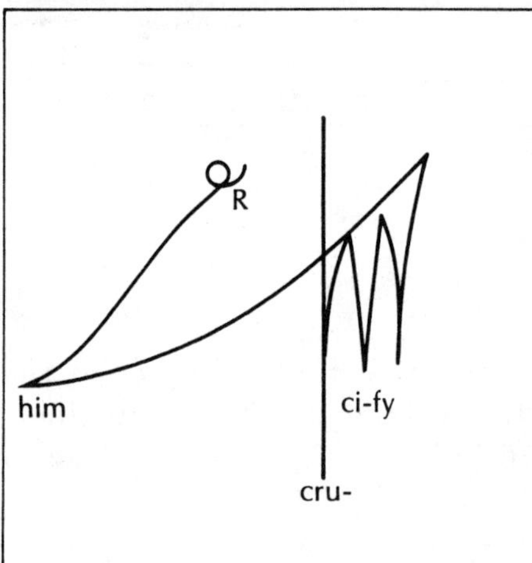

Exercise 16–2

BACH: Away With Him, Away (*The Passion According to St. John*)

When the *ritardando* occurs in the middle of the music, which then returns *a tempo,* as in Example 16-3, the type of gesture you use depends on how much you slow down. If you slow down only slightly, you may be able to conduct the *ritard.* with angular stop gestures. If you slow down considerably, you may be forced to move into a subdivision of the pulses for as long as the last two pulses of measure 2 (Diagrams 16-5a and 16-5b).

The downbeat of measure 3 must be in the original tempo. Eye contact throughout the *ritardando* and the return to the original tempo is essential. An angular gesture in measure 3 may also be necessary until the ensemble is comfortably reestablished in the original tempo.

Example 16-3:

Diagram 16–5a

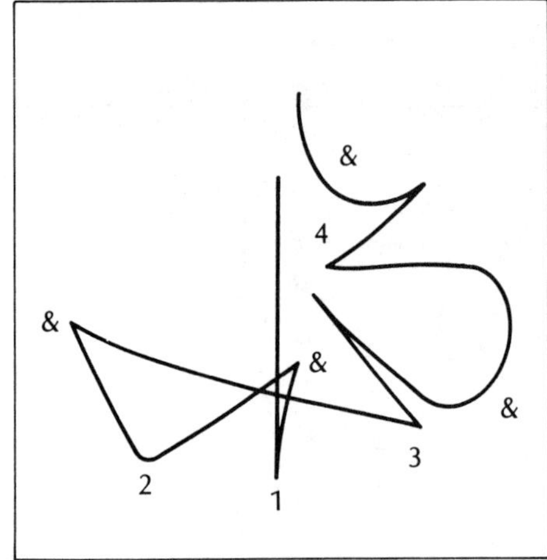

Diagram 16–5b

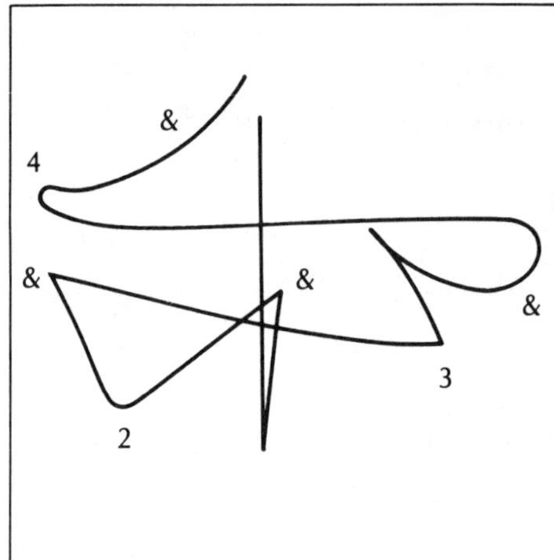

Conduct Exercises 16-3 to 16-7.

Exercise 16-3

Exercise 16-4

Exercise 16-5

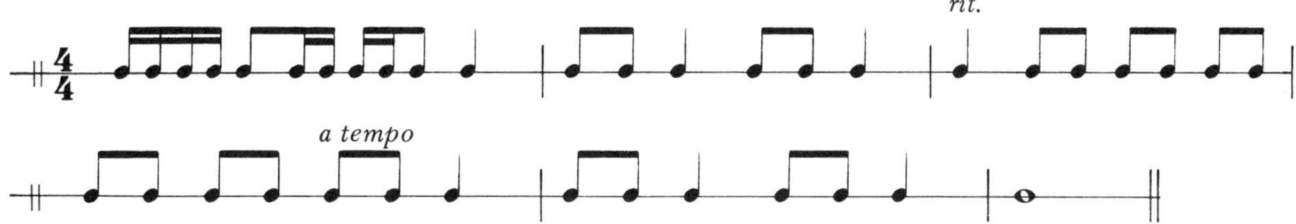

Exercise 16-6

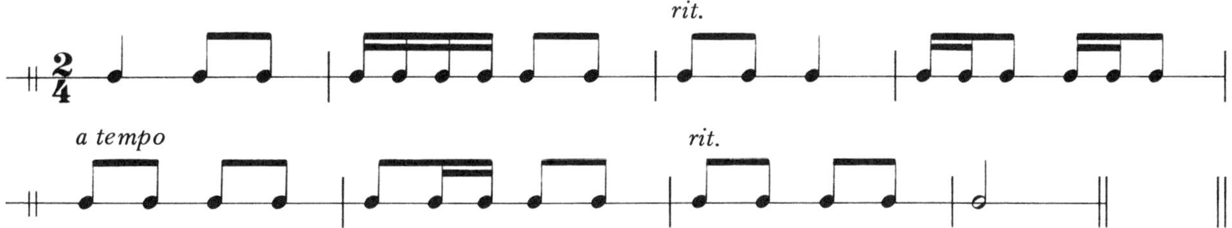

Exercise 16-7

BACH: From the tangle of my transgressions (*The Passion According to St. John*)

The Accelerando

An *accelerando* is often used to heighten the drama of the text or to move into a new musical section. A clear conducting pattern is essential. Prepare the ensemble by eye contact, changing your stance, bringing your left hand into play, or changing the size of the pulse pattern.

In Example 16-4 the *accelerando* is followed by a slight *ritard.* As the *accelerando* begins, the pulse becomes much more angular so that the performers can sense the growing speed of the subdivision. Intensity should also increase. If the *ritard.* is minimal, a very angular pattern may suffice. If the *ritard.* is considerable, each note should be subdivided so that the singers know exactly when each note is to be performed.

Example 16-4:

In Example 16-5 the pulse gestures become more angular throughout. There should be no *ritard.* at the end. Urge the tempo forward. Care must be taken to achieve the effect of acceleration rather than just jumping into a new tempo. Do not slow down at the end. Continue to urge the tempo forward at an even rate. Be certain, however, not to push the tempo beyond the ability of the ensemble.

Example 16-5:

Conduct Exercises 16-8 to 16-10.

Exercise 16-8

Exercise 16-9

Exercise 16–10

SREBOTNJAK: Come, Sweetheart (*Two Macedonian Folk-Songs*)

17 Conducting Triplets and Abrupt Tempo Changes

Triplets

Performers must usually be taught a mental process before they sing triplets accurately. Conductors do not necessarily depart from the metrical pattern they are using before the triplets begin. Rather, they allow the performers to sing the triplets on their own. However, for some ensembles it may be necessary to conduct the triplet values as they are being learned.

The Quarter-Note Triplet

When performing the quarter-note triplet in $\frac{4}{4}$ (Example 17-1), the conductor and performer must begin to think eighth-note triplets in the previous measure. The triplet eighths are then tied in the manner shown in the "mental process" part of the example. Each pair of tied triplet eighths in measure 2 represents a quarter note in the quarter-note triplet. A six pattern would be used to conduct the two groups of quarter-note triplets in measure 2.

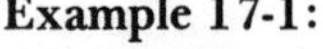

Example 17-1:

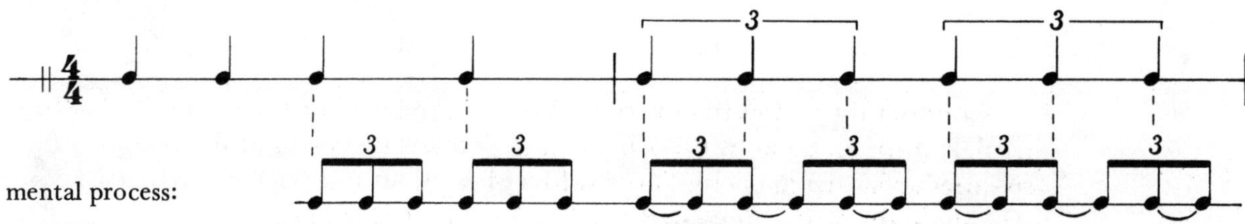

Conduct the following exercise. Your performers are just learning the quarter-note triplet. In order to help them (and yourself) understand the mental process required, conduct the actual note values of the quarter-note triplets in measures 2 and 3. The first measure sets up the underlying triplet feeling. The mental process suggested is given below the exercise.

Exercise 17-1

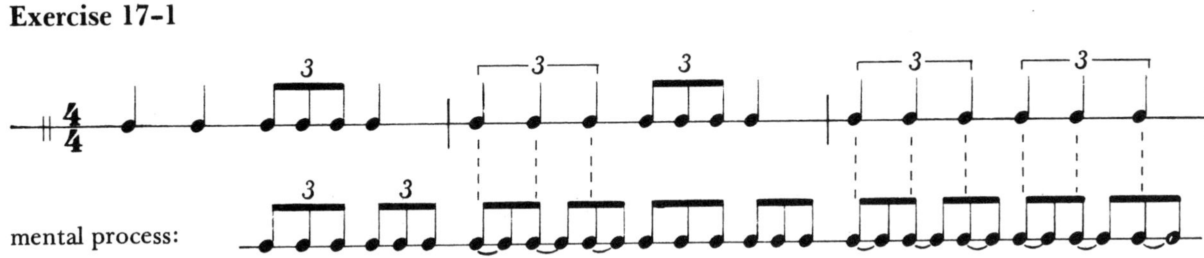

The conducting pattern for the second measure would be the same as if conducting a $\frac{2+2+2+3+3}{8}$ measure, while the third measure would be conducted as a $\frac{2+2+2+2+2+2}{8}$ measure.

The Half-Note Triplet

The mental process for performing the half-note triplet is similar to the process for singing the quarter-note triplet. In the previous measure you must begin to think eighth-note triplets (Example 17-2). The eighth notes are then tied in groups of four, each group representing a half note in the half-note triplet.

Example 17-2:

Conduct the following exercise. Your ensemble is just learning the half-note triplet. In order to help the singers and yourself understand the mental process required, conduct the actual note values of the half-note triplets where they occur. The mental process suggested is given below the exercise.

Exercise 17-2

Example 17-3, a chart of triplet relationships, may be helpful.

Example 17-3:

As the performers learn the feeling of these triplets you should no longer conduct the actual note values. The metric pattern should be maintained wherever possible.

Supplementary Conducting Exercises: Triplets

PAGE: Your Countenance (*Six for Song*)

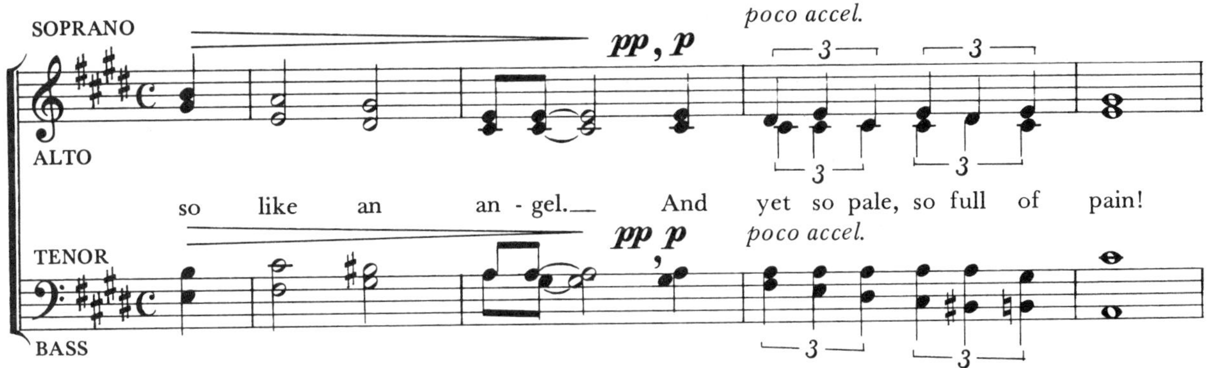

WILLAN: The Spirit of the Lord

Lento

SOPRANO *p*
The Spir - it of the Lord fill - eth the world;

ALTO *p*
The Spir - it of the Lord fill - eth the world;

TENOR *p*
The Spir - it of the Lord fill - eth the world;

BASS *p*
The Spir - it of the Lord fill - eth the world;

Lento
[PIANO-for rehearsal only]
p

Abrupt Tempo Changes

Tempo is one of the most important aspects of music. The vitality of a performance often depends on the tempo chosen for a particular work. The conductor must consider several variables when establishing the essentially correct tempo for a work.

1. *The composer's wish.* Tempo designations such as *allegro* and *largo* usually leave fairly wide latitude for the conductor to establish an appropriate tempo. However, ♩ = 60 is very specific. The conductor must know how fast ♩ = 60 is.

2. *The acoustics of the performance area.* Works may be performed somewhat more slowly in rooms with much reverberation so that words and musical lines will be heard clearly and distinctly. In rooms with little reverberation tempos tend to be faster.

3. *The shortest note value.* The ensemble must be able to perform the shortest note value in the work cleanly and precisely.

4. *The ensemble's ability.* The conductor has an obligation to perform music in a manner which would be acceptable to the composer. However, this obligation must sometimes be altered in order to provide certain kinds of musical experiences to students in an educational setting. Students may not be able to sustain a very slow passage or sing a particular melisma as rapidly as performance practices might ordinarily require. In these instances alteration of tempo would be appropriate to provide a musically satisfying experience for these students. Problems with tempos should not necessarily be a reason for denying access to certain works of great composers.

Common Tempo Changes

Most conductors carry a primitive type of metronome: a wristwatch with a second hand. The metronome marking ♩ = 60 means the equivalency of sixty quarter notes per minute, or one quarter note per second. A tempo of ♩ = 120 would be twice as fast (the equivalency of two quarter notes per second), and a tempo of ♩ = 30 would be twice as slow.

In the following exercises a suggested mental process is indicated to ensure that the new tempo to be established is absolutely accurate. As you approach the measure where the tempo change occurs, begin to think the subdivision given in the "mental process" portion of each exercise. That subdivision will then become the pulse in the new tempo.

Do not guess at setting tempos and changing tempos in these exercises. It is very important that the new tempos be executed accurately.

2-to-1 Proportional Change

Exercise 17–3

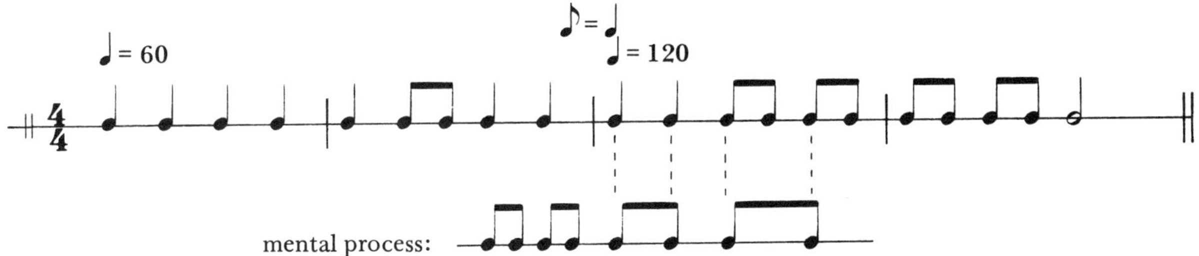

In measure 2, subdivide the pulse into note values that are twice as fast as the pulse. The eighth note in the mental process then becomes the pulse in the new tempo. Conduct the four pattern using the mental-process eighth note as the new pulse. *Note: The eighth note in the mental process remains constant throughout.*

3-to-1 Proportional Change

Exercise 17–4

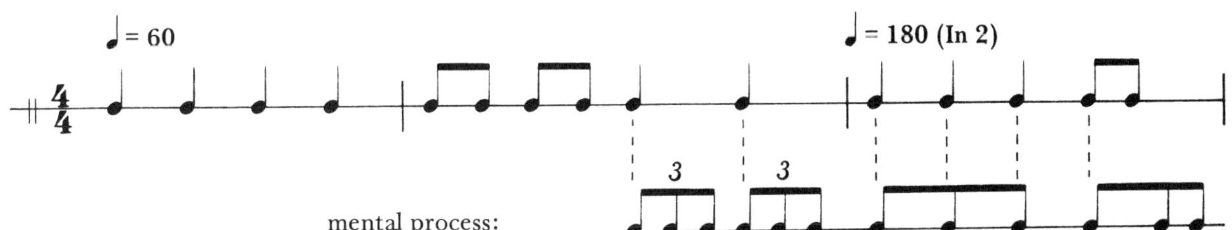

Since the new tempo will be three times as fast, subdivide the pulse into note values that are three times as fast as the pulse. The eighth note in the triplet figure will become the new pulse. Because the new tempo will be very fast, combine two of the triplet eighths into a single conducting gesture. Measure 3 should be conducted very angularly so that the duple subdivision is felt early in the measure.

1-to-2 Proportional Change

Exercise 17–5

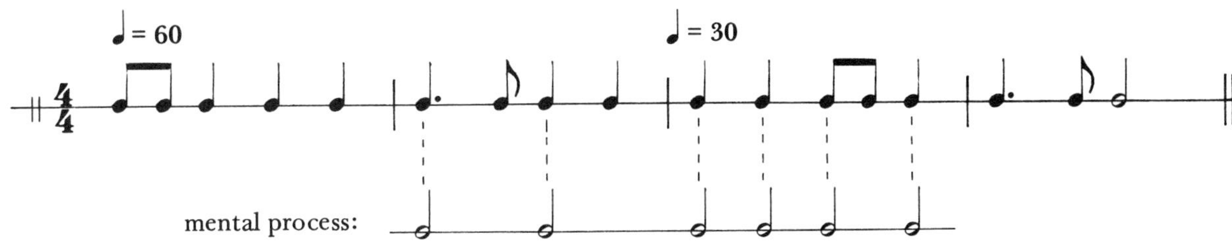

Since the new tempo will be twice as slow, combine two of the original pulses to create the new pulse in measure 3. Conduct a subdivided four pattern with the half note of the mental process as the new pulse.

3-to-2 Proportional Change

In Baroque and Renaissance choral music it is common to switch from $\frac{4}{4}$ to $\frac{3}{4}$. The tempo changes proportionally. Conduct the following exercises. The suggested mental process is indicated under each exercise.

Exercise 17-6

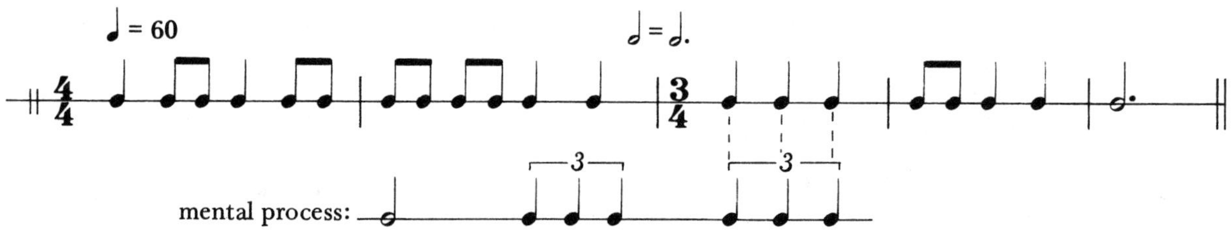

If the tempo is fast enough it may be possible to actually conduct the second measure using a two pattern ($\frac{2}{2}$), thereby setting up the half-note feeling and the following triplet. The ratio of change is 3 to 2, or three pulses in the new tempo to two pulses in the previous one.

Exercise 17-7

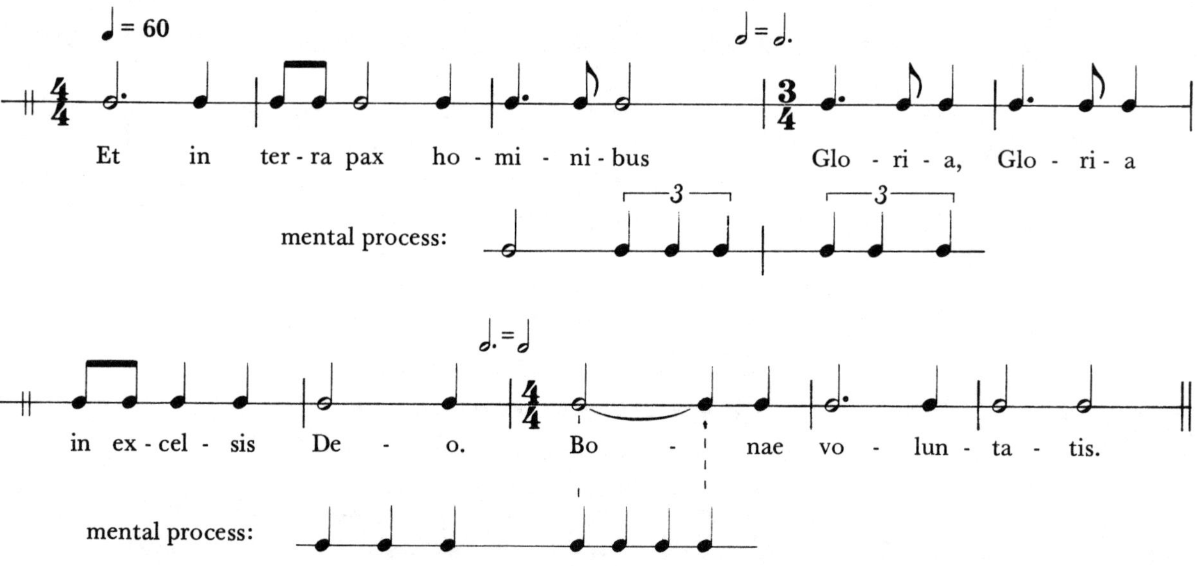

When moving from $\frac{3}{4}$ back to $\frac{4}{4}$ in the above exercise, the first measure of $\frac{4}{4}$ ("Bonae") should be conducted very angularly so that the duplet feeling is strongly established.

Exercise 17-8 Conduct the following excerpt from Hassler's "Cantate Domino." Conduct the change in tempo as indicated.

At other times this same proportion may be given with metronomic markings, changing from ♩ = 60 to ♩ = 90. The ratio of change is 3 to 2. For every three notes of a particular duration in the original tempo there will be two notes of the same value in the new tempo (Example 17-4). As you approach the measure of tempo change, think triplets and then transfer the speed of these triplets to a duplet sensation. The triplet eighth note remains constant throughout the mental process.

Example 17-4:

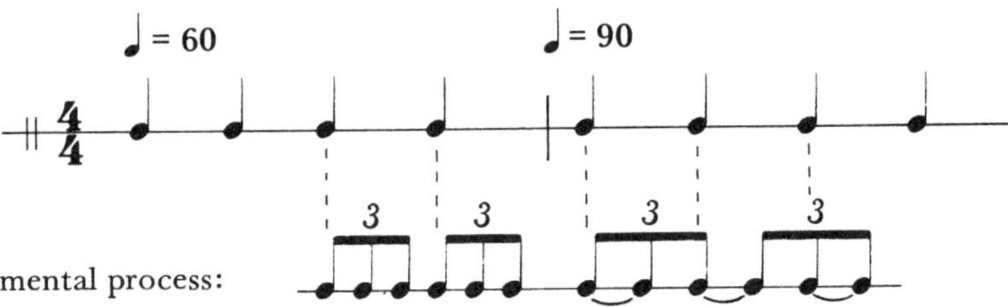

Exercise 17-9 Conduct the following.

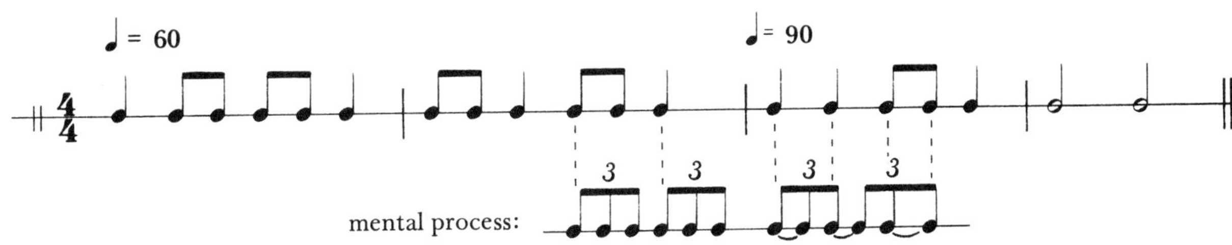

2-to-3 Proportional Change

The reverse process must be used when going from ♩ = 90 to ♩ = 60. The ratio is 60 to 90, or 2 to 3. For every two notes of a particular duration in the old tempo there will be three notes of the same duration in the new tempo (Example 17-5). In the measure before the tempo change, subdivide the pulse into eighth notes. Three of these eighth notes will become equivalent to the pulse in the new tempo.

Example 17-5:

Exercise 17-10 Conduct the following.

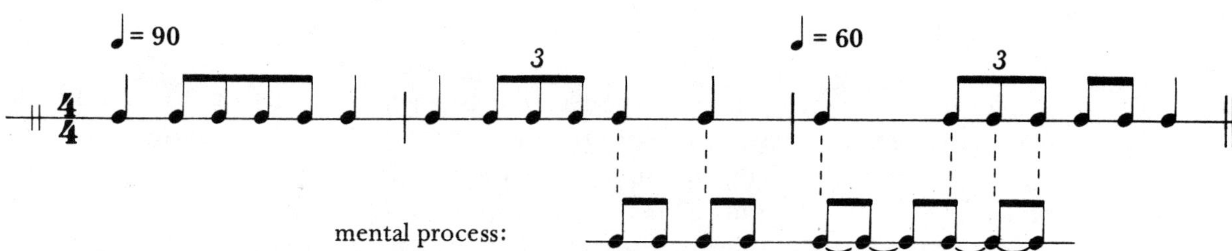

Note that throughout the mental process the duration of the eighth note remains constant. The double eighth-note figure in measure 3 should be conducted very angularly to establish the duple feeling.

4-to-3 Proportional Change

When changing tempo from ♩ = 60 to ♩ = 80, the ratio is 80 to 60, or 4 to 3. For every four notes of a particular duration in the original tempo, there will be three of the corresponding value in the new tempo (Example 17-6). In the measure before the tempo change, think subdivisions of four sixteenth notes per pulse. Three of these four sixteenth notes will then become equivalent to the pulse in the new tempo.

Example 17-6:

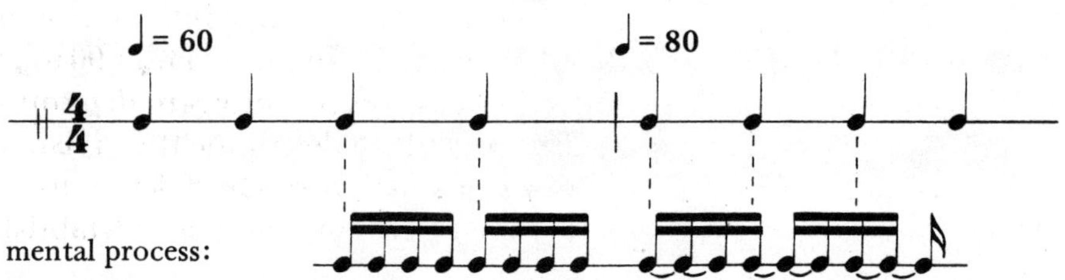

Exercise 17-11 Conduct the following exercise.

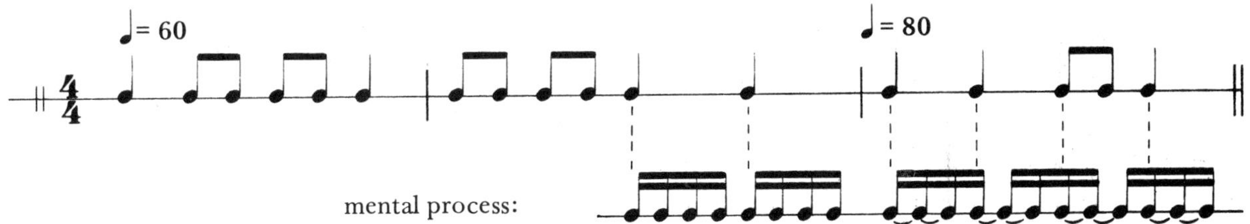

Remember that in the mental process the sixteenth-note duration remains constant.

3-to-4 Proportional Change

If you are changing from ♩ = 120 to ♩ = 90, the ratio is 90 to 120, or 3 to 4. Thus, for every three notes of a particular duration in the original tempo there will be four notes of the same duration in the new tempo (Example 17-7). In the measure before the tempo change, think triplet eighth notes to the pulse. Four of these triplet eighth-note values will be equivalent to the pulse in the new tempo.

Example 17-7:

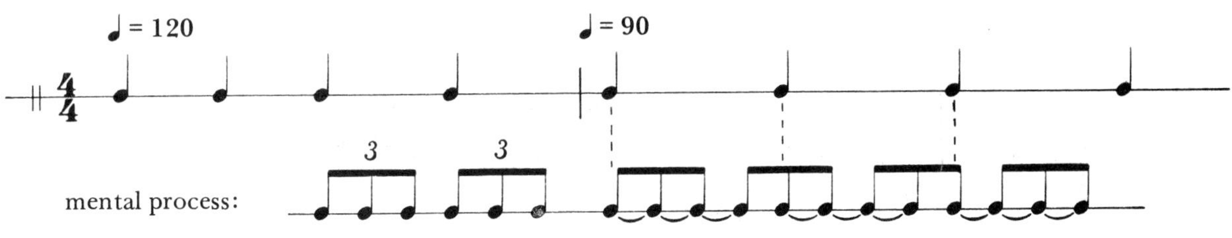

Exercise 17-12 Conduct the following.

Remember that in the above exercise, the eighth note remains constant throughout the mental process.

Other combinations of tempo changes are possible, although ratios may become approximations rather than exact. Changing from ♩ = 90 to ♩ = 84, a ratio of 84 to 90 or 14 to 15, would cause certain complications in determining the exact subdivision. It is mathematically possible to determine the division of the pulse. However, to *feel* the large number of subdivisions and determine accurately the new tempo is quite different. It is best to use a metronome to establish the relationship of these tempos.

18 Nontraditional Notation

Contemporary composers have sought new means of expression. With these new types of expression have come new notation systems which have not yet become totally standardized. When learning works in nontraditional notation you must often rely on the composer's key or legend prefacing the work to indicate intended performance practices. When this key is not available you must rely on your own creative abilities to decipher the notation. Some composers deliberately leave the notation vague so that the conductor and ensemble must exercise some creative input in the performance of the work. This added creativity results in interest and freshness in each performance. Other works are strictly based on chance or randomness and each performance by design will be different from all others.

Nontraditional works are often foreign to both ensemble and conductor, and therefore difficult to comprehend. The ensemble's reaction may be negative. Only through your careful guidance can the performers begin to appreciate many of the nontraditional works of this century. You should remember that these works were conceived in all seriousness. Your performance should reflect the aesthetic result desired by the composer.

Probably the greatest reason for performing nontraditional works is because they exist. As an educator it is your responsibility to educate performers and audiences in the creative means of today.

The following exercises in nontraditional notation each involve the solution of a basic conducting problem. The interpretation of the work and its performance medium is left to you. You are to decide what sounds the ensemble is to make and the manner in which these sounds are to be uttered. Your explanation of the performance requirements must be precise and as short as possible. Each exercise should take no more than one minute to perform. Some of these exercises, like other nontraditional works, may require nontraditional conducting gestures. You will have to explore a new series of gestures to express these nonmetric mini-works.

Exercise 18-1

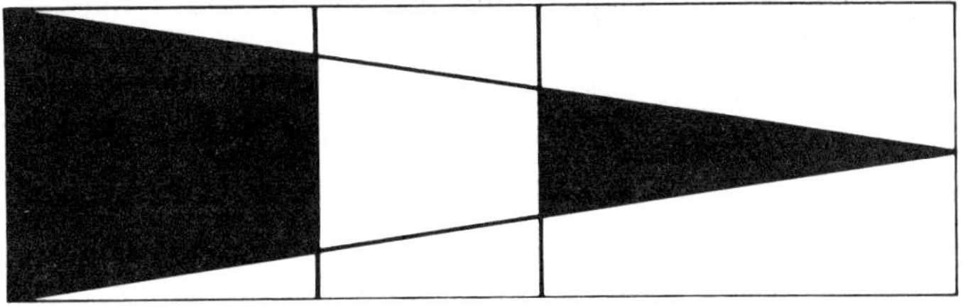

Exercise 18-2

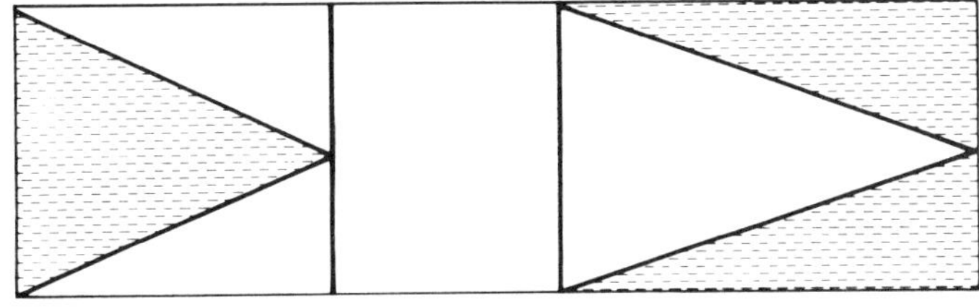

Exercise 18-3

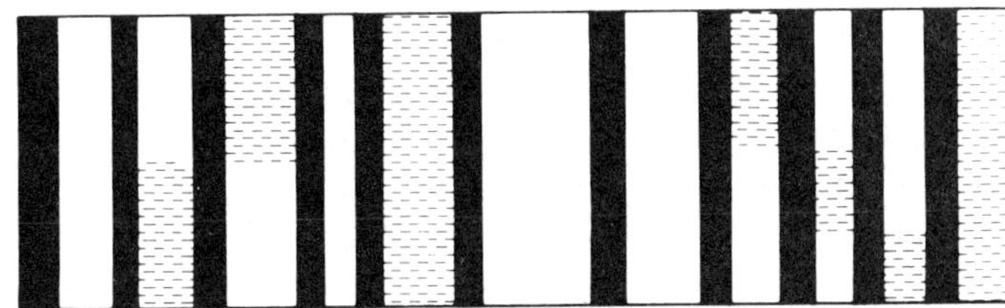

Exercise 18-4

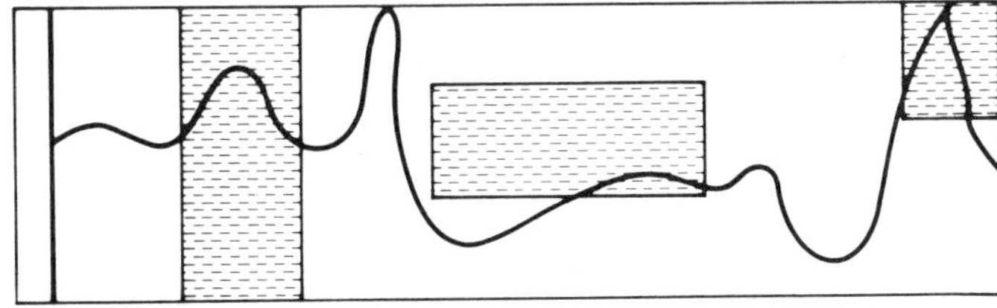

Exercise 18-5

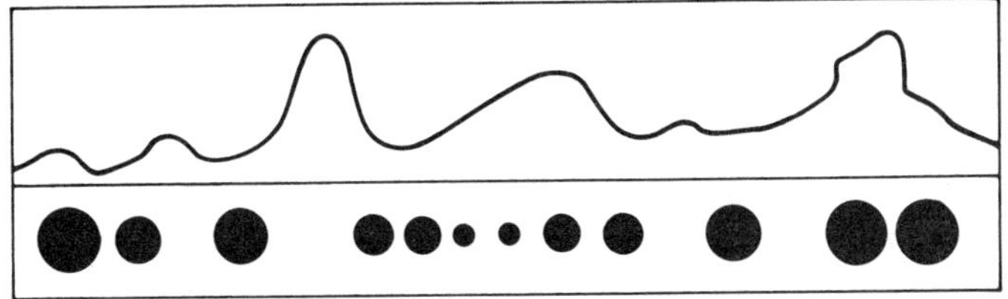

Exercise 18-6

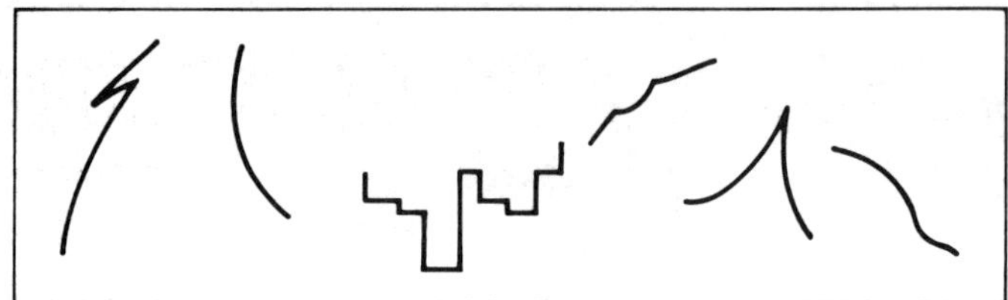

Exercise 18-7

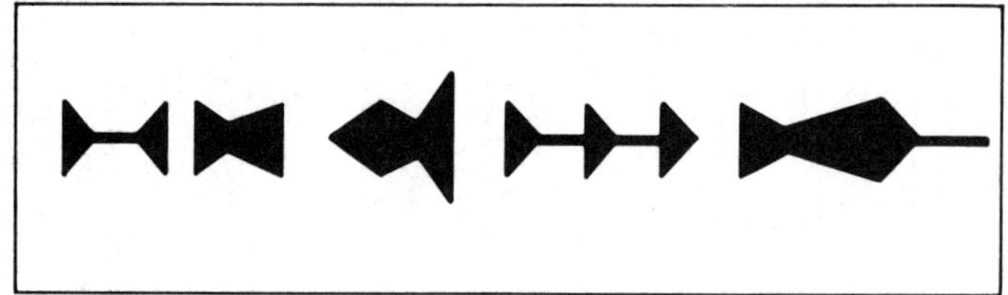

Exercise 18-8

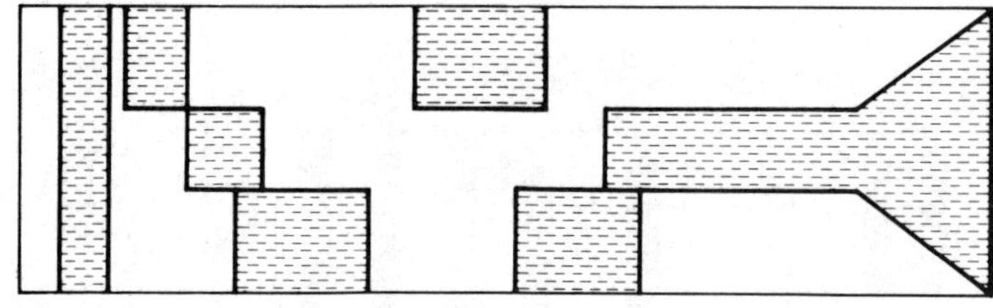

19 Advanced Conducting Exercises

Conduct Exercises 19-1 to 19-12. As you study each exercise, determine the pattern to be used for each measure.

Exercise 19-4

Exercise 19-5

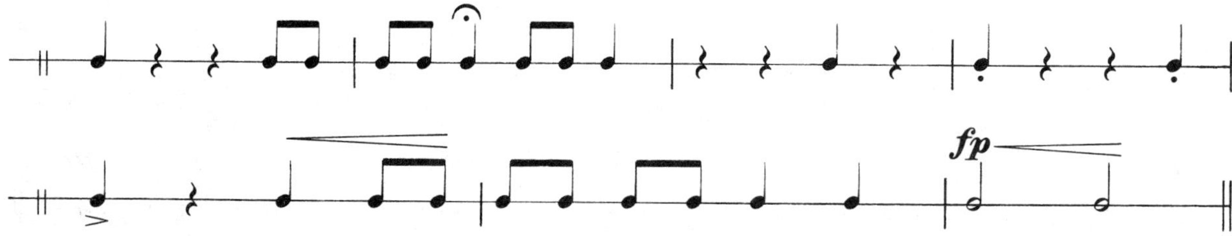

Exercise 19-6

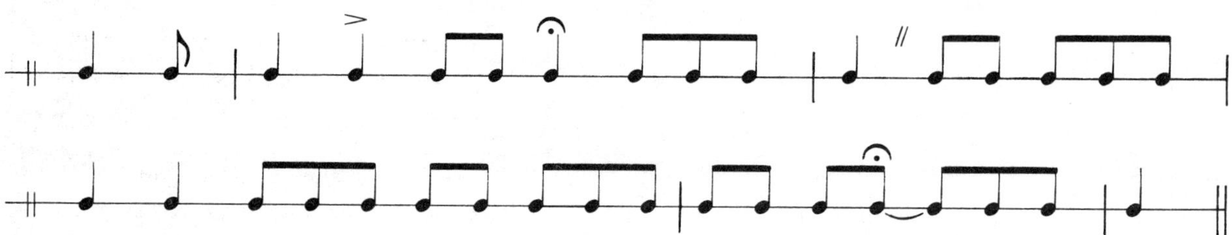

Exercise 19-7

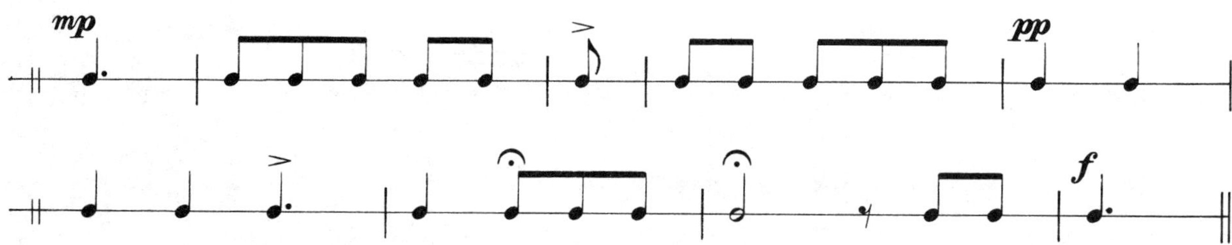

Exercise 19-8

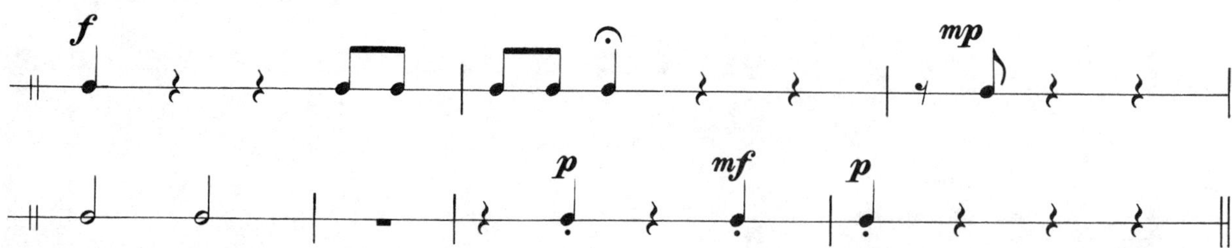

Exercise 19-9

Exercise 19-10

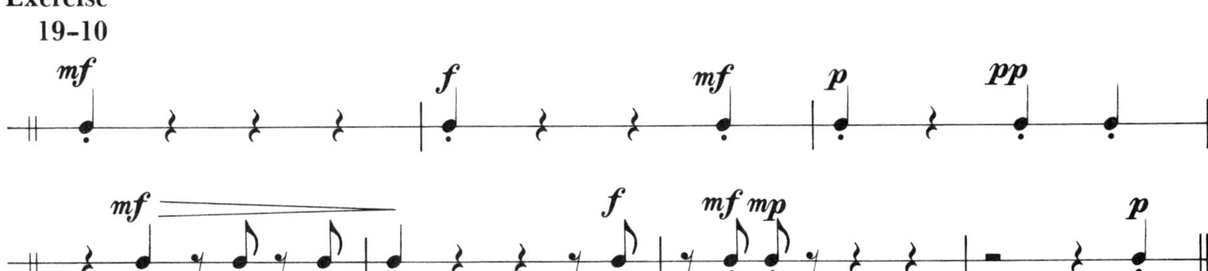

Exercise 19-11

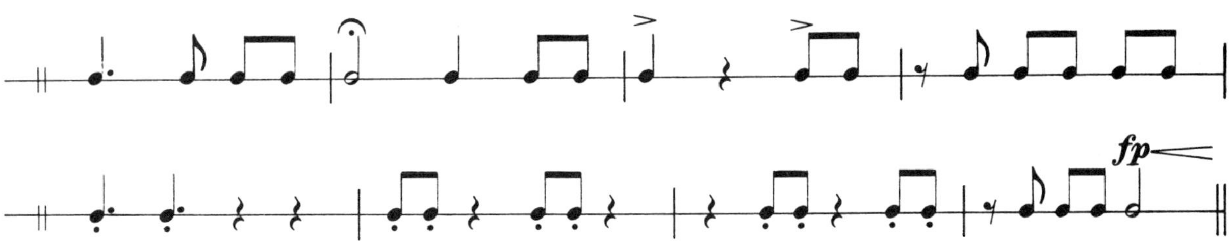

Exercise 19-12

PART III

The Conductor as Organizer and Teacher

20 Organizing and Rehearsing The Ensemble

Organizing the Ensemble

Two major functions will be pertinent to your role as conductor: organizing and teaching. Your success as a conductor will be based on your competence to perform these two functions.

In school settings the teacher usually has to justify the establishment of new ensembles. With budget problems besetting school districts, even existing ensembles are being carefully scrutinized. The purpose of any ensemble should be carefully stated. A show choir and a concert choir exist for different reasons. Professional choirs and church choirs exist for still other reasons. The purpose of the ensemble will greatly affect (1) auditioning procedures, (2) selection standards for membership, (3) the size of the ensemble, and (4) conductor-member relationships.

The Audition

Singers are usually frightened by auditions. They come to an audition because their desire to sing outweighs their fright. You must disarm their fears with your own approach: a smile, a kind word, even a few personal questions to set them at ease.

Often those seeking admittance to a volunteer choir come without a proper warm-up. Your first exercise should help warm up the voice as well as allow you to hear a variety of its characteristics. A melodic exercise using 1-3-5-3-1 or 1-2-3-4-5-4-3-2-1 moving up or down by half or whole steps will not only be a good warm-up but will also allow you to hear almost all of the vocal characteristics important for the particular ensemble. You will have to determine which of the following characteristics are important for *your* ensemble.

1. *Range.* The extreme high and low of the singing voice.
2. *Tessitura.* That portion of the range where the voice sings most comfortably. For some the tessitura may encompass a fourth or fifth, for others as much as an octave.
3. *Tone quality.* Determined by those portions of the overtone series the particular voice emphasizes. These overtones give the voice its lightness or darkness, its flutiness or reediness.
4. *Agility and flexibility.* "Agility" refers to the ability to sing rapidly and still maintain accuracy. Lighter voices tend to move more rapidly, although training and conscious effort may result in considerable agility on the part of heavier, darker voices. "Flexibility" refers to one's ability to use all areas of the voice with ease, to move from high to low, and to shift directions easily.
5. *Legato and staccato.* "Legato" refers to the ability to sing a musical line smoothly with no interruptions in the flow. "Staccato" involves the singer's ability to stop and start the tone accurately and quickly.
6. *Intonation.* The singer's ability to sing in tune.
7. *Vowel formation.* The singer's ability to form and pronounce vowels correctly, thereby enhancing the acoustical resonance of the voice.
8. *Dynamic control.* Important in some types of small ensembles. Using a single sustained tone, have the singers begin pianissimo, crescendo to fortissimo, and then return to the original dynamic level.
9. *Vibrato control.* Some types of literature require a straighter tone than others. Begin by having the singer sustain a tone without vibrato. Gradually he or she should warm the sound by adding vibrato, then reverse the process by removing the vibrato until the initial sound is reproduced.
10. *Bright-Dark control.* Using a sustained bright "ah" vowel, the singer should gradually darken the vowel quality to an "aw" and then reverse the process until the initial sound is reproduced.

Auditions should also determine the singer's tonal memory: what the singer can reproduce after hearing a melodic fragment. Begin with short tonal fragments and make them increasingly longer and more complex (Exercise 20-1).

Exercise 20-1

Reading ability is essential in many choirs. The required level of reading depends on the purpose of the ensemble. Some conductors couple reading exercises with intervallic drills, asking the singer to sing certain intervals both up and down from a given pitch. Reading rhythms may also be included in this part of the audition.

The format of the audition is based on the purpose of the ensemble and on the time you have available for auditioning. If speed is critical (you have sixty junior high students in your classroom during third period waiting to be auditioned), you will have to determine which portions of the audition can give you the most information in the least amount of time. Group auditions of four to five singers at the same time are possible. On the other hand, professional auditions may last thirty minutes or longer for each performer. If you gave thirty minutes for auditions to every student in a school choral program, the semester would be almost over by the time auditions were completed. Your audition organization depends on time and on the body of information you need immediately to select the personnel and place them within your choral ensemble organization.

Even if several of your ensembles do not require a formal audition for membership, it is recommended that all singers go through the audition process. You will want to know what each voice is capable of and what you will have to teach in order to improve the singing ability of each person in your ensemble program.

Seating

Once the selection of choir members is complete, they must be placed in a section within a choral setting. Seating members often demands much experimentation to get maximum blend and balance. You may wish to place softer voices next to more dynamic voices, reedy voices next to flute-like voices, good readers next to poor readers. How you place singers within the section determines the overall sound. Voices that tend to stick out should never be placed on outer edges of the section. Rather, they should be surrounded with voices that blend well.

The best criterion for placing a voice within a section is tone quality. However, many school conductors face difficult decisions with voice placement. Students may have the range to sing either alto or soprano, tenor or baritone. Even if a girl's voice has a definite soprano quality, she may be placed in the alto section because she has the range and the reading ability needed to strengthen the section. Unfortunately, expedience and need often prevail in placing voices. Many baritones are "kicked upstairs" because of the scarcity of tenors. When young choristers are singing out of their normal voice section you must:

1. Teach them how to sing more easily at extreme ranges
2. Watch and listen for strain
3. Not ask for too much from these singers
4. Choose music sensibly on the basis of voices within the ensemble
5. Remind singers not to push

TO RUIN A YOUNG VOICE IS A CARDINAL SIN.

Whether sopranos go to the left or right of the conductor is a matter of personal preference. The seating configuration you choose should be purposeful. It is also recommended that for various purposes you have two or three different seating arrangements available. Diagram 20-1 shows some common seating arrangements.

Diagram 20–1

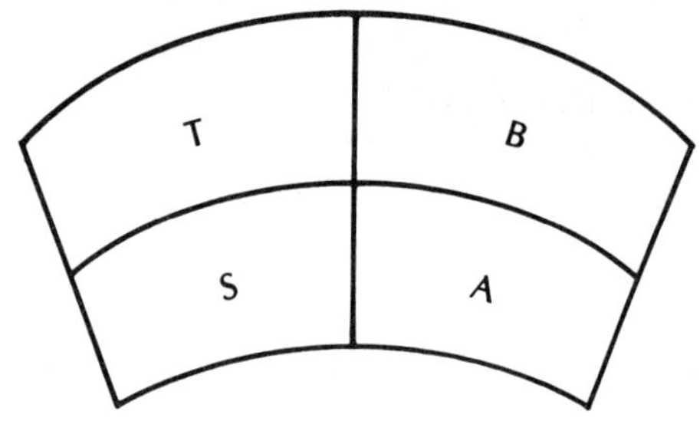

High voices to the left (right), low voices to the right (left); highest and lowest polarized for good intonation stability; a common seating arrangement.

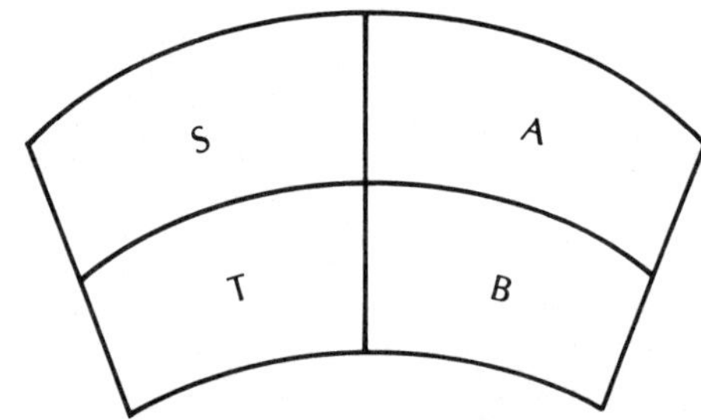

Men and women reversed. Particularly good if you wish to concentrate on what the men are doing. Also helpful if the men are not as strong as the women.

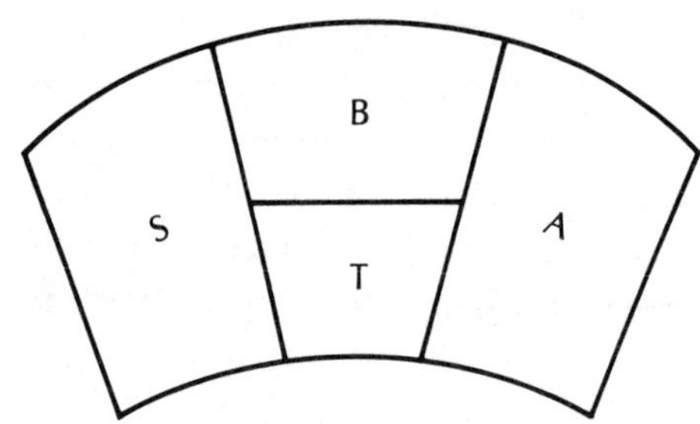

Good for a smaller male section; men blocked in center for solidity rather than spread out across the back or front.

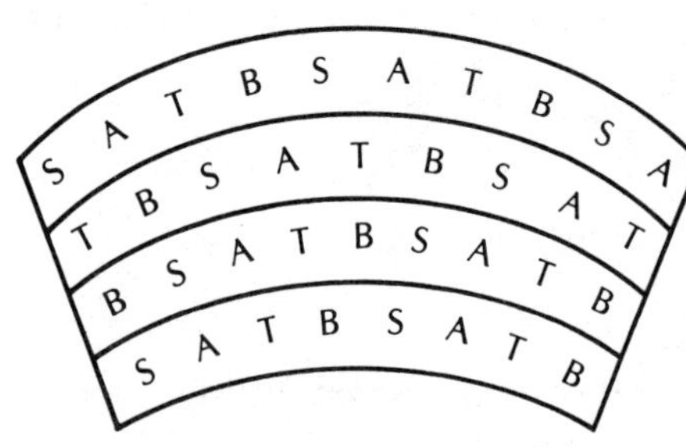

Quartets. Forces independence. Usually improves blend and balance when all parts are secure. Security of parts is essential, since all cues from conductor are made generally rather than specifically to a section.

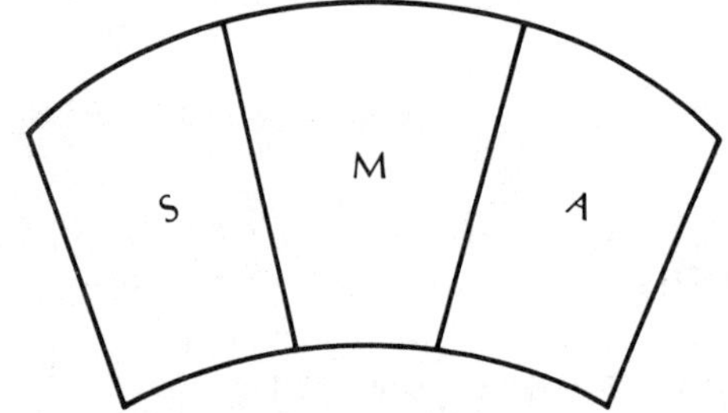

Good for three-part mixed music or small men's section in which all the men sing the same part.

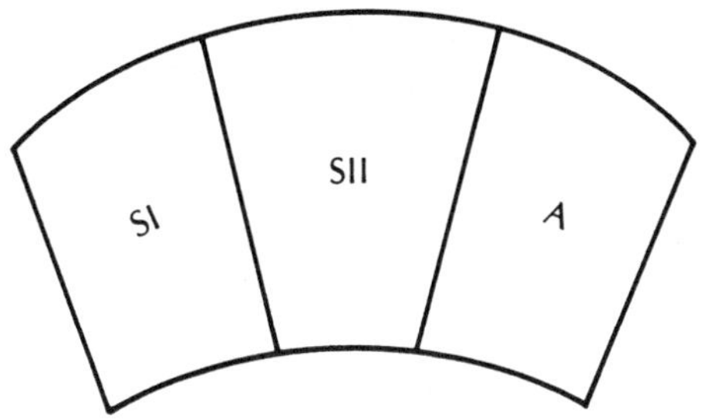

Common arrangement for women's three-part choir; high-low voices are polarized to the outside.

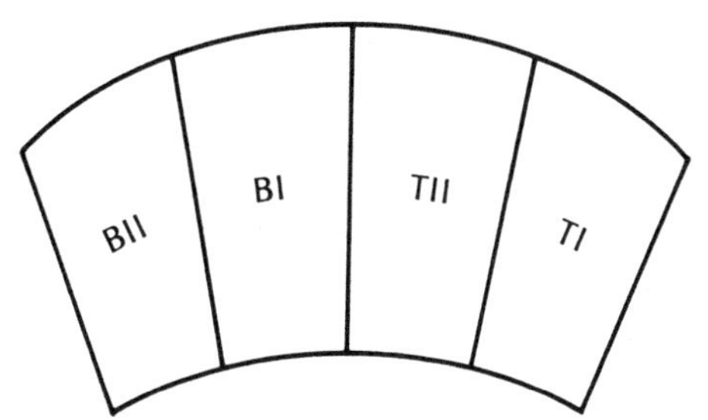

Common arrangement for men's chorus; high-low voices are polarized to the outside.

The Conductor's Responsibilities

Preparing the music is only one component of concert preparation. Although you may delegate certain organizational details to others, ultimately all aspects of a concert, from publicity to setting up the stage, remain your responsibility. It is your responsibility to verify that such tasks have satisfactorily been completed. That is simply a fact of musical life.

Your responsibilities as a conductor begin with selecting and training the singers and end with a successful performance. The following list of responsibilities is only partial but will give some idea of their scope.

1. Selecting and training singers
2. Selecting an accompanist
3. Selecting music
4. Purchasing equipment: pianos, music stands, uniforms, music folders, risers, acoustical shells, library supplies, sound system
5. Publicizing the ensemble
6. Selecting concert dates and sites
7. Preparing printed programs
8. Advertising concerts through newsletters, radio, newspapers, TV, and posters
9. Preparing and selling tickets
10. Handling ensemble finances (fund raising)
11. Rehearsing the ensemble
12. Recruiting responsible persons to help in the operations of the ensemble

For the actual performance the conductor must be certain someone will be responsible for:

1. Running the sound system
2. Operating the lights
3. Passing out programs
4. Taping the concert
5. Setting up the stage area
6. Tuning the piano
7. Being sure music stands, chairs, and podium are available
8. Selling tickets
9. Pulling curtains

A basic checklist such as the one shown in Diagram 20-2 may help the conductor ascertain that all tasks are completed:

Diagram 20–2 **CONCERT PREPARATION CHECKLIST**

Place: School Auditorium
Date: November 15
Time: 8:00 p.m.
Accompanist: Marcy
Assistant Conductors: Jacque Melody

Ensembles: Concert Choir
Legionnaires

Pre-Concert Needs

Printed Programs: Date: Nov. 3

News Releases: Newspaper Nov. 5 — Printed Nov. 15
Radio Nov. 5 — Reviewed Nov. 13, 14, 15
TV Nov. 5 — Viewed

Posters Marcy, Janie, Nov. 8
Newsletter none
Ticket Printing none
Piano Tuned contact Rod, Nov. 10

Stage Set-up (diagram)

Concert Choir

Legionnaires

Concert Needs

Music stands 5
Chairs 4
Piano grand & upright
Risers 4 sections
Podium yes
Sound System Bill, sound crew

Ticket Takers Mavis, Samantha, George
Curtains none
Programs Girls Glee, Marsha Melody
Lights Harry (stage staff)
Taping My machine, wife
Platforms 3

Advanced Rehearsal Techniques

The good ensemble conductor runs an efficient, effective rehearsal. The goal of any rehearsal is developing musicality, not just drilling notes. Often certain techniques help the conductor become a better rehearsal technician. The following techniques are intended to strengthen your rehearsal skills.

1. Know your music. Don't sight-read in front of the ensemble.
2. Expect an exciting rehearsal. Be positive. Expect musical things to happen.
3. Be prepared to deal with style, tempos, harmonic considerations, blend, balance, technical difficulties in singing and playing, performance practices, mood, and interpretation of the text. Anticipate where problems will occur and be prepared to deal with them.
4. Start the rehearsal exactly on time. Expect the performers to be in their places when the rehearsal begins. End the rehearsal exactly on time.
5. Post the rehearsal order of the music so that the performers can arrange their music correspondingly before the session begins. Fumbling and hunting for music wastes valuable time.
6. If necessary, specify the amount of time you will spend on each work in your rehearsal plan. This allotment of time keeps you task-oriented.
7. Set up the room before the rehearsal begins.
8. Vary the warm-up exercises. Compose new ones when those in current use begin to loss their effectiveness.
9. Encourage the performers to listen rather than talk when you are giving directions or teaching them something. You will accomplish much more when the ensemble listens to what you have to say.
10. Wherever possible, direct instructions to the entire ensemble, not just to a section or an individual. The entire ensemble should listen intently to all other parts as they are rehearsed.
11. The pace of the rehearsal must keep the ensemble members alert. Don't get bogged down by rehearsing a section over and over again with diminishing returns.
12. Concentrate on the music and the learners. Don't wander from the subject. Discipline your mind to stay on task.
13. Conduct as *much* as possible, talk as *little* as possible. A short demonstration may save many words.
14. Let the ensemble rehearse the work occasionally without a conductor. This forces the performers to listen more carefully and react like an ensemble.
15. Deal with only one problem at a time. Rehearse each problem intensely before going on to the next.
16. Teach the ensemble to stop when you stop. You must remind the performers to place their music in such a way that you are always visible.
17. Vary the rehearsal approach to a work. Don't always begin at the beginning and work to the end. Occasionally begin with small sections at the back of the work. This also ensures that the end of the work is adequately rehearsed.
18. Teach the ensemble to trust the preparatory gesture. Don't "count off" a full measure before beginning.
19. Teach the ensemble the meaning of your gestures. This will save hours of misunderstanding.

20. Some a cappella works of the Renaissance and Baroque periods can be raised and lowered in pitch until a suitable ensemble pitch is found. This is consistent with known performance practices. Raising a work a half step will often cure intonation problems.
21. Give a reason for repeating a section or a phrase. Tell the performers what needs to be corrected and how to make those corrections.
22. Be positive. Positively reinforce what was done well.
23. Work for an aesthetic experience during each rehearsal. Work at perfecting something, even if it is one phrase or even one chord.
24. Don't sing with the ensemble. Listen.
25. Give directions only once. Do not get in the habit of repeating directions.

21 Developing Choral Sound

Blend

In any choral setting one of the first tasks of the conductor is to instill within the ensemble the desire to produce a good sound. A good sound is absolutely essential if the singers are to have an aesthetic experience.

Each singer within a section produces a unique sound. Blend occurs when two or more performers singing in unison produce a sound which is perceived as a single tone. Because the vowel is the primary carrier of tone, blend is ultimately the result of the unanimity of vowel production. Blend is not a quality the composer can write into the score.

Achieving blend is a matter for trained ears. It has been said that the fine choir is one that "sings with its ears." The ear must be trained and sensitized to hear blended tones. Each singer must perceive minute differences in vowel formation and make subtle adjustments to improve the blend. For example, there is a major difference between the vowel sounds "ah" and "uh." Many singers do not hear the difference and will sing "uh" in place of an "ah." As a teacher you must demonstrate the effect of incorrect vowel conception and take measures to improve vowel unanimity. Training the ensemble to watch the conductor will not automatically improve blend.

The effects of blend may be observed by having one person sing the vowel "o͞o." Then add the other voices one by one in the section, asking each person to enter with the same vowel sound at the same dynamic level. Voices which enter with a different vowel sound, such as a modified "uh," will stand out immediately. It is most important that the singers, not just you, hear the difference.

Eventually the singers who are not blending properly must be the ones to make the minute adjustments. Ask these singers to modify the vowel sound so that it more nearly matches the sound of the section as a whole. Work to achieve blend on all vowels.

Slow, sustained chordal music which demands concentration on blend should be selected early in the year. Often, if this music does not require extremes of range, it can be used as a warm-up. Use the tape recorder to make people aware of problems with blend.

Balance

Balance depends on proper control of dynamics. There are essentially two types of balance: balance within the section and balance between sections. Each voice within the ensemble must sing at basically the same dynamic level. This is very difficult in young choirs, since some voices will be very soft and others more powerful. Timidity, as well as the degree of natural vocal strength, may make it difficult for some voices to sing as loudly as others. These softer voices are still valuable to the ensemble since they add body and depth to the sound.

The well-balanced section is one in which all singers are capable of producing exactly the same dynamic level. Problems arise when, for example, one tenor is much stronger than the three modified baritones in a section. When this happens the establishment of balance, as well as blend, is much more difficult, but not impossible.

Have one singer sustain a neutral pure vowel such as "o͞o" or "ah." Over the sustained vowel add the other voices one by one. Achieving balance, like blend, is a matter for trained ears. Each singer must listen carefully to the dynamic level and make adjustments to balance with others. Begin softly, then work through the middle dynamic ranges. Many problems occur at louder dynamic levels, since softer voices simply cannot match the volume of bigger voices. In any section of the ensemble, the dynamic level just before balance collapses and individual voices become prominent is the optimum dynamic range for that particular section.

Balance also exists within the entire ensemble. This means, for example, getting the entire alto section to sing as loudly as the soprano section. The singers' ears must be brought into play again, since only the ears can tell how much energy must be supplied to the tone dynamically. Singers should be expected to listen across the choir as well as within their own section.

Problems arise when the acoustics of the performance or rehearsal hall make listening across the ensemble difficult. If, for example, the sopranos cannot hear the altos because of the acoustical properties of the room, balance will be difficult to achieve. The conductor then becomes the regulator of balance.

No voice should ever be required to sing at maximum volume. Solidity of sound, giving the illusion of power, can be achieved by exploiting the other end of the dynamic scale. If the choir cannot sing *ffff*, the more subtle gradations along the entire dynamic scale must be achieved. Since dynamics are relative, the ensemble that learns to sing a very soft, intense tone will give the illusion of having greater power at the forte level. THE ENSEMBLE IS ONLY AS STRONG AS ITS WEAKEST SECTION. Whatever the weakest section can produce well dynamically sets the dynamic level of the entire ensemble.

Voice placement within the section can play an important part in gaining maximum blend and balance advantages. Experiment with voice placement to determine where everyone makes the greatest contribution. Very strong singers should be placed within the ensemble rather than on the ends or in the front. In this position they will be able to hear the total sound and make adjustments in dynamics as needed.

Singing in quartets within the ensemble is probably the best blend-balance technique (see Diagram 20-1), but some singers simply cannot handle the quartet arrangement. They need the security of the section. Placing strong voices next to weaker voices may help the weaker voices develop strength. Placing softer, flute-like voices next to more nasal, reedy voices may help the reedy voices develop a more diffused tone quality.

A soprano who stands at the end of the section hears the ensemble differently than one who stands next to the tenor section or within the bass section. Shift the performers around occasionally to give them new perceptions of how the ensemble sounds from various positions within the choir. You force singers to listen more critically and make adjustments as needed by putting men in front and women in back or singing in quartets (see Diagram 20-1).

In many choirs the conductor makes all adjustments for blend and balance, as well as for pitch. However, if you never ask your singers to use their ears and to make these adjustments themselves, they will never develop critical listening skills. You will be forever adjusting blend, balance, and pitch and you may never have the chance to make music. Although each voice is unique, it is also an amazingly flexible instrument. Coupled with a good ear, the voice is very versatile. Good choral singers must give their voices to the ensemble. That is, each voice may have to give up some of its individuality when developing a good choral sound. Usually not everyone can sing in any fashion they wish. Modifying vocal timbre and vowels and controlling pitch accuracy, dynamic level, and vibrato for the good of the ensemble is part of the choral experience. The voice can make these adjustments if the ear is trained to listen critically.

Vocal Exercises

Just like long-distance runners, vocalists should always warm up before performing. Vocal exercises help build the voice and improve technique, as well as aid the ensemble in singing a particular work better.

Singers need training in six general areas:

1. Blend and balance
2. Tone-quality development
3. Range development
4. Flexibility and agility
5. Diction and articulation
6. Control of air supply

The reason for using any exercise you do should be apparent to the singers.

Exercises should begin in the middle range of the voice, where singing is most comfortable. Work the voice to the outer portions of the range. If strain occurs, return to a more moderate range. Repeat the process until range limits are reached that will allow the voice to sing the next one or two works comfortably.

Exercises are learning tools. Listen carefully to how the ensemble performs them. When necessary, stop the ensemble and make corrections. Build lines and phrases. Don't allow the ensemble just to sing notes. Musicality should be stressed in all exercises.

Two schools of thought exist regarding warm-ups. One school suggests the use of abstract exercises, while the other advocates using material from the music being learned. It is recommended that either or both be employed as the situation dictates. At certain times an abstract exercise may be used to concentrate on a specific vocal problem. At other times the music may be used to place the solution of the vocal problem in context. Remember: No one method is better than the other. Analyze the needs of your singers and decide what will solve their vocal problems most efficiently.

The exercises given throughout this chapter are useful in solving certain types of vocal problems. They are not just dull, boring warm-ups.

Blend and Balance

Blend depends on uniformity of vowel production among all singers in the ensemble. Singers should use only pure vowels. The sound "uh" should not be a substitute for "ah." Balance depends on unity of dynamics. Each section must balance within itself so that no voices stick out. The section should sound like a single voice. The sections of the ensemble must also balance with each other so that no section overpowers another.

Exercise 21-1

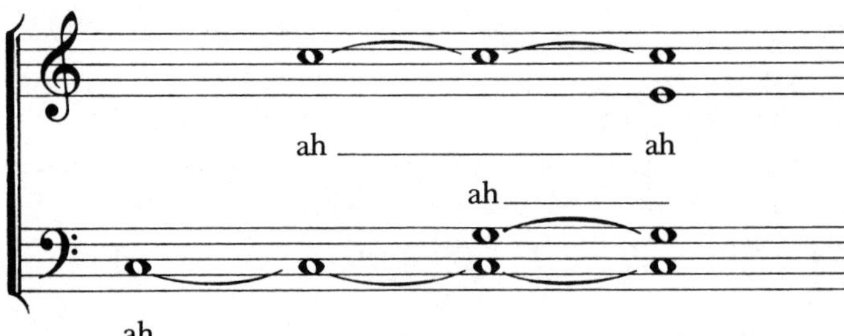

Be certain octave is in tune. Then add fifth and check intonation. Use all pure vowels. Listen for a consistency in vowel production.

Exercise 21-2

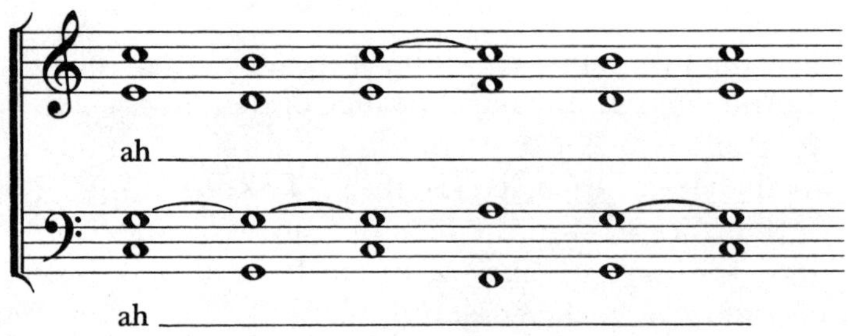

Exercise 21-3

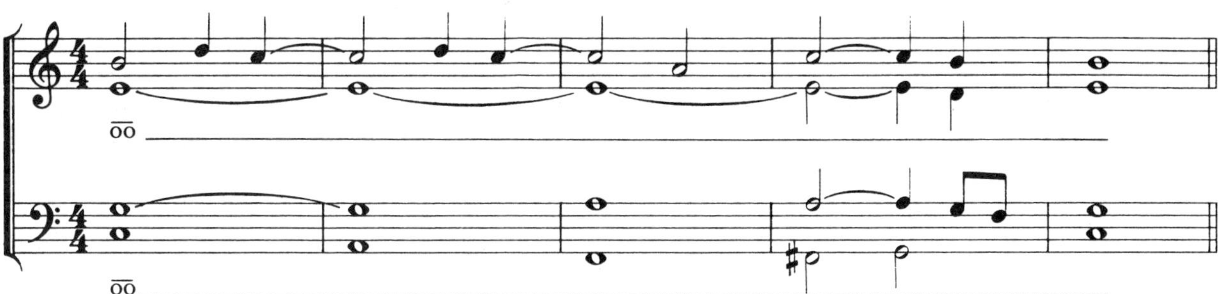

Tone-Quality Development

Strive for an open, forward sound. Relaxation of the vocal mechanism is essential. The inside of the mouth acts as a resonator. It should be made as large as possible without tensing the jaw. The tongue should remain low and forward in the mouth when singing vowels. There should be no visible signs of tension. There are certain places in the vocal range where timbre changes occur. These are called lift points, registers, or breaks. The good singer is one who learns to sing across these breaks with no noticeable change in quality. Exercises may be used to smooth out these changes in quality and develop a more homogeneous sound throughout the range. Use only pure vowels. Work to decrease tension in the vocal mechanism.

Exercise 21-4

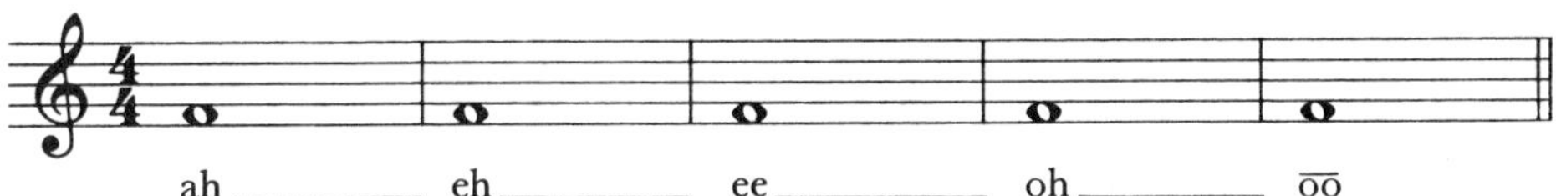

Exercise 21-5

Exercise 21-6

Range Development

Both the top and bottom of the singers' ranges should be developed. Move exercises up and down either by half steps or by whole steps. Start in a moderate range at a moderate tempo and dynamic level. Remind the singers to (1) take a deep breath; (2) listen critically to interval relations; (3) supply added energy as pitches are extended toward the extremes, without tightening the vocal mechanism or pushing; and (4) sing with the best tone quality and musicality they are capable of.

Exercise 21-7

Exercise 21-8

Flexibility and Agility

The singer who is flexible and agile moves the voice quickly and accurately through all portions of the range using a variety of articulations. In the following exercises speed is important, but not at the expense of everything else. Good tone quality and musicality are still essential. Begin slowly at ♩ = 60 and increase the speed to ♩ = 120. Perform each exercise with a variety of consonant and vowel combinations.

Exercise 21-9

Exercise 21-10

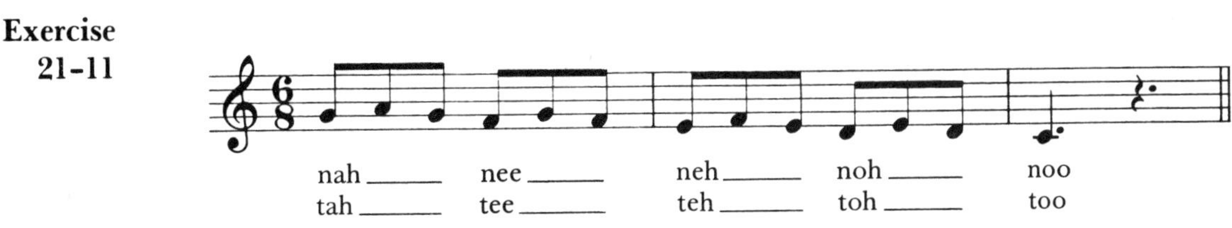

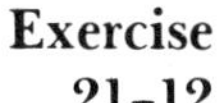

dah meh nee poh too lah bay dah meh nee poh too lah bay dah meh nee poh too lah bay dah

meh nee poh too lah bay dah meh nee poh too lah bay dah meh nee poh too lah bay dah meh.

Diction and Articulation

Diction and articulation depend on clarity of consonants and purity of vowels. Singers must energize consonants so that they project, and must also unify vowel production (as discussed earlier in "Blend"). In the following exercises, concentrate primarily on (1) the energy level of the various component sounds of each syllable; (2) the intelligibility of the syllable as a whole; and (3) the precision of attack and release. Use a variety of consonant and vowel combinations.

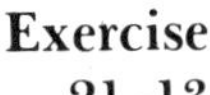

Exercise
21-14

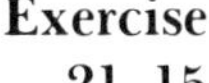

Exercise 21-16

Control of Air Supply

Each singer must learn to control the breath by releasing only as much air as needed to produce a tone appropriate to the musical line being sung. Inexperienced singers may tend to squander air, resulting in a breathy tone quality. Breathing deeply is essential. Shoulders must stay down. Common statements to singers include: "Breathe deeply." "Fill up like a 500-pound canary." "Breathe to the toes." "Breathe low around the middle." "Push the air down into your body." Singers should expel only as much air as needed for proper phonation, i.e., energy level at initial articulation and sustaining of the vowel at an adequate dynamic level. Exercises should emphasize singing long, sustained tones; controlling the air supply; and maintaining purity of vowels. Stress the importance of breathing *before* the need for a breath occurs, because by the time the need for air arises, the tone has already suffered a loss of intensity, a loss of focus, or a drop in pitch.

Exercise 21-17

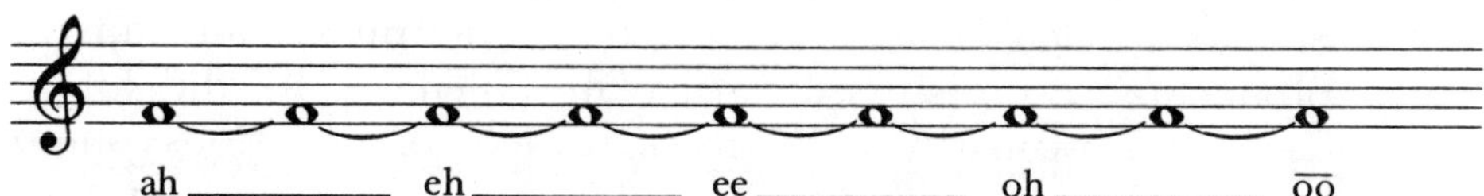

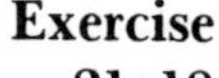

Exercise 21-18

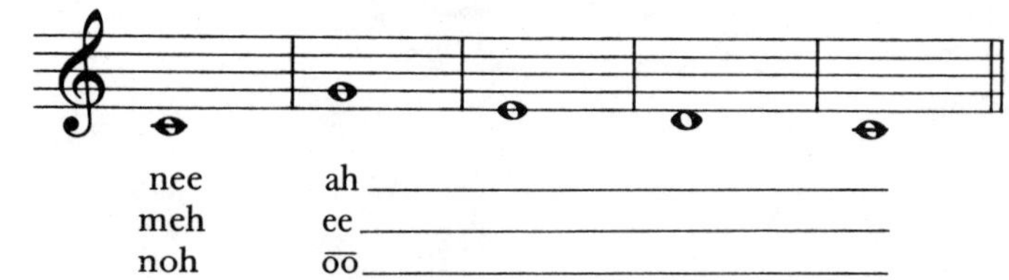

Exercise 21-19

Singers count while sustaining a single tone. Each time they should try to extend the length of time they can sustain the tone.

When practicing staggered breathing, stress three basic rules:

1. Breathe anywhere but at a bar line or anyplace else that would be obvious
2. Sing the tone, release the tone to take a quick catch-breath, and then reenter on the same tone if possible (Example 21-1)

Example 21-1:

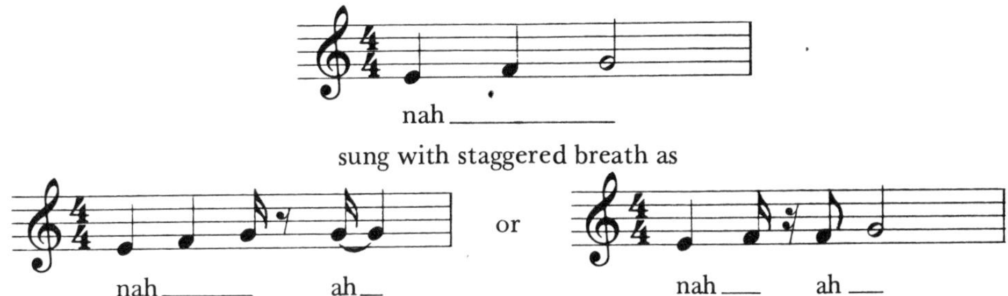

3. Do not reenter louder than when singing ceased before the breath

Intonation

An ensemble sings in tune because (1) the conductor has sensitive ears and (2) he or she has trained the ears of the singers. Most people do not automatically sing in tune. They have to be taught to concentrate on the fine points of tuning.

The causes of out-of-tune singing are many. Singers tend to make descending intervals too large. They generally do not make ascending intervals large enough. Many singers find repeated tones unexciting and relax the intensity of the musical line, allowing the pitch to sag. The unsuspecting singer is trapped at every turn.

The Piano

Many conductors tune their choirs exclusively with the piano. The piano, however, is tuned using equal temperament, which means that certain intervals are slightly out of tune so they can be accommodated in all keys. Many choirs tuning to the piano have pitch problems when singing music a cappella because they do not sing pure intervals. The third and seventh degrees of the scale tend to be sung too low. You must give conscious attention to correcting intonation problems with these two scale degrees.

Solutions. Do as much singing without the piano as possible. Even exercises should be done a cappella. Constantly remind the singers to listen. Pay close attention to the third and seventh degree of the scale. Emphasize singing them high. Be certain you concentrate on developing your own critical listening skills.

Rehearsal and Performance Space

The rehearsal or performance space itself may cause intonation problems. Rooms with little reverberation leave singers feeling as if they are singing a solo. Too much reverberation results in lack of clarity and definition to the sound. Singers tend to get tired more quickly when the room is stuffy, warm, or humid. Rooms may also have a prevailing pitch (the result of air-conditioning or boiler room noise) which tends to pull singers away from actual pitch.

Solutions. Singers must be instructed so that they can cope with all types of acoustical settings. Critical listening is especially important in rooms with little reverberation. The ensemble should rehearse in a variety of acoustical settings, which should be well ventilated and on the cool side. With conscious effort it is possible to concentrate so that an ambient noise in the room is successfully ignored. You should occasionally perform works against an intentionally added impeding sound. If the ensemble is singing in the key of F, play something softly in the key of E-flat at the same time. You must insist on concentration and critical listening.

The Singers

Singers often come to rehearsals mentally and physically tired. They lack the strength to throw off their fatigue. Some tired singers may dread an hour or two of rehearsal. Under such circumstances, it is not surprising if intonation is a problem. Poor posture and bad vocal habits also cause intonation problems. You may have ensemble members who cannot sing in tune, perhaps because they can't match pitches or because they are overly concerned with the mechanics of singing, such as placing the vowel, keeping the tongue down, or deep breathing, that they do not pay adequate attention to pitch accuracy.

Solutions. You must constantly stimulate the performers so that fatigue and boredom become inconsequential. Each singer also must mentally prepare himself or herself to be "up" for each rehearsal and performance. Both you and the singers have responsibilities to challenge and motivate one another. You must insist that the ensemble uses appropriate posture conducive to good singing. Since you are also the voice instructor, you must teach the ensemble how to sit and stand, how to breathe, how to sing, and how to enunciate the text clearly and precisely. You will have to devise tone-matching games where needed.

The Music

Difficult or unfamiliar intervals, high tessituras, unusual voice leading, and chromatics in the music may cause choristers to sing out of tune. When they are first learning a work, certain interval relationships may be difficult for the singers to duplicate. Although the altos, for example, may be able to sing their musical line alone, the inclusion of other parts against that alto line may cause the altos to sing out of tune.

Sustained high singing can result in vocal fatigue. The voice loses its sustaining power and sings flat. Chromatic movement may result in loss of tonality. The singing of a major sixth ("do" to "la") may suddenly become much more difficult if those same pitches are "mi" to "di" in a new tonal framework. Insecurity may cause singers to undercut the upper pitch by as much as a minor third.

Solutions. The music selected for the ensemble should be within its ability. Difficult lines and intervals should be learned independently, then combined with other voice parts. Use warm-up exercises that stress the difficult intervals. Transpose difficult lines to a more comfortable range when necessary. Listening to intervallic relations within the line and between parts should be stressed. You want the ensemble to be challenged by each work that you select, but not so challenged that the work can never be mastered. If singers sense that a work is beyond their grasp, intonation problems may persist. If the work is within the ability of the ensemble, familiarity with the work will eventually solve many problems.

Responsibilities of the Conductor

It is not enough merely to tell a choir that it is flat. You must diagnose the problem and prescribe or demonstrate a solution. A choral ensemble will rarely fix intonation problems just because it knows it is out of tune. You must train the ears of the choristers. Fine singers do not automatically make a fine choir. Solutions to intonation problems can only be accomplished with trained ears.

Diction and Interpretation

The text—its literal meaning, its interpretation, and its intelligibility to the listener—must be of concern to every choral conductor. You must (1) study the text as poetry, seeking its interpretive essence; (2) read the text aloud to yourself, feeling the words as they form in your mouth; and (3) seek expressive nuances for each word. In rehearsal you may recite portions of the text to give its literal meaning and to demonstrate its interpretation. Simply reading poetry is not enough. It must be spoken interpretively. Words must be articulated differently according to the expressive content desired.

Sung sound is the medium by which the text is conveyed to the listener. The text itself is a series of individual sounds which, when connected, contain meaning and potential beauty of expression. Letters of the alphabet, as such, are of no consequence. Only the potential sounds they represent are of concern to the conductor.

It has been said that consonants are the rhythm makers in choral music whereas vowels sustain tone. Consonants and vowels are both very important in expressing choral music. You must decide how words will be sung by the ensemble. You must determine the exact sound and vowel color desired.

1. Read the text over several times until you understand its basic content.
2. Decide on the mood of the text. Is it majestic, sad, introspective, joyful?
3. Is the main idea of the text to tell a story, describe a situation or an object, profess a national ideal, or paint a picture?

4. Decide which words need special emphasis. What words are key to understanding the text?
5. Say these words expressively within the mood of the text.
6. Decide how each sound component of these words will be sung. How long will each component be and how much vocal energy will be needed to project these sound components over a long distance? Two main properties of expressive singing are the prolongation of various sound components and the amount of energy applied to the components.

Consonants must be energized both mentally and physically. When singing the word "moon," the result is usually

m O O n

The "m" and the "n" sounds are slighted and the result is a grossly exaggerated "$\overline{oo}$" sound. In order to project the "m" and the "n," the singer must mentally conceive the individual sound components of the word "moon" to be of equal weight. The physical energy behind these consonant sounds must be increased. The result will be a word in which all sound components are projected with more nearly equal weight.

M O O N

"M" and "n" and "l" are referred to as liquid consonants because they may be sustained on a pitch. They must be energized to ensure proper projection. You must determine the method of attack and release of these consonants. The liquid consonant sounds may be initiated by forcing the air quickly and solidly behind the lips ("m") or tongue ("n" and "l"), causing an abrupt, accented attack; or the air may be started more gently, giving a more liquid attack. You must decide, on the basis of the interpretation of the word, which attack is more desirable. The release of the "m" may be made by quickly releasing the energy behind the lips and "exploding" into the vowel, or the lips can be gently parted, as if supplying a counterforce of energy to the airstream, thus providing a much more liquid release. The release of the "l" and "n" into the vowel may be accomplished by literally releasing the tongue from the hard palate in a quick, forceful manner or by gently releasing the tongue in almost slow motion. The differences may be characterized as shown in Example 21-2. In the dramatic example the "l" is exploded. In the sensuous example the "l" is dragged out, elongated, and gently released.

Example 21-2:

THE VOWEL IS SUNG DIRECTLY ON THE PULSE.

Thus, initial consonants must begin before the pulse. The length of the consonant is determined according to the interpretation sought. "I love you" may be sung in the ways illustrated in Example 21-3. In each instance the "l" is given more prominence. In Example 21-3a the "l" is added quickly; in Example 21-3c the "l" takes up half of the previous pulse.

Example 21-3a:

Example 21-3b:

Example 21-3c:

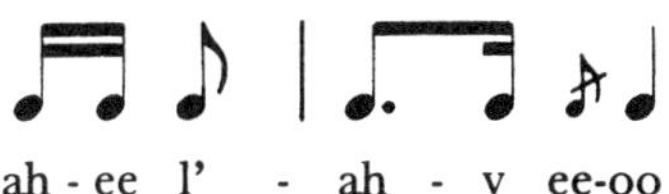

At this point attention has been given only to the "l." Since the "v" sound is sustainable, it is possible to give the "v" added weight by lengthening its duration, as in Example 21-4. In Example 21-4b the "v" sound occupies almost half the pulse. Decisions must be made about these "micro-rhythms" within the words themselves. It is these rhythms that give the words added meaning and character. Usually the rhythm is not so precise that note values can be assigned as has been done above. However, as a conductor you must think about the energy of the consonant and the duration of the sound.

Example 21-4a:

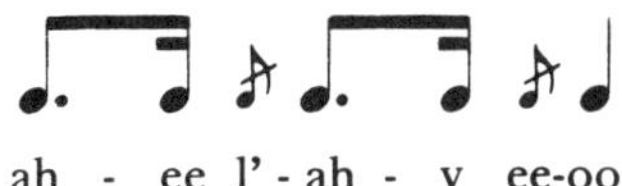

Example 21-4b:

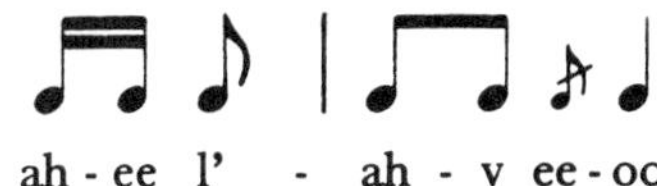

When the phrase "Oh, please" is said in a very pleading manner, the "p" sound is not clipped in duration, but rather is extended somewhat, as is the "l" sound. In fact, there may be a sense of space being left between the "p" and the "l" sounds. If the tongue is being used to stop the air, a slowly lowered tongue will result in air escaping before the tongue leaves the palate area, thus elongating the consonant.

Energy growth behind the articulator stopping the air flow is essential. The articulator—the tongue, for instance—may then act like a drawbridge. If pressure is applied to the drawbridge, it may slowly unwind its chain and release the pressure, or the chain may snap and the drawbridge slam to the bottom. At least in phonation the singer can control whether the consonant is exploded into existence, like a sudden release of energy, or is freed gently.

Consonants

Because of the stress put on singing beautiful vowels, consonants tend to be relegated to a position of little importance. Without consonants, however, words have no meaning. Consonants are the springboard into vowels. Often if vowel sounds are sung incorrectly the reason can be traced to incorrect singing of the consonant sound preceding the vowel.

Consonants may be classified by the way they are formed in the mouth; for example, they may be dental, labiodental, palatal, and so on. Our concern, however, is not so much with how the consonants are formed, but rather with what the singer should do expressively to consonants in the process of singing.

There are two sets of related consonants, each pair being formed exactly the same way in the mouth. In the voiced set of consonants the vocal cords are actually set in motion for a portion of the sound. The other set is unvoiced, meaning that the vocal cords are not used. Either the tongue or the lips are used to stop the air and then release it without any assistance in phonation by the vocal cords.

Voiced	Unvoiced
b	p
d	t
g	k
j	ch
v	f

Voiced consonants seem to start lower in the throat. Unvoiced consonants seem to originate in the mouth.

Prolonging these consonants is more difficult than prolonging the liquid consonants. Most reference sources dealing with diction suggest that consonants be uttered quickly, moving directly to the vowel. This technique, however, denies the expressive qualities of the consonant. Because the air flow is stopped by the tongue or lips it is possible to store vocal energy by continuing to increase the pressure behind the stopping articulator. As with liquid consonants, how the consonant is sung will depend on how the articulator releases the energized air column. If the lips are exploded apart or the tongue snapped down, the result will be a sharply attacked and released consonant. If, on the other hand, the lips or tongue are gently released or, more correctly, slowly released, the result will be an elongated, "more liquid" consonant.

Troublesome Consonants

The "r." The "r" sound can be ugly. The initial "r" of a word or syllable can be elongated in the manner explained above, although most conductors find the sound so offensive that they choose to get through the consonant as quickly as possible. The "r" should not be overly accentuated. A slight flip of the tongue is often used. Your ear must be the judge. The final "r" is off-glided or simply omitted. The off-gliding of the "r," as in the word "fire," keeps the word from taking on an ugly cast.

fah-ee-uh(r)

The "r" is almost completely eliminated. Indeed, some sources suggest that the "r" be eradicated from such words. The same is true of "r" in combination with other consonants (as in "world" and "word"), when the "r" can easily be slighted or almost completely eliminated without losing the intelligibility of the sung text.

Sibilants. The sibilants "s" and "z" and their associated sounds—unvoiced "sh" (*sh*ould) and voiced "sh" (vi*s*ion)—can become ugly hisses. You must decide the duration of these sounds and what emphasis will be placed on them. Multiplying the hiss by fifty choir members usually forces most word-sensitive conductors to back off from this sound, even to the point of having only a few singers sound the final "s."

The "x" is a combination: "k" plus "s." The "s" is the prolonged sound, so the rules applied to the sibilants may also be applied to "x." It is possible to extend "k" and "s" by storing energy behind the blockage of the tongue, then releasing the tongue from the back of the palate to the front of the palate either suddenly for a dramatic attack or more subtly for a more sensitive, gentle attack.

Aspirants. The aspirant "h" can be elongated by expelling energized air, or sung quickly with rapid air escape. The desired emotional impact determines how the "h" should be sung.

The aspirant "w" is formed by shaping the mouth for an "o͞o" sound, then forcing air through the shape. In the word "when" the vocal cords are activated as the initial "wh" sound is pronounced. In "what" the "wh" combination is voiceless. Elongation is possible by prolonging the air flow so that there is more aspirant sound before the vowel component is phonated.

Vowels

The most complex and complete system for dealing with vowel sounds is the International Phonetic Alphabet (see Appendix I). Another system is the Bell Vowel Chart (see Appendix II). For simplicity, a basic vocabulary of pure vowel sounds is given here:

Pure Vowels.

ah	as in father
ă	as in man, pan
aw	as in awful
ee	as in mean, beet
eh	as in set, met
ih	as in miss, kiss
oh	almost never found in English without the "o͞o" off-glide. The word "obey" comes about as close as possible to representing this sound.
o͝o	as in book
o͞o	as in boot
uh	as in mother

These ten pure vowels constitute the primary basic vowel sounds found in English. They may be modified in the process of singing to provide an unlimited palette of dark and light vocal colors.

Diphthongs

Diphthongs are made up of two consecutive pure vowel sounds, one of which is sustained, the other placed quickly before or after the sustained vowel component. The sustained vowel component in each of the diphthongs below is underlined.

<u>ah</u>-ee	as in fight, light, my
<u>ah</u>-ōō	as in now, cow
<u>aw</u>-ee	as in boy, toy (Madeleine Marshall* gives this combination as "aw-ih")
<u>eh</u>-ee	as in bay, day (the "eh" component is actually somewhat brighter than the "eh" in set and met)
ee-<u>ōō</u>	as in few, beautiful (this is the only diphthong in which the second component is sustained)
<u>oh</u>-ōō	as in no, road

Triphthongs

There are also a few triphthongs made up of three consecutive vowel sounds.

ah-ee-uh(r)	as in fire
ah-ōō-uh(r)	as in our
ee-ōō-uh	as in fewer, fuel
oh-ōō-uh(r)	as in four

The sounds are at times approximate when dealing with vowel coloration. The spelling of words is not of concern, only the sounds that are made.

Problems in Pronunciation

Discrepancies in pronunciation will exist no matter what system of classification is used. Certain questions will always arise. Is the word "you" sung as a diphthong (ee-ōō) or does the "y" have a unique sound of its own? Does the word "your" actually have four vowel sounds (ee-oh-ōō-uh)? Is the "wh" in "when" a diphthong (ōō-eh) with an extra burst of air or does the word start with "w," a unique consonant sound? "W" and "y" are consonant sounds, but one would have difficulty denying the vowel component of the sound. They are generally treated as consonants because the sung sound precedes the pulse like other consonants. If they were vowels, they would be sung on the pulse.

*Madeleine Marshall, *The Singer's Manual of English Diction* (New York: G. Schirmer, 1953), p. 170.

Definitions

Pronunciation: The correctness of the sounds used in the utterance of a word. A standard dictionary may be used to verify pronunciation. Conductors must be wary of regional pronunciation differences.

Articulation: The use of the tongue, teeth, lips, and jaw in the utterance of sounds. Lazy use of these articulators results in lack of energy and unintelligible words.

Enunciation: The clarity with which sounds are uttered. Of necessity, pronunciation, articulation, and enunciation are closely linked in the singing process. Good diction in singing is a result of concentration on all three aspects. There should be maximum emphasis on making the text intelligible to listeners.

22 Concert Preparation

Criteria For Music Selection

Finding just the right works for an ensemble takes considerable patience. The criteria for selection must be applied each time a work is considered.

1. *Musical worth.* Is the music worth buying? Can the text be made intelligible to the ensemble? Is the musical setting appropriate to the text? Will the ensemble still like the piece of music after many hours of rehearsal? Will they like it at all?
2. *Singableness.* Can the ensemble master the music? Is the voice leading logical? Are ranges and tessituras appropriate? Can difficult rhythms and intervals be mastered? Can ensemble sections be divided if there are divisi passages?
3. *Accompaniment.* Do you have an accompanist who can play the score—both the accompaniment and the open score? How long will it take *you* to learn the accompaniment? Will the accompaniment have to be reduced or simplified?
4. *Budget.* Will purchase of the music fit within the budget?
5. *Universality.* Will the music still be worth performing five years from now? Twenty years from now?
6. *Programming.* Can the work be programmed with other materials you have selected for the year? What will precede and follow it in concert? Can technical problems, such as the need for instruments, sound system, or split choir, be solved? Is there audience appeal?
7. *Educational value.* Does the work fit the educational needs of the ensemble? Is there something to be learned from performing it? Will the audience learn something from it?

8. *Library concerns.* Does this music fill a niche in the choral library? Are a range of composers, periods, and genres (masses, motets, etc.) adequately represented in the library?
9. *Editions, arrangements, and transcriptions.* Is the version you choose in keeping with the composer's original intent? How much has been changed to bring this particular edition to its present form?
10. *Special considerations.* Are works for particular holidays, seasons, or contests needed? What special criteria must this music fulfill?

Finding good music appropriate for your ensemble needs is difficult. You will study many scores to find those few works that will fulfill the needs of your ensembles. Attending reading sessions and national, regional and state choral conferences, festivals and contests can be excellent sources for finding appropriate literature. Conductors with years of experience may also provide you with titles of works that have been useful to them.

Establishing Program Order

The purposes of establishing program order are:

1. To arrange the progression of the concert so that one work does not overshadow another
2. To maintain audience interest
3. To educate the audience and raise its level of music appreciation
4. To provide an aesthetic experience for both ensemble and audience
5. To entertain the audience
6. To demonstrate the ability of the ensemble

A good choral concert, like a good composition, must have unity and variety. Unity may be achieved by providing the concert with a theme, arranging the music historically, performing all sacred or all secular music, or performing the music of one composer or one text set by many composers. The danger of too much unity is boredom.

Variety may be achieved by performing music of varying historical styles, composers, and forms, as well as solos, duets, trios, and polychoral works. Physically rearranging the ensemble provides visual variety. Dynamic, tempo, and mood contrasts also provide interest.

The following are basic guidelines for organizing a good concert?

1. Provide a variety of key and mode relations. For example, don't program two pensive works in the key of C minor successively.
2. Vary moods within each section of the program.
3. Provide each group of works with a climax. Then provide the entire concert with a climax. Remember: Not all climactic works must be loud and bombastic. Some very soft, intense works have as much dramatic potential as those that are loud.
4. Consider your audience. Today's audiences have grown up under the kaleidoscopic influence of television—many people will no longer sit for

two hours listening to an ensemble sing sixteenth- and seventeenth-century English madrigals. A wide variety of literature will not only instruct your audience but also hold its attention.

5. Consider the singer's durability. Program for moments of relaxation for the singers. Most singers cannot maintain a high-dynamic, high-intensity, and high-pitch level in work after work. Contrast is essential to give the singers a chance to recuperate before their next vocal challenge. Not all works demand an equal amount of effort from the singers. It is better to program several easier works at the beginning of the concert rather than to tire the singers with the very first work.
6. Use a variety of voicings, such as duets, trios, SSA, and TTBB works.
7. Use instruments in contrast to voices a cappella.
8. Feature soloists from the various ensembles.
9. Program a variety of styles and composers.

When more than one choral ensemble is on the program, variety is built in. Less accomplished groups should be placed before more competent ensembles. The strongest ensemble should perform last, although there may be exceptions to this rule. The type of literature performed may dictate which ensemble should perform last. It may be preferable to program a select chamber choir performing eight madrigals before a concert choir closing with the "Hallelujah" chorus. *Most important,* the audience should leave the concert with a very positive feeling about the music and its performance.

Performance Preparation

Acoustics

Each choir should rehearse once, and preferably twice, in the room where the concert will be held. Prepare the singers to handle difficult acoustical problems by rehearsing in a variety of settings. The large expanse of a gymnasium, the starkness of a cafeteria, a stage with sound-eating curtains, and even a rest room with maximum reverberation all provide singers with opportunities to cope with a variety of acoustics.

In each acoustical situation you must carefully explain the types of adjustments singers must make. When performing in rooms where there is little reverberation (e.g., an auditorium with heavy curtains and carpeted floor):

1. Tempos may need to be faster.
2. Musical lines must be more sustained.
3. More energy is required to sustain long lines.
4. Rhythms must be crisply executed.
5. Tone quality may need to be brighter to enhance projection.
6. Singers must listen more critically.

In spaces where there is considerable reverberation (rooms with hard, reflective walls and floors):

1. Tempos usually need to be slower.
2. More separation is needed between notes in melismas. In some quicker-moving runs each note may need to receive a slightly new articulation.
3. Lines must be more detached.
4. More care must be taken with diction so that the text is not muddled or blurred.

Often singers have to move from their cozy choir rehearsal room to a much larger and acoustically much deader auditorium. They should not try to outsing the space, but instead should adapt their singing to its acoustical properties.

The Dress Rehearsal

The dress rehearsal should include a straight run-through of the performance without stopping. This is easier said than done. Unlike an orchestra or a band, singers must practice ensemble stage deportment: walking onto the stage, getting onto the risers, standing, raising the choir folders to singing position, holding the folders, turning pages, and exiting. If the performers are to come from an area in the audience and return to the audience following their performance, the system of movement must be mapped out in advance. Each student must know exactly where to sit, how to get to the stage area, and how to return to his or her seat. Mixups cause embarrassment and slow concert flow. You must decide which hand the music should be carried in. These matters will consume a considerable portion of the dress rehearsal time unless you have dealt with them earlier.

Unlike instrumental concerts, the choral concert begins when the ensemble moves toward the performance area and becomes visible to the audience. The audience expects a certain amount of uniformity from a choral ensemble. Although it is a matter of personal taste, it is customary to let the first row of singers move into position on the risers first. Be sure to decide which end of the row is to enter the stage area first. It is embarrassing to discover that the ensemble is standing on the risers in exactly the reverse order of its usual position. At least some of the riser climbing, tripping on hems of choir robes or dresses, stumbling, or catching heels in the risers is hidden from the audience when the first row is already in place. The next row of singers to enter the stage area would be the top row, followed by each succeeding row in descending order.

The Pre-Concert Warm-Up

The members of the ensemble should assemble from thirty minutes to one hour before the concert begins. Hold a short warm-up session. The singers may not need a warm-up, but they do need to get back in touch with you musically. Include several familiar warm-ups as well as an exercise or two that demands close attention and concentration from the singers. You may also wish to begin and end each selection on the program. Your comments should be positive and encouraging. Your confidence will breed assurance among the singers.

Five minutes before concert time the singers should line up exactly as they will appear on stage. Any last-minute instructions should be given at this time. Remind them to watch you and to listen to each other. Quickly check the appearance of the choir members and remind them of the hand in which the choir folder is to be carried. Then give a final word of encouragement.

Once the ensemble is onstage, pause for a moment before you enter the stage area. After the ensemble is set in position and the audience is quiet, take a deep breath and walk purposefully to the center of the stage. If the audience applauds, recognize it with a bow from center stage. Now you are ready for the concert to begin.

The Final Release

The audience should be treated to a good ending. It has been said, although somewhat facetiously, that the beginning and ending are the most important places in a musical work, and that what happens in between is experience. If your performance begins well, it will probably end well. If the work ends well, the audience may excuse many musical transgressions which have occurred during the performance.

The conclusion of a work is more than just the end. After the conductor has given the final release and the ensemble no longer produces physical sound, music still exists in the air. It is still reverberating off the walls and being absorbed by the people in the audience. This "presence" of music seems to travel through the fiber of the audience, even through the walls of the auditorium and beyond.

The ending of a musical work is thus more than just the cessation of sound. At that moment the essence of the work as a whole may become manifest to audience, performers, and conductor alike. Through many weeks of study and rehearsal you and the ensemble have diligently searched for the aesthetic qualities of the music. You have taken the work apart and rehearsed small sections. You have heard and rehearsed the work many times. The audience, however, hears the work only once. You must reach through the dimension of conducting technicalities into the dimension of communicating the enriching qualities of this music as a whole to those who will hear the work just once.

The conclusion of the music should not be rushed. As the work comes to a close, the release must match the musical character and mood that are to remain with the audience. The final release allows the work to make its last and most powerful statement. After the release your hands should either stop or float very slowly through the air. They should do nothing which might distract the listeners—no sudden gestures or big, flowery movements. When your hands, visible to the audience, stop or move only slightly following the release, they let the sound complete its journey and hold the audience in suspension. Rather than bursting into applause, the audience tends to wait for more. Only after you sense that the journey is complete should your hands move to your side—*in the character of the music.*

Your acknowledgment of the applause should also be in the character of the music. Serious works demand serious acknowledgment; joyous works demand a smile and a pleasant face. All movement made by the conductor, from the moment of music's birth through the acknowledgment of applause, should be in the character of the music.

The final release has implications for the performers as well. After it is given they should become motionless. They should not turn pages, close their music, or turn to their neighbor. Performers must also be receptive to music's final inaudible statement. The fact that they have closed their mouths does not close the performance. The performers should maintain the mood and character of the music as long as is judiciously feasible after the final release. The conductor will usually signal the ensemble by change of facial expression, physical gesture, or body attitude that the ending is over. The ensemble is then to relax or to change the mood in preparation for the next work to be performed.

The process of listening beyond the final release must be taught. The ensemble which breaks its discipline loses that fleeting moment when a work speaks its last to us. The ensemble must be as disciplined as the conductor to continue participation in the music beyond the final release.

APPENDIX I Basic International Phonetic Alphabet Sounds Found in English Pronunciation*

IPA	Sound	Examples
		Vowels
ɑ	ah	father [fɑðɚ]; pot [pɑt]; follow [fɑlo]
æ	ă	fat [fæt]; catch [kætʃ]; master [mæstɚ] In singing æ, the student should avoid placing the sound too far forward in the mouth. A dropped jaw will help.
e	ā [ae]	plate [plet]; inflate [ɪnflet]; ape [ep]
ɛ	eh	fed [fɛd]; met [mɛt]; better [bɛtɚ]
i	ē	heat [hit]; green [grin]; please [pliz]
ɪ	ih	pin [pɪn]; it [ɪt]; hymn [hɪm]
o	ō	broke [brok]; float [flot]; token [tokɛn]
ɔ	aw	haul [hɔl]; gloss [glɔs]; talk [tɔk]
ʌ	uh	in stressed syllables only. under [ʌndɚ]; public [pʌblɪk]; shut [ʃʌ t]
ə	uh	in unstressed syllables only. until [əntɪl]; machine [məʃin]; undone [əndʌn]
u	oo	booth [buθ]; tomb [tum]; zoo [zu]
ʊ	o͝o	book [bʊk]; foot [fʊt]; took [tʊk]
		In singing ʌ or ə, it is best to drop the jaw and lean toward the ɑ[ah] sound.
		Diphthongs
ɑɪ	ah-ih	mine [mɑɪn]; buy [bɑɪ]; untie [əntɑɪ]
ɑʊ	ah-oo	town [tɑʊn]; crowd [krɑʊd]; power [pɑʊɚ]
ju	yoo	youth [juθ]; new [nju]; few [fju]
ɔɪ	aw-ih	toy [tɔɪ]; employ [ɛmplɔɪ]; noise [nɔɪz]

The following diphthongs may be used to clarify the sounds inherent in the single IPA letter, if desired.

IPA	Sound	Examples
ɛɪ	eh-ih	say [sɛɪ or seɪ]; play [plɛɪ or pleɪ]; obey [obɛɪ or obeɪ]
or		
eɪ	a-ih	These diphthongs, along with the IPA vowel e [a], are essentially the same sound in English, differing in the stress and color given to the second, or fade-out, vowel, and the brightness of the initial ɛ or e part of the diphthong.
ou	oh-o͝o	sew (sou]; blow [blou]; throw [θrou]

The r

The pronunciation of the r is a matter of some concern for choral musicians. The question is often raised whether or not to actually pronounce it, or to simply sing the vowel sound immediately preceding it, omitting the r, leaving it to be supplied by the "ear" of the listener. With the r omitted: fear [fiə]; there [ðɛə]; perhaps [pɚhæps]. The use of the IPA character ɚ, which for clarity's sake includes the r sound, may be substituted for the ə: fear [fiɚ]; there [ðɛɚ]; perhaps [pɚhæps]. There are also occasions when an r sound within the word may also be omitted: charm [tʃam]; garden [gadɛ n]. This is at the discretion of the conductor in keeping with the diction problems of his particular choir. The r before a vowel sound must always be pronounced, however.

Triphthongs

ɑɪɚ	ah-ih-uhr	fire [fɑɪɚ or fɑɪθ]; tire [tɑɪɚ or tɑɪθ]; inspire [ɪnspɑɪɚ or ɪnspɑɪθ]
or		
ɑɪə	ah-ih-uh	
ɑuɚ	ah-ōō-uhr	tower [tɑuɚ or tɑuə]; hour [ɑuɚ or ɑuə]; power [pɑuɚ or pɑuə]
or		
ɑuə	ah-ōō-uh	
ɔɪə	aw-ih-uh	oil [ɔɪəl]; boil [bɔɪəl]; royal [rɔɪəl]

The following triphthong may be used if desired, to clarify the sounds inherent in the single IPA letter, o, when connected to the final ɚ or ə sound.

ouɚ	oh-ōō-uhr	ore [ouɚ or ouə]; roar [rouɚ or rouə]; more [mouɚ or mouə
or		
ouə	oh-ōō-uh	

Consonants

IPA	Sound	Examples
b	b	best [bɛst]; baritone [bɛrɪton]; bellow [bɛlo]
d	d	diction [dɪkʃən]; under [ʌndɚ]; dock [dɑk]
f	f	flag [flæg]; flute [flut]; pharmacy [fɑrməsi]
g	g	get [gɛt]; negate [nɪget]; bag [bæg]
h	h	hill [hɪl]; hath [hæθ]; behold [bihold]
ʤ	j	judge [ʤʌʤ]; gently [ʤɛntli]; job [ʤɑb]
k	k	kiss [kɪs]; cantata [kɑntɑtɑ]; choral [korəl]
l	l	love [lʌv]; all [ɔl]; length [lɛŋθ]
m	m	major [meʤɚ]; diminish [dɪmɪnɪʃ]; gem [ʤɛm]
n	n	note [not]; unto [ʌntu]; machine [məʃin]
ŋ	ng	sing [sɪŋ]; anger [æŋgɚ]; watching [wɑtʃɪŋ]
p	p	practice [præktɪs]; peace [pis]; escape [ɛskep]
r	r	run [rʌn]; glory [glori]; children [tʃɪldrɛn]
s	s	sit [sɪt]; cross [krɔs]; blessing [blɛsɪŋ]
ʃ	sh	shush [ʃʌʃ]; shall [ʃæl]; patient [peʃɛnt]
tʃ	ch	church [tʃɚtʃ]; clutch [klʌtʃ]; riches [rɪtʃɛz]
t	t	tooth [tuθ]; yet [jɛt]; posture [pɑstjuɚ]
ð	th [voiced]	breathe [brið]; this [ðɪs]; then [ðɛn]
θ	th [unvoiced]	breath [brɛθ]; eighth [eɪθ]; think [θɪnk]
v	v	very [vɛri]; voice [vɔɪs]; every [ɛvri]
w	w	west [wɛst]; well [wɛl]; waltz [wɔlts]
j	y	yet [jɛt]; young [jʌŋ]; yellow [jɛlo]
z	z	zero [ziro]; bays [bez]; xylophone [zɑɪləfon]
ʒ	zh	azure [æʒjuɚ]; vision [vɪʒən]; pleasure [plɛʒjuɚ]
hw	hw	where [hwɛr]; when [hwɛn]; wheat [hwit]
ɚ	ur or er	early [ɚli]; maternal [mətɚnəl]; singer [sɪŋɚ]

Ray Moore, "Toward a Better Concept of Choral Diction Through the International Phonetic Alphabet," *The Choral Journal*, Sept. 1972, pp. 22-23.

APPENDIX II

The Bell Vowel Chart

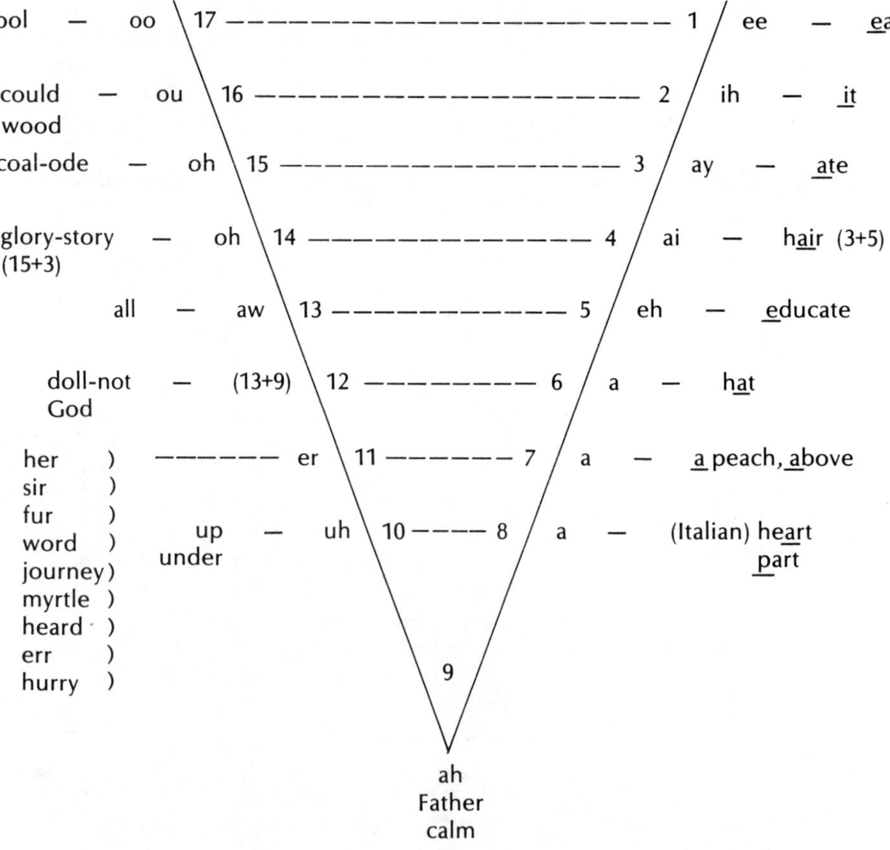

Louis H. Diercks, "A Guide to Improving the Diction and Tone Quality of the Choir," *The Choral Journal,* Oct. 1974, pp. 9-10.

Index

F

H

I

L

M

N

O

P

R